GLASS HALF FULL

GLASS
HALF FULL

THE DECLINE AND REBIRTH
OF THE LEGAL PROFESSION

Benjamin H. Barton

OXFORD
UNIVERSITY PRESS

OXFORD
UNIVERSITY PRESS

Oxford University Press is a department of the University of Oxford.
It furthers the University's objective of excellence in research, scholarship,
and education by publishing worldwide.

Oxford   New York
Auckland   Cape Town   Dar es Salaam   Hong Kong   Karachi
Kuala Lumpur   Madrid   Melbourne   Mexico City   Nairobi
New Delhi   Shanghai   Taipei   Toronto

With offices in
Argentina   Austria   Brazil   Chile   Czech Republic   France   Greece
Guatemala   Hungary   Italy   Japan   Poland   Portugal   Singapore
South Korea   Switzerland   Thailand   Turkey   Ukraine   Vietnam

Oxford is a registered trade mark of Oxford University Press
in the UK and certain other countries.

Published in the United States of America by
Oxford University Press
198 Madison Avenue, New York, NY 10016

© Oxford University Press 2015

Library of Congress Cataloging-in-Publication Data
Barton, Benjamin H., 1969– author.
Glass half full : the decline and rebirth of the legal profession / Benjamin H. Barton.
p.   cm.
Summary: "A counterintuitive and optimistic reconsideration of the crisis in the American legal
profession"— Provided by publisher.
ISBN 978–0–19–020556–0 (hardback)
1. Practice of law—Economic aspects—United States. 2. Lawyers—United States—Economic
conditions—21st century. 3. Legal services—United States. I. Title.
KF315.B37 2015
331.7′613400973—dc23

2014042512

1   3   5   7   9   8   6   4   2

Printed in the United States of America on acid-free paper

CONTENTS

PART II: LAW SCHOOLS

PART III: BIG PICTURE AND THE GLASS HALF FULL

ACKNOWLEDGMENTS

—————

I received a great deal of help in writing this book. Glenn Reynolds and Brannon Denning talked over much of this material with me during lunches and happy hours and then they read and rewrote swaths of the book for me. Their thoughts on the legal profession and law school are ever-present in these pages. Ashby Jones, Nancy Levit, Russell Pearce, Dana Remus, and Deborah Rhode all edited multiple drafts and sharpened my work immeasurably. I am also extremely grateful for comments from my colleagues Wendy Bach, Doug Blaze, Iris Goodwin, Paula Schaefer, Maurice Stucke, Penny White, and David Wolitz. The University of Tennessee College of Law is a great place to work.

The book is based in part upon a paper I presented at George Mason University's Unlocking the Law Conference, which was a celebration of the scholarly work of the late, great Professor Larry Ribstein. I learned much from Larry about these topics and the life of a legal scholar. The comments and reactions at the conference inspired this book. Bruce Kobayashi, Bill Henderson, Thomas Morgan, Todd Henderson, and Daniel Currell were especially helpful.

My family was enormously supportive. My wife Indya read and edited the book and cut me a lot of slack as I wrote. The book is dedicated to my two lovely daughters Dahlia and Georgia.

I have always been lucky to have excellent student research assistants and this book was no exception. Thanks to Mason Smith, Sarah Watson, Robert Wheeler, and Anna Xiques for their work. Last, but not least, Dave McBride of Oxford University Press was a great believer in this project from the start and guided me through the process with kindness and patience.

I

Introduction

CHARLES DICKENS WROTE *Bleak House* as a serial in the 1850s and published it as a single volume in 1853.[1] It is a blistering assessment of the English Chancery system and remains one of the most trenchant critiques of the common law system. It is also, like most Dickens serials, a ripping good yarn.

Given the bewildering series of technological and societal changes over the last 160 years, there is something remarkable about Dickens's portrait of lawyers in *Bleak House*: it is utterly familiar to a modern reader. Chapter 1 takes us on a tour "In Chancery." Dickens describes the Judge (the Lord High Chancellor), the lawyers (barristers), and the various court hangers-on. At the end of the chapter the Chancellor interrupts a lawyer—aptly named Mr. Tangle—to see if he has almost concluded his argument in the never-ending case of *Jarndyce and Jarndyce*. Mr. Tangle responds "Mlud no—variety of points—feel it my duty to submit—ludship" before the Chancellor cuts him off for good.[2]

Similar scenes recur every day in courts all over the United States of America. Individual lawyers, representing clients by the hour, appear in person before judges to make arguments based upon a "variety of points." If Mr. Tangle visited a contemporary court he would be puzzled by cell phones, iPads, and laptop computers, but as soon as a lawyer stood and addressed the court Mr. Tangle would know *exactly* what was happening.

Bleak House portrays a legal profession little changed from then to now. Dickens describes lawyers meeting in person with clients, or drafting papers, or investigating their cases. English lawyers in 1850 practiced an individualized and bespoke[3] professional service that consisted of paying a lawyer for his time, sometimes in court, sometimes in consultation, sometimes in drafting documents or conducting research.

Legal practice has changed in tools (computers notably) and in scope (today's large American law firms are without historical parallel), but not in kind. Law may have changed less than any other area of the economy between 1850 and today. The same basic product is being sold and the same basic service is being performed. The practice of law is notoriously resistant to change, and law schools have likewise remained largely the same over the last century.

No one dodges the reaper forever. The industrial revolution brought mass production to manufacturing and the information revolution has seen knowledge workers replaced by computers. In multiple areas of the economy computers now handle work once done on an individualized basis by highly paid professionals.

The pattern for these changes began in the industrial revolution and continued in the information revolution. Bespoke work done by individuals for other individuals is replaced by standardized and then commoditized products, which are mass produced and much cheaper.[4] The total number of people needed to create the good goes down, as does the average wage earned by those in the industry. The few at the top, who control the process or design the product, however, make much more than any single provider of customized services ever could.

This has contributed to what economists Robert Frank and Philip Cook call "the winner-take-all society."[5] The individuals who own the computer processes that replace individual humans become very wealthy. The same is the case with the professionals who can do the work that is too complicated or important to outsource or computerize. Those individuals will be in high demand and will also make an excellent living. The humans who used to do the work that has been computerized or outsourced fight it out in a fiercely competitive market, and earn much less. Growing income inequality reflects this phenomenon. The middle of various industries is being destroyed, leaving only a small top and a large bottom.[6]

This book explains how these changes have come to the American legal profession. In homage to the late Larry Ribstein's seminal piece, *The*

Death of Big Law,[7] these trends are called the four "deaths": death from above, death from below, death from the state, and death from the side.

"Death from above" assesses the challenges facing Big Law (the large and highly lucrative American law firms that serve corporate clients). Big Law has grown exponentially in size and profits since 1980. Some of the strategies that fueled that growth are killing (or at least injuring) the goose that laid the golden egg. Big Law was built on "reputational bonding."[8] Clients seek out large corporate law firms because these firms have presumably done the work to select the most able lawyers for the most complicated work. Over time Big Law has been mortgaging its reputational capital and its firm cultures in the relentless pursuit of increased profits per partner and size. Law firms have increased leverage (the ratio between partners and associates), aggressively pursued lateral hiring, and raised hourly rates and hourly billing targets. These have been very successful short-term strategies, but are corrosive long term.

Corporate clients have responded to the higher prices by pressing for fixed price billing and using insourcing, outsourcing, and computerization for more straightforward legal work. Paradoxically, they have continued to pay more for true "bet-the-company" transactional and litigation work. This is consistent with the winner-take-all economy: the most profitable firms and most in-demand lawyers get richer doing the truly specialized work and everyone else falls backward toward the pack.

"Death from below" uses Clayton Christensen's theory of disruptive technologies to describe how computerization is replacing bread-and-butter legal work. *LegalZoom, Rocket Lawyer,* and others are horning in on traditional areas of practice like drafting incorporation papers and wills. Websites offering free or very inexpensive legal advice have also proliferated. So far, these websites and virtual law firms have largely avoided prosecution for the unauthorized practice of law (UPL), and some, like *LegalZoom,* have grown so large and prevalent that the time to quietly nip them in the bud has passed.

Computerization will not replace in-court work anytime soon, however, because that is the area most jealously protected by judges and lawyers. Just like Big Law, there will always be some "bet-the-family/small business" cases that require expensive and individualized representation. As in Big Law, there is already ferocious competition over these cases and there is not enough of that work to support the current number of lawyers.

"Death from the state" describes the ways that courts and legislatures have reined in litigation since the 1980s. Tort reform and limitations on class actions, damages, and lawyer's fees have proliferated. These changes have chased non-specialists from the market and consolidated the remaining work for a smaller group of lawyers. This trend has also hit the defense bar. Because tort or class action cases are worth less and the downside risk is often capped, defendants and insurance companies are less interested in rolling up bills litigating, and plaintiffs are more likely to settle quickly.

The ultimate example is the rise of the settlement mill, where a few lawyers front a mass of non-lawyers who work solely on getting settlements for as many clients as they can, and where the lawyers rarely, if ever, litigate. Specialists soak up the remaining work, and the small-firm and solo practitioners who used to dabble in this area have been pushed out.

Government hiring, a steady source of lawyer employment for years, has stalled at the worst possible moment. The fees paid for appointed work as a defense lawyer have also stagnated.

"Death from the side" analyzes the thirty-year decline in small-firm and solo practitioner earnings. Recent coverage of the legal profession describes the market for lawyers collapsing, starting in 2008. That year does mark the start of Big Law's struggles (the portion of the legal market generally covered by the press), but the majority of American lawyers who work in small firms or as solo practitioners have faced grim prospects since the mid-1980s. Between then and now solo practitioners have seen a 37 percent decline in real income. According to IRS data drawn from actual tax returns, the average solo practitioner earned $46,560 in 2010.

Why? There are too many lawyers and too many law school graduates. A comparison of the number of law school graduates, the number of licensed lawyers (not all of whom work as a lawyer), and the Bureau of Labor Statistics (BLS) estimate for the actual number of lawyers shows that there are many more law school graduates than there are personsemployed as lawyers, and there have been since the 1980s. If you use the BLS count of lawyers, almost half of the individuals who earned a JD in the last forty years are not currently working as a lawyer. The National Association of Legal Placement (NALP) data over the same period demonstrate that roughly one in three law school graduates were unable to find work that required a JD post-graduation.

But if underemployment is such a problem for lawyers, why are legal services often too expensive for middle- and low-income Americans? If there is an oversupply of JDs why has it not solved America's access to justice problem? The answer is that lawyers at the low end of the market earn so little that it makes more sense to leave the profession and take another job suitable for a college-educated adult than to charge even less for individualized legal services. When the *average* salary of a solo practitioner is $46,500 it is easy to imagine that many JD holders would rather work as an insurance adjuster or run their own business than scrape by as a lawyer.[9]

If you want to understand what has happened in the legal market over the last thirty years, there is one chart that explains it quite crisply. Since the 1960s the IRS has gathered and published the tax return data for all lawyers who file partnership income tax returns and all lawyers who file as sole practitioners. These categories are not as neat as they sound. For example, the partnership returns include many lawyers in small partnerships that more closely resemble solo practitioners than Big Law partners. Likewise, the partnership count does not include professional corporations, so some Big Law salaries are left out. Nevertheless, these two categories have been measured since the 1960s and Figure 1.1 well demonstrates what has happened in the market since then.

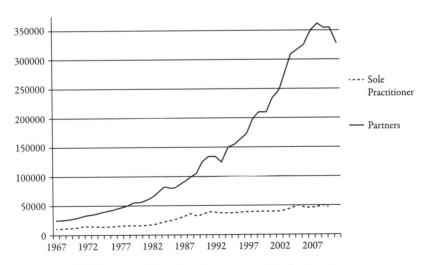

FIGURE 1.1 IRS Income Data for Partners and Sole Practitioners

Consider just how much the earnings for these two categories have grown apart over the years. In the 1960s partners earned about twice what a solo practitioner did. In 2010, *after* the Great Recession, partners earned more than seven times as much. There is a clear split into two professions and the gulf has widened considerably since the mid-1980s.

Solo practitioners have done miserably since the 1980s. Adjusted for inflation to 2010 dollars, the average solo practitioner earned $69,955 in 1988 and $46,560 in 2010, a 34 percent decline in buying power. The years from 2008 to 2011 have been bad for law partners. They have seen almost a 16 percent decrease in real earnings over just a three-year period, easily the worst stretch in the forty-four years of data.

Despite the fact that the last thirty years have been lean ones for the majority of American lawyers, more law schools opened, and existing schools relentlessly raised tuition and accepted more students. Between 1987 and 2010, the number of ABA-accredited law schools increased from 175 to 200 and total JD enrollment rose from 117,997 to 147,525. Over the same period law school tuition rose over 440 percent for in-state residents at public institutions and 220 percent at private institutions. Student debt loads have increased substantially as well.

The fall of Big Law in 2008 finally brought public attention to the employment numbers for law graduates, and applications and attendance at law schools have fallen steeply since 2010. The downward trend is so marked that unless it reverses in 2014–15 fewer students may *apply* to law school than *enrolled* in 2010–11. In 2013 only 39,674 first-year students enrolled in ABA-accredited law schools, the lowest number since 1977. Some law schools may close, but a much likelier result is that law schools will risk disaccreditation by admitting anyone they can and cutting costs rather than actually closing the doors. This may mean closing the law library altogether or replacing the bulk of the tenured faculty with adjuncts. It is inexpensive to run a skeleton law school that has few administrators and is taught by adjunct faculty.

The question then shifts to what the ABA would do. The ABA has never disaccredited a fully accredited American law school, and the legal and public relations ramifications of such a move are unclear.

Things sound grim, no? Most of the work on this subject has, in fact, been negative. It has also been written by the parties most likely to suffer, law professors and Big Law partners. Many recent books by law professors and Big Law partners grimly describe the changes: *The Lawyer Bubble, Failing Law Schools, Declining Prospects, Don't Go to Law School (Unless).*[10] In contrast, this book attempts to fairly describe the many challenges and still present the glass-half-full case.

Consumers are the obvious beneficiaries of these changes. Whatever else is coming in the future, it seems likely that legal services will be more widely available to more people and businesses at lower prices. This trend starts at the top with corporate law firms and bubbles up from the bottom with *LegalZoom* and other forms providers. Lawyers and legal fees are what economists call "transaction costs." When transaction costs fall, more transactions occur, and goods and services are more likely to end up with their highest-value users.

The benefits will be especially marked for the poor and the middle class. Most middle- and low-income Americans cannot afford to hire a lawyer. This means that many Americans cannot afford to have a will or get divorced or change child-custody arrangements or defend themselves in eviction/foreclosure proceedings.[11] Bar associations and advocates for the poor have argued for years that increased legal aid funding, required *pro bono* service, and a civil *Gideon* right are the answers to these problems—that is, more bespoke legal services by more government-supported or volunteer lawyers. These are deeply backward-looking, 1960s-era solutions to a very serious problem.

Fortunately, except for the in-court portion of the problem (which could theoretically be solved by *pro se* court reform), computerization is on the verge of bypassing the legal profession altogether. Non-profits and governments have put almost all of the raw materials of American law online, from case law to statutes to regulations. *Google* and other search engines have made that law easier to find than ever. An American with a smartphone now has easier access to legal sources than most lawyers did in the 1980s, let alone the 1880s.

Free and low-cost legal documents are widely available. State supreme courts and legal aid societies have put reams of forms and instructions online, covering areas as diverse as name change actions and divorces. *LegalZoom* offers more than 160 different documents for sale for as low as $14.95. Cheap or free legal advice is offered through sites like *Avvo* or *Lawpivot*. Even dispute resolution is offered online as a route around expensive court proceedings and legal fees.

First-generation online services may not be as good as a live lawyer (although everyone knows a lawyer whose work is already worse than what *LegalZoom* provides), but over time they will continue to improve. *LegalZoom* and *Rocket Lawyer* are already superior to nothing, which is all most poor and middle-income Americans can afford.

Even in-court work will grow cheaper as lawyers take advantage of forms and virtual offices. They will need to use these tools to survive, because more lawyers competing for less work will continue to drive prices down. The lawyers who continue to be dislocated from Big Law and the new graduates from the 201 ABA-accredited law schools will need to work somewhere. Unless they leave, or never enter, the profession, there will be downward pressure in every legal sector as displaced lawyers and new law graduates fight over lower-paying jobs.

Between technology, outsourcing, the flood of new law graduates, and the displaced lawyers now willing/forced to work for lower salaries, customers will suddenly (and for the first time in recent history) be paying much less for legal services. If you have enjoyed the digital revolution in music and photography, you will likewise enjoy the legal market in ten to twenty years. Legal services will be cheaper, more accessible, *and* better. That is bad for lawyers in the same way digital photography was bad for Kodak. It is, however, outstanding news for the country as a whole.

After a wrenching period of change the profession itself will be improved. The profession will benefit greatly if fewer students enter law school, and if those who do indeed go to law school arrive with a more realistic view of what lawyers do and what they earn. Fewer law students also means less competition for the remaining jobs.

Current law students came in spite of a headwind, rather than because they were history majors with no other plans. They haggle more over tuition and try to borrow less. One of the hidden causes of rampant lawyer unhappiness is that too many lawyers were not thoughtful about coming to law school and are later disappointed with their choice. The realistic students who decide to go to law school despite the current negativity are much likelier to enjoy law school and practicing law. Lowered expectations are a key ingredient to happiness. That alone will be a boon to a profession that has had too many disappointed and disillusioned members. The college graduates who do *not* go to law school will also be better off, pursuing work for which they are better suited.

The actual job of being a lawyer will also improve. The best of times for Big Law profits has been the worst of times for the lawyers themselves. Big Law has led a boom in both remuneration and misery. The changes ahead will slow or even shrink some portions of Big Law. They will also force "alternative billing" for many projects, encouraging creativity and efficiency rather than the grind of maximizing hourly billing. Much of the less interesting work will be computerized or outsourced, leaving only the most challenging work. Competition from *Axiom* and other virtual law firms will allow creative lawyers flexibility in the terms and conditions of their employment, allowing some lawyers to do Big Law–type work on their own schedules. Surveys have regularly shown that Big Law lawyers would take less money in return for more free time and autonomy. That sort of work will become increasingly available. This will make those lawyers happier and will enhance quality, because creative humans do better when given autonomy in problem solving.

Today's challenges will push some parts of Big Law back to the future. Some of the firms that survive will more closely resemble the American law firms of the past: true partnerships where lawyers work together without an eye toward lateraling in or out; where they work to build firm reputation and serve clients well by providing value and insight, not just billed time.

The same trends will make those small-firm and solo practitioners who survive better off. First, some portion of Big Law will separate from the most profitable firms and fall back to the pack. This may result in a rejoining of what now resembles two separate professions (Big Law and everyone else). Right now a graph of the starting salaries of law graduates is a double hump, one high salary hump for Big Law at around $160,000 and a much larger hump for everyone else near $60,000. Turning the double hump back into a bell curve would do much for the sanity of the profession and the happiness of non–Big Law lawyers.

Second, as with Big Law, much of the most basic legal work will be lost, but the work that remains will be complicated and intellectually stimulating. To use Richard Granat's phrase, lawyers will practice "at the top of their licenses." At every level of the profession, entrepreneurialism will be required. Lawyers will not be able to count on hanging a shingle and serving clients who *have* to see them. Instead, the lawyers who survive will be the lawyers who can demonstrate the value of their insight and services. This will be hard but satisfying for the lawyers who make it.

It will be a galvanizing time for the profession and that will draw all lawyers together, putting other concerns into perspective. It seems likely that in ten years the managing partners of large and small law firms and the deans of American law schools will gather over drinks to discuss with bemusement the rankings and other silliness that obsessed the profession during the 1990s and 2000s.

This book takes the broadest possible view of these changes, considering the past, present, and future of small-firm and solo practitioners, Big Law, and law schools, rather than just addressing one or the other piecemeal. Each of the trends identified herein is worthy of its own book and rich in detail, but in order to draw the strands together some generalizations are necessary and helpful.

This book also situates the legal profession within a broader context. For example, short-term thinking, competition, and venality are the cause of much of the current crisis. Big Law and law schools have each been engaged in their own self-destructive rankings competitions (over the *Am Law 100* and *U.S. News* rankings, respectively). The battle to inch up in these rankings has twisted the core values of longstanding institutions, ruined internal cultures, and encouraged cheating. This process of corner-cutting, eschewing long-term planning, and destroying reputational capital in return for a quick payoff are part of a bigger American trend, as the spate of recent financial crises and fraud demonstrates.

Similarly, law schools are facing a crisis of confidence from current and potential students over employment numbers, tuition, and debt levels. Law school appears to be a bad choice for many college graduates. Yet there are few good choices for the millennial generation. The days when a college or graduate degree could guarantee steady employment and a middle-class lifestyle appear, at least for now, to be in the past.

The law school crisis is just part of a broader higher education crunch. Glenn Reynolds has called law school the canary in the coal mine for the higher educational bubble.[12] Law schools are currently facing close scrutiny about their return on investment, but those same questions will trickle down to other graduate and undergraduate programs that cost much more than they did a generation ago, generate a mass of student loan debt, and do not offer great career prospects.

The book is divided into three parts. Part I covers American lawyers, focusing on the private practice of law. Historically (and still) there are four different legal professions: lawyers who work in small firms or solo practice, lawyers who work for the government, lawyers who work in-house for corporations, and lawyers who work in big firms (firms of fifty lawyers or more). Before 1876, the great bulk of American lawyers worked in small firms or as solo practitioners. Large firms and corporate counsel were unheard of.

From the industrial revolution forward, the number of government, corporate, and big-firm lawyers grew, with an especially large boom after World War II. This book is mostly about the private practice of law, but the recent significance of corporate counsel and government lawyers is mentioned throughout.

Part I starts with a brief history of the American legal profession, highlighting four eras. The first era is the mid-nineteenth century period of Jacksonian democracy. Anti-elitism and hostility to lawyers resulted in a period of near deregulation for the legal profession. Bar associations ceased to exist. Entry regulation collapsed. The industrial revolution brought lawyers back from the brink and launched the modern profession.

The second era is the Depression, when lawyer incomes cratered, law schools closed, and there were complaints of too many lawyers and non-lawyers competing over a limited amount of work. During that period bar associations and state supreme courts laid the regulatory groundwork for today's legal profession, with most states requiring an undergraduate degree, three years of ABA-accredited law school, and a written bar examination to become a lawyer. These regulatory changes and the booming post–World War II economy rescued lawyers once again.

The third era is the boom years from 1960 to 1990, when a rising tide lifted all boats. From 1960 to 1990, the number of lawyers grew from 250,000 to 850,000 and earnings grew 6.6 percent annually. The profession more than tripled in size *and* lawyer salaries ran ahead of inflation.

In the last, most recent era, Big Law boomed and small-firm and solo practitioners, who have always made up the majority of American lawyers, fell backward. Between 1986 and 2011 the size of the firms in the *Am Law 100* more than tripled. Over the same period profits per partner also tripled. Eight firms from the original 1986 *Am Law 100* topped 1,000 percent growth in revenues and 500 percent growth in profits per partner. So Big Law continued the trend: it got bigger *and* more profitable. In comparison, solo and small-firm practitioners earnings declined by as much as 34 percent over the period.

Part I then describes the four deaths the legal profession now faces and concludes that law will become more of a winner-take-all market. In-court work and bet-the-company/household matters will remain the province of bespoke lawyers. More straightforward, out-of-court work will face brutal competition.

Part II describes the other half of the equation, law schools. It starts by briefly describing the history of the American law school, starting with the creation of the case and Socratic methods at Harvard in the late nineteenth century. Initially, this elite model struggled to vanquish apprenticeship and cheaper, more practice-oriented law schools that students could attend at night. In the Depression, state supreme courts, the ABA, and the American Association of Law Schools (AALS) teamed up to end the competition by requiring graduation from an ABA-accredited (read: elite model) law school.

After World War II, the legal profession grew and law schools followed along. The growth through the 1970s was rational and reflected increased demand for legal services. The growth since the 1980s, however, has occurred despite poor employment numbers outside of Big Law. Part II ends by discussing the current slowdown in applications and attendance and predicting how law schools will adjust to the new normal.

Part III discusses some big-picture parallels between law schools and the legal profession and then lays out the glass-half-full scenario. For example, Big Law and law schools are largely staffed and run by the same people, lawyers who finished at or near the top of their class in an elite law school. These lawyers are naturally competitive, hierarchical, and path dependent, which explains much of their puzzling behavior. It explains why law schools and (to a lesser extent) Big Law still run on models from the nineteenth century: the Langdell/Harvard model for law schools and the Cravath model for law firms.

It also explains why law schools as well as Big Law have been obsessed with self-destructive rankings competitions. The lawyers who run these institutions are the same lawyers who sweated their class rank and law review membership at a top-10 law school.

The rankings competition is just part of the story. Law schools, Big Law, and plaintiff's-side law firms have all been operated for short-term gain and maximum profit, to the detriment of these institutions' reputations and their future.

Part III also responds to some objections. Lawyers and bar associations claim that computerized legal services and the work of nonlawyers are too dangerous to be trusted and that the low price hides the hidden cost of later litigation to fix errors. Unsurprisingly, they consider the only safe alternative to be a licensed lawyer.

The alleged shortcomings of computerization are overstated. First, the claimed harm is quite speculative. Lawyers have long railed against (and prosecuted) UPL based on consumer protection. Yet, most of the UPL complaints have come from lawyers, not injured clients. Similarly, the complaints and lawsuits against *LegalZoom* have come from lawyers and have generally not alleged any specific harm to consumers other than UPL. If there were a flood of complaints or injuries from *LegalZoom*, then there would be a mass of lawsuits or significant publicity by bar associations or both.

Second, the Internet itself offers significant protection, because there are so many forums for disappointed customers to complain and online retailers are particularly sensitive to online reputation. *LegalZoom*, for example, brags repeatedly about its customer satisfaction and Better Business Bureau ranking.

The irony is that online legal services are likely *more* responsive to consumer complaints than bar associations. Bar complaints are handled in secret and more than 50 percent of complaints are dismissed without investigation. In 2009, there was roughly one complaint to a bar disciplinary agency for every ten American lawyers. Only 5 percent of those complaints resulted in any public sanction and only 0.6 percent resulted in disbarment.

In a similar vein, some critics argue that cheaper legal services may harm society. Perhaps cheaper law will result in increased litigation or some other unforeseen problem. First, in-court legal services are likely to be the least affected by computers and technology. UPL is best policed in court because judges are there to enforce it and because of judicial hostility to *pro se* litigants. This will tamp down any litigation explosion.

Second, the legal services that will become cheaper and better through computers may actually lower litigation rates. If more people had wills, then probate matters would be easier or nonexistent. If more businesses had LLC or partnership documents, then litigation over dissolutions or ownership would decline.

Part III also discusses some changes that are not likely to happen. As long as state supreme courts and the ABA are in charge of regulating the legal profession and law schools, neither institution is likely to radically change. This is because many of the ideas for change—a two-year law school program, tiered licensing, more allowances for non-lawyer practice—might make an already tough market worse for existing lawyers. Lawyer regulators will not want to rock the boat in a time of turmoil and decreased demand.

The best we can hope for from lawyer regulators is desuetude, with continued non-enforcement of UPL and growth in non-lawyer and computerized legal services. The worst-case scenario is Depression-era tightening on entry and stepped-up prosecution of UPL. Ideally, the online provision of legal services is mature and widespread enough that lawyer regulators will try to hold on to the areas they can still protect and allow non-lawyers, computers, and outsourcing to continue to provide out-of-court legal work.

This book is quite explicitly predictive but not prescriptive. I am attempting to describe and analyze the past and predict the future, not to say what individual lawyers or law schools should do in response. Aside from the obvious advice that lawyers will need to be more entrepreneurial and to more clearly determine and state their value proposition, this book is about the shape of the market as a whole rather than how lawyers or law schools should proceed.

Nevertheless, the book closes with the most basic reason for optimism. The American legal profession has faced much worse and come roaring back. Through much of the book the profession appears to be relatively passive and unprepared for the brave new world of computerization and international competition. There are pockets of the profession that will refuse to change and some of those lawyers and law firms will likely fail. There is, however, a long American tradition of lawyer creativity and entrepreneurialism. We live in a complicated world governed by extraordinarily complex legal regimes. American lawyers have long been well-paid guides to this world. If history repeats, lawyers will find ways to remain relevant and employed for as long as legal complexity remains.

A brief history of other downturns demonstrates the extraordinary resilience of the American lawyer. Jacksonian democracy explicitly attempted to break the profession and failed. Lawyers resuscitated bar associations and the industrial revolution created more legal work than lawyers could handle. The Depression presented a much starker collapse in the demand for legal services and lawyer earnings, and post–World War II saw a boom for lawyers that lasted sixty years for Big Law and thirty years for the profession as a whole. De Tocqueville had it right in the 1830s: for better or worse lawyers are part of the DNA of this country. Sharp-elbowed and ambitious, tomorrow's lawyers will find a way to overcome and eventually to triumph. They have before. They will again.

Part I

THE MARKET FOR LAWYERS

2

Birth, Death, Rebirth, Near Death
American Lawyers from 1776 to 1950

THIS CHAPTER IS AN abbreviated history of the American legal profession that places the current trends into perspective. While today's challenges of technology and globalization are without precedent, the American legal profession has waxed and waned significantly over the years. This history can serve as a prologue to analyzing the current crisis.

There are two historical periods that inform our current predicament. The first is the era of Jacksonian democracy, the most recent time that the requirements for becoming a lawyer in America slackened. In the mid-nineteenth century every state loosened their entry requirements, and many states allowed any citizen to appear in court or practice law. This period is relevant because a number of current factors make deregulation of the profession suddenly seem possible. Both the U.K. and Australia have relaxed their regulation of lawyers, American state and federal governments are seeking ways to cut expenses, and politically both the extreme left and right are pushing anti-elitism. The rise of online legal services also raises the possibility of de facto deregulation. These dynamics and the roil in the profession create fertile ground for the first loosening of entry to the profession since the mid-nineteenth century.

The second period is the Great Depression, which was the last time the legal profession faced a similar sustained shrinkage in earnings and what felt like an existential crisis. Bar associations and courts reacted to the Depression by ramping up their regulation of the profession, strongly tightening entry standards, and enshrining the ABA-accredited law school. Bar associations and state courts also stepped up the prosecution of the unauthorized practice of law (UPL). Because today lawyers are again facing a crisis there will be pressure from bar associations and other lawyer interest groups to enforce prohibitions of UPL more aggressively or to make it harder to become a lawyer. Thus, competing and countervailing forces buffet the bar and it is unclear which will prevail, although chapter 13 of this book argues that the status quo or increased regulation is likelier than a revival of deregulation.

We begin in the eighteenth and nineteenth centuries. The earliest American legal historians were generally lawyer-scholars who took a partisan and pro-bar association view. These scholars divide the early history of American lawyers into three periods. In the first period, lawyers grew in expertise, prestige, and importance into the "golden age" of the bar in the early nineteenth century.[1] The golden age was followed by the dark days of Jacksonian democracy, when populist deregulation caused the "demoralization" of the American bar. Finally, the reemergence of bar associations and a rise in lawyer prestige in the late nineteenth century marks the return to excellence.[2] Readers less sanguine about the rise of lawyers in America may wish to provide their own spin on this story.

A.   1776–1830—The Birth of the American Legal Profession

Lawyers became more common in the middle of the eighteenth century as the American economy grew larger and more complex and the profession was well established by the American Revolution.[3] The legal profession was guild-like and locally run. Lawyers worked as solo practitioners or in small partnerships; large firms were unknown.

Lawyers frequently were businessmen or farmers, or held multiple jobs at once. For example, Supreme Court Justice James Wilson was a lawyer and a land speculator in Philadelphia before joining the Court.[4] Likewise, before their respective appointments to the Court, Justices John Blair and John Rutledge served in significant government posts while also practicing law.[5]

Lawyers entered practice through apprenticeship and local court admission.[6] Early bar associations controlled entry regulation, sometimes quite tightly. For example, in Hartford, Connecticut, lawyers founded a bar association in 1783. The bar association created rules for the admission of apprentices and minimum requirements for legal training and admission to practice, because "after the Revolution the number of attorneys increased rapidly and perhaps unreasonably."[7] The New York Bar Association "to prevent inroads upon their practice, made an agreement not to receive into their offices, as clerks, any young men who intended to pursue the law as a profession."[8] There was no formal regulatory control over lawyer behavior,[9] other than the traditional common-law court power to disbar or sanction and the social opprobrium possible in small, tight-knit communities.[10] Some states had attorney deceit statutes that punished fraud on the court with imprisonment or treble damages.[11]

The legal profession grew in prominence and social status throughout this period and served leading roles in the revolution and the formation of the new country. De Tocqueville famously described American lawyers as the closest thing this country had to aristocracy. As of 1831 this was likely true.[12]

B. 1830–1870—Jacksonian Democracy and the "Dark Ages"

In the early and mid-nineteenth century the era of Jacksonian democracy included a broad-based populist attack on elites. The legal profession and the judiciary were natural targets. State governments dismantled not only many barriers to entry but also formal regulation of the legal profession. During this period New Hampshire, Maine, Wisconsin, and Indiana abolished their requirements for appearing in court.[13] In 1800, a set period of preparation for admission was required in fourteen of the nineteen states or territories. In 1840, it was required in eleven out of thirty. By 1860, it was required in only nine of thirty-nine.[14]

As an example of this period's approach to bar admissions, consider this first-hand description of Abraham Lincoln's examination of a potential attorney in Illinois as Lincoln lounged in a bathtub:

> He asked me in a desultory way the definition of a contract, and two
> or three fundamental questions, all of which I answered readily, and
> I thought, correctly. Beyond these meager inquiries . . . he asked

nothing more. . . . The whole proceeding was so unusual and queer, if not grotesque, that I was at a loss to determine whether I was really being examined at all.[15]

Lincoln then wrote a letter to a Judge Logan recommending bar admission: "Examine him, if you want to. He's a good deal smarter than he looks to be."[16]

During the same time period, states moved rapidly from appointed to elected judiciaries. In 1832, Mississippi amended its Constitution to become the first state to elect all of its judges, including those on courts of appeals. Every state that entered the Union before 1845 did so with an appointed judiciary. By contrast, from 1846 to 1959 each new state had some form of judicial elections. In 1850 alone, seven states adopted popular election of judges.[17] By 1865, twenty-four of the thirty-four states elected their judges.[18]

Legislatures in the middle of the nineteenth century launched a significant law reform effort and attempted to codify the common law and eliminate special pleading forms.[19] Consistent with the general populist flavor of the time, codification was meant to simplify the law and break the lawyers' monopoly on court pleadings.

The resulting legal profession was virtually unregulated, quite small, and populated by solo practitioners. Bar admission standards were low and bar associations were mostly unknown.[20] Few lawyers worked for the government or directly for businesses. Many lawyers struggled financially. Many "rode circuit" with the judges, picking up cases as they went.[21] Specialization or partnerships of multiple lawyers were relatively rare and litigation and court appearances dominated.[22]

In each of these reforms state legislatures, rather than courts or bar associations, led the way. This is not to say that courts or lawyers were silent. To the contrary, handwringing was common. One former Mississippi Supreme Court Justice stated that because of elected judges "[o]ur constitution is the subject of ridicule in all the States where it is known. It is referred to as a full definition of mobocracy."[23] Consider this from a lawyer in 1847: "The voice of the multitude is against the legal community. . . . The bar finds no favour at the ballot box. . . . A cry is going out over the land. Radicalism is infectious as the pestilence. The tide of popular will must soon sweep away our prerogative, unless we stay its waters."[24]

C. 1870–1930—Don't Call It a Comeback

Between 1850 and 1900 the United States shifted from an agricultural to a manufacturing economy. The economy grew threefold and by 1900 the annual income of manufacturing was more than twice that of agriculture.[25]

It was a time of radical growth and change for the American bar as well. Lawyers grew in both absolute and proportional numbers. Early (and rough) estimates suggest that in 1850 there were 22,000 lawyers in the United States. That number roughly quintupled to 114,000 by 1900.[26] By 1930, there were 160,000 lawyers.[27] The ratio of lawyers per person in the United States fell in this period from 1 lawyer per 969 Americans in 1850, to 1 in 696 in 1900, but rose to 1 lawyer per 764 in 1930 (because of population growth from immigration rather than from a shrinking profession).[28] Despite the growth in absolute and proportional numbers, lawyer incomes remained relatively high throughout this period.[29]

As the economy changed, the practice of law changed with it. Lawyers spent less time in court and more time in their offices, often working for businesses and corporations rather than for individuals. By 1900, even solo and small-firm lawyers spent more time doing office work than riding circuit or appearing in court.[30] Roscoe Pound noted in 1909 that the leaders of the bar were "client caretakers" whose "best work is done in the office, not in the forum."[31]

In 1872, there were only fourteen law firms in the entire country with four lawyers or more.[32] From 1870 forward the corporate lawyer emerged: first in New York, then in Chicago and throughout urban areas.[33] Table 2.1 (displayed on p. 24) shows this growth by counting the number of "large firms" (defined as four or more lawyers) in the ten most populous American cities of the time.[34]

These "large" law firms worked hand in hand with corporate clients. Rather than serving a revolving set of clients in various litigations, these lawyers built their businesses by serving the same large clients over time. They handled litigation (as lawyers always had), but they also worked to avoid litigation. They drafted contracts and created corporate entities and worked on tax issues. They grew prosperous along with the companies they represented.[35]

TABLE 2.1 Number of Firms with Four or More Lawyers

CITY	1872	1882	1892	1903	1914
New York	10	23	39	64	85
Chicago	2	2	4	23	41
Boston	0	2	2	13	18
Cleveland	0	0	2	8	13
Kansas City	0	0	1	8	13
Detroit	0	1	3	6	12
Philadelphia	0	0	1	5	12
Milwaukee	1	1	2	6	8
Cincinnati	1	1	2	6	8
Buffalo	0	0	3	4	7
TOTAL	14	31	58	141	216

1. The Cravath System

The turn of the twentieth century also saw the creation and propagation of a new kind of law firm management, the so-called "Cravath system," named for Paul Cravath and his law firm, Cravath, Swaine, and Moore. Like other contemporary law firms, the Cravath system relied on longstanding relationships with several large corporate clients, with the firm handling most of their legal work.

Cravath's big innovation was in hiring and training. Most contemporary law firms consisted only of partners. Insofar as lawyers who were not partners worked in these offices, their associations tended to be temporary and non-exclusive, or long term as clerks, without hope of advancement.[36]

Cravath insisted on hiring lawyers straight out of law school rather than finding partners or hiring laterals.[37] These hires had top grades from the top law schools and a well-rounded education. Once hired, Cravath partners trained the associates in the practice: "At the outset of their practice Cravath men are not thrown into deep water and told to swim; rather, they are taken into shallow water and carefully taught strokes."[38] Compensation was (and still is at Cravath) generally lockstep within the firm by seniority, and starting salaries were often set in conjunction with other leading firms.

"Every lawyer who enters the Cravath office has a right to find his life career there—but only by attaining partnership."[39] Those associates who did not advance to partnership were expected to leave the firm, because a "man who is not growing professionally creates a barrier to the progress of younger men." Efforts were made to find soft landings for departing attorneys, at other firms or with corporate clients. Lateral hires were extremely rare, so young partners and associates were "seldom subjected to the discouragement of seeing someone come in over them from the outside."[40] This partnership "tournament," the competition among associates for the possibility of becoming a partner, became the defining feature of the American corporate law firm and the pumping heart of the Cravath system.[41]

History is written by the winners, so it is likely an exaggeration that Cravath truly invented the "Cravath system." Much of it was based on Cravath's own work as an associate for William S. Carter.[42] Likewise, Louis Brandeis reformatted his Boston law firm along similar lines during the same period.[43]

The Cravath system has proven remarkably durable since its inception and despite much fraying around the edges it still forms the basic DNA for Big Law. If you doubt the ongoing vitality of the Cravath system, just read the firm's own website, which trumpets the history and basic tenets outlined above.[44]

2. Industrialization and Technology

Changes in the economy, the law, and technology drove the growth. The rise of the corporation as the dominant structure for business organization, as well as the sheer scale of many of the new corporations, created a raft of complicated and new legal transactions, along with new government regulations.[45] There was thus more lucrative and complicated legal work. Similarly, the invention and popularization of the typewriter and the telephone made it to necessary to have a staff and larger offices, and this allowed for more collaborative legal work.[46]

The law firms of this era were quite different from today's, as they were much, much smaller. In 1872 the largest recorded firm had six lawyers. At the turn of the century the largest recorded firm had ten lawyers. As Table 2.1 shows, a firm of four or more lawyers counted as "large" at the turn of the twentieth century.[47] Also, the ratio of associates to partners was much lower than now; there were generally more partners than associates.[48] The firms worked long term with many of their clients.

Lawyer or client defections were rare. The lawyers who worked in these firms were well paid, but hardly rich. At the turn of the twentieth century, the starting associate's salary at Cravath was $360 a year ($30 a month),[49] a federal district court judge made $5,000, a Supreme Court Justice $10,000,[50] a survey of law professors showed an average salary of $2,564,[51] and a law firm partner in Houston earned $3,000.[52]

Outside of these few "large firms," the vast majority of lawyers still worked in small or solo practices.[53] From the dawn of the American legal profession until the present day a majority (or plurality) of lawyers have worked in small or solo practices representing individuals and small businesses. Corporate law firms were (and are) wealthy and prominent, so their footprint within the profession has always outstripped their head count.[54] As late as 1947, the average American law firm included only 1.64 lawyers and less than 5 percent of law firms had 8 lawyers or more.[55]

To get a flavor for how unusual big-firm experience was in the nineteenth century, consider the backgrounds of Supreme Court Justices. The experience of these Justices is helpful because it establishes that even the most elite members of the nineteenth-century profession generally worked as solo practitioners or in small partnerships. As Figure 2.1 establishes, no Supreme Court Justice had any experience working in a large law firm before the late nineteenth century and law firm experience did not become dominant until the mid-twentieth century.

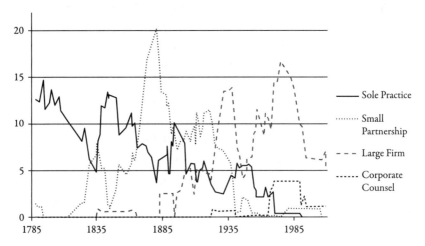

FIGURE 2.1 Pre-Appointment Years Spent in Practice Settings per Justice

The path to entry into the legal profession also changed. Before 1880, lawyers overwhelmingly entered the profession by way of apprenticeships with practicing lawyers.[56] In the late nineteenth and early twentieth centuries, entry shifted from apprenticeships to law schools. In 1870, there were 28 American law schools with 1,600 students. There were 54 schools with 6,000 students in 1890, and 100 schools with 13,000 students by the turn of the century. In 1870, one-quarter of new bar admittees were law school graduates, but by 1910, two-thirds were.[57]

The number and types of law schools exploded.[58] There were full-time, high-prestige law schools attached to major universities; part-time schools; and YMCA night-law schools all operating in the same market. Women and African Americans were largely excluded, but the poor, middle class, and immigrants were frequently able to attend the lower-cost law schools and enter the profession.[59] The massive growth in the number and types of lawyers necessitated the end of the apprenticeship system. It would have been impossible to supply all of the lawyers needed in the new economy through apprenticeship.

The education of Supreme Court Justices demonstrates how uncommon a law school education was in the early and mid-nineteenth century, even for the elite of the profession. Figure 2.2 shows that undergraduate education was somewhat prevalent, but law school did not overtake apprenticeship/reading the law until after the turn of the twentieth century.[60]

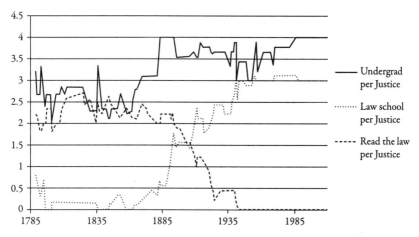

FIGURE 2.2 Education Years Per Justice

3. The Rise of Bar Associations and State Supreme Court Regulation

The 1870s also saw the rebirth of bar associations, first in local, city bar associations and later in state and national associations.[61] The members of these new bar associations were drawn by invitation from the "elite" of practice. For example, the ABA was founded in 1878 in Saratoga, New York, by "seventy-five gentlemen from twenty-one jurisdictions, out of approximately 60,000 lawyers then practicing in the United States."[62]

From its inception the ABA, like other early bar associations,[63] pilloried the undesirable element in the bar and proposed a tightening of bar admission standards. They believed that low admissions standards had contributed to "extraordinary numbers" of the "ignorant" and "unprincipled" becoming lawyers.[64] This subject "received more attention from the Association during the Saratoga era than any other."[65] Much of this criticism was, in fact, aimed at immigrants, African Americans, and Jews who had been able to enter the profession.[66]

The desired changes did not take hold until the twentieth century, but the blueprint was laid quite early. In 1891, the ABA Committee on Legal Education produced a remarkably prescient sixty-page report on entry to the profession. The report recommended a number of changes that would eventually come to fruition, including state supreme court control over entry, written bar exams, a three-year requirement for law schools, and specific law library and facility requirements.[67] The report's very first resolution was to "strongly recommend that the power of admitting members to the Bar, and the supervision of their professional conduct, be in each state lodged in the highest courts of the State."[68]

The ABA's regulatory revolution came in fits and starts, but there were two big events that paved the way. First, state supreme courts all over the country claimed an inherent authority over the regulation of lawyers. Second, the Depression, which crushed lawyer incomes, galvanized the profession and the courts to drastically tighten entry.

State supreme court inherent authority is the most important and least understood aspect of lawyer regulation, so a brief explanation will be helpful. Since the middle of the twentieth century, state supreme courts rather than legislatures have handled almost all regulation of lawyers.[69] This regulatory structure is unique. Every other profession in the United States, from doctors to architects to hair stylists, has to push their regulatory structures through legislative bodies. This is a distinct advantage for lawyers, and helps explain why lawyers can persuasively claim to be the only truly self-regulated profession in the United States.[70] Predictably, self-regulation has proven very helpful to the legal profession over the years.[71]

In most cases state supreme court control over lawyer regulation derives from constitutional decisions claiming an inherent authority over the regulation of lawyers. Because this state court authority is constitutional, the power of the courts cannot be overturned by simple legislation; a constitutional amendment would be necessary. As a result, state supreme courts have broad and almost unreviewable authority in this area.

Exclusive state supreme court control over lawyer regulation is relatively new. In the eighteenth century, courts and legislatures worked together on admission to the profession. Courts always had the power to disbar, but legislatures regularly set the qualifications for practice.[72] As an example of the former legislative power, consider the virtual abandonment of entry requirements by most states during the mid-nineteenth century. That deregulation was driven by legislatures, not courts.

At the turn of the twentieth century, and at least partially at the behest of the ABA and state bar associations, this all changed. *In re Day*[73] is probably the best-known inherent authority case. In 1897, the Illinois Supreme Court, acting on its own inherent authority, decided to raise entry standards and required three years of law school and a written bar exam.[74]

Students from existing two-year law schools (who would have been automatically licensed under the previous regime and who were currently disenfranchised) petitioned the Illinois legislature for assistance. The legislature obliged by passing a law exempting these students from the new rules. When these applicants petitioned the Illinois Supreme Court to be licensed the Court invalidated the Act because the legislature had "assumed the exercise of a power properly belonging to the courts."[75]

In re Day, as well as most of the other inherent authority cases, is based upon the principle of the separation of powers. Article III of the Illinois Constitution stated that "[t]he powers of the government of this state are divided into three distinct departments—legislative, executive and judicial; and no person, or collection of persons, being one of these departments, shall exercise any power properly belonging to either of the others, except as hereinafter expressly directed or permitted."[76] Based on this language, the Court asked whether the power to admit attorneys to practice law was properly in the legislative or judicial department, in other words, is regulating entry to the legal profession a judicial or legislative power?[77] The Court argued that the admission of attorneys was an essential judicial power, because lawyers served as "officers of the court" and are closely involved in the administration of justice.[78]

In re Day was favorably featured in a contemporaneous *Harvard Law Review* article and was widely cited and imitated afterward.[79] By 1936, the inherent authority of state supreme courts over lawyer regulation was well settled enough that the *ABA Journal* published an article on the matter, and courts were using their inherent authority to investigate, and even *sua sponte* prosecute, UPL.[80]

D.   1930–1948—Bust Times

The arrival of the Depression made this inherent authority significantly more important. Courts and bar associations reacted to the changed fortunes of lawyers by clamping down on admission to the bar and UPL.

The Depression was even more calamitous for lawyers than for the country as a whole. The absolute number of lawyers and their incomes shrunk from the Depression until the end of World War II.[81] Median lawyer income shrunk 8 percent between 1929 and 1933[82] and real earnings per lawyer were lower in 1940 than in 1929.[83] According to one survey of New Jersey lawyers, new lawyer salaries shrank from $2,850 in 1925 to $950 in 1937. Senior lawyers grossed $10,425 in 1928, but only $4,850 in 1938.[84] Figure 2.3 (displayed on p. 31) presents the census data for non-salaried lawyers from the relevant period.[85]

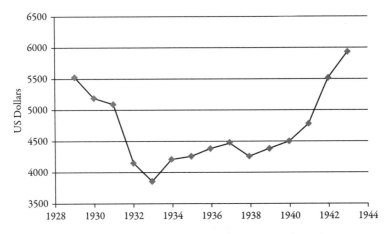

FIGURE 2.3 Average Annual Net Income for Non-Salaried Lawyers

The average net income for a non-salaried lawyer fell from $5,534 in 1929 to $3,868 in 1933. The first time that lawyer income rose above the 1929 average was 1943, when non-salaried lawyers earned $5,945.

Between 1940 and 1948, the absolute number of lawyers fell from 179,000 to 169,000.[86] Attendance in law school declined as well, from over 40,000 students in the late 1920s to 30,000 students in 1940. The number bottomed out at 6,000 in 1943, at the height of the war effort.[87]

Seventy law schools went out of business between 1930 and 1950, and sixty-nine of them were unaccredited.[88] Many of these unaccredited law schools went out of business because of new state supreme court requirements.

Entry standards, which had been rising since the turn of the twentieth century, became more stringent and uniform during the Depression. By the end of the 1930s, most states required some years of college prior to law school, graduation from an ABA-accredited law school (instead of apprenticeship), a set number of years (usually three) of law school, a formal character and fitness test, the elimination of the diploma privilege, and a harder, written bar exam run by a central authority under the unified bar or the state supreme court.[89]

The Depression also saw a ramp up in the shift to the unified, or integrated, bar. A unified bar requires every licensed lawyer in the state to be a member of, and pay dues to, the state bar association. Today, the bar is unified in thirty-six states and the District of Columbia.[90] Many of these unified bars were created during the Depression by state supreme courts exercising their inherent authority.[91]

Obviously, a mandatory bar association has significant benefits for the legal profession. In many of these states, supreme courts ceded control over the profession to the unified bars.[92] Further, like a closed union shop, the mandatory collection of dues and the associated political clout of having *all* lawyers be members of the bar association provided significant advantages to the profession.

The Depression was enormously difficult for lawyers. The gains in self-regulation and the tightening of entry standards, however, meant that when growth resumed after World War II, the profession was well placed to profit. By the end of World War II, the modern legal profession was largely in place. There were high barriers to entry, including graduation from an undergraduate institution (or three years of undergraduate education in some states), three years of ABA-accredited law school, a written bar examination that was long and difficult, and an extensive review of character and fitness. There have been some additional tweaks (like the requirement of taking the Multistate Professional Responsibility Examination (MPRE), regular continuing legal education [CLE], etc.), but the basic structure was already set. There were also strong protections against UPL.

There was a developing, but still fairly lax, set of conduct regulations. Law was (and remains) a profession that is hard to get in to, and harder still to get removed from. Disbarment has always been rare, generally limited to the most easily provable and egregious violations.

The governance structure was also basically set. State supreme courts controlled licensure and discipline in all fifty states, often exclusively and constitutionally under their inherent authority. In a majority of states, the bar was unified, which meant that all lawyers in those states were members of a mandatory bar association. Lawyers were thus poised for growth as the country pulled out of the Depression.

3

From Boom, to Two Professions, to Big Law's Slump

American Lawyers from 1950 to the Present

THE DEPRESSION WAS HARD on lawyers, but the post-war years saw a boom that ran for more than three decades. Between 1945 and the 1980s the legal profession grew exponentially. There were more total lawyers, more lawyers per capita, more law schools, more law students, and more law school faculty and staff. Even as the size of the profession tripled, lawyer income, from solo practitioners to Big Law, rose steadily through the 1980s and frequently outpaced inflation. The absolute amount spent on legal services grew, and legal services grew as a percentage of the Gross Domestic Product (GDP).

From the mid-1980s until 2008 the profession divided. Small-firm and solo practitioners saw their real income shrink, while Big Law continued a spectacular period of growth. By the mid-2000s the private practice of law was more divided than it had ever been. Big Law was rolling and everyone else lost ground or stagnated.

A. 1950–1990—Boom Times Again

The post–World War II boom is exceptional by any measure. The ABA has recorded the number of licensed American lawyers since 1880, as shown in Figure 3.1 (displayed on p. 34).[1]

The number has increased steadily, but especially recently, as demonstrated in Figure 3.2 (displayed on p. 34). Between 1960 and 2011 the number of American lawyers increased by 320 percent.

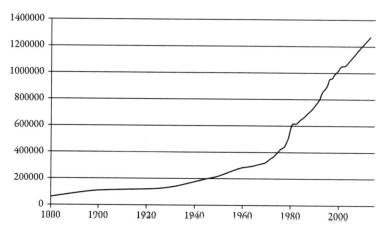

FIGURE 3.1 Number of Licensed American Lawyers—1880–2013

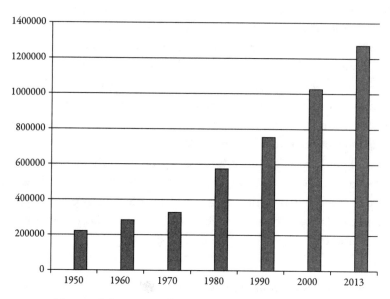

FIGURE 3.2 Licensed American Lawyers—1950–2013

The per capita number of lawyers has grown as well. Consider Figure 3.3 (displayed on p. 35). In 1930, there was roughly 1 lawyer for every 885 Americans.[2] By 1950, it was 1 to 687 and by 2011, it was 1 to 254. The steepest decline occurred in the 1970s. One in 627 Americans were licensed lawyers in 1970; 1 in 396 were in 1980.

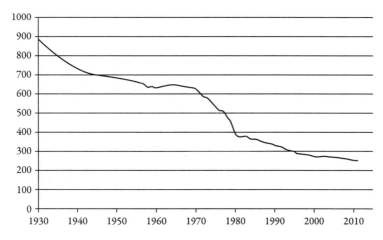

FIGURE 3.3 The number of Americans per lawyer

As the profession grew exponentially, incomes rose as well. From 1920 to 1951, lawyer earnings lagged behind the country as a whole and those of other professionals: the incomes of physicians increased 157 percent, all full-time workers grew 112 percent, and lawyers only increased 58 percent. The period from 1950 to 1978 told a different story, however, as lawyer incomes grew by 544 percent, well above the figure for all industries or for physicians.[3]

How did the profession grow and earn more? Through increased expenditures and demand for legal services. Between 1929 and 1940, America's personal consumption expenditures (PCE)[4] on legal services were basically flat, rising from $402 to $423 million, for a growth rate of 0.5 percent. Between 1940 and 1976, PCE rose to $8.6 billion, 51 percent growth.[5]

Lawyers increased their share of personal expenditures and of GDP at the same time that the economy as a whole was growing rapidly. Figure 3.4 (displayed on p. 36) shows the trend. On the eve of the Depression, legal services were 0.5 percent of PCE.[6] In 1959, it was 0.6 percent, rising to a peak of almost 0.85 percent in 1990 and 2003, and then falling under 0.7 percent in 2011. The last time that legal services were under 0.7 percent of PCE was 1984.

Between 1960 and 1985, legal services' portion of GDP more than doubled (in constant 1982 dollars) from $15 billion to $35 billion. Legal services' proportion of GDP rose from 0.59 percent to 1.17 percent across the same period.[7]

FIGURE 3.4 Legal Services as a Percentage of PCE

When an industry claims a growing percentage of a growing economy, incomes rise. Figure 3.5 demonstrates that between 1975 and 1990, lawyer earnings grew at 6.6 percent annually, and rose almost every year.[8]

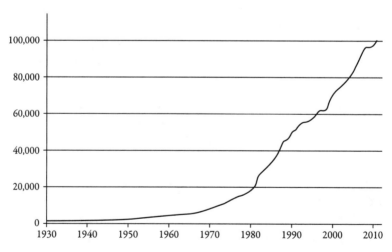

FIGURE 3.5 Legal Services Employee Compensation in Real Dollars

The inflation-adjusted chart (Figure 3.6), however, shows basically flat compensation from 1929 to 1947, a valley again in the 1970s, a boom in the 1980s, and another relatively flat period in the 1990s and since 2008.

FIGURE 3.6 Legal Services Income in 2012 Dollars

Figures 3.5 and 3.6 lump Big Law lawyers in with everyone else. As we shall see, the growth in lawyer compensation has not been evenly distributed since 1990, and virtually the entire rise since the mid-1980s has come from Big Law. Nevertheless, the growth from the 1950s through the early 1990s is impressive because, as Figure 3.7 displays,

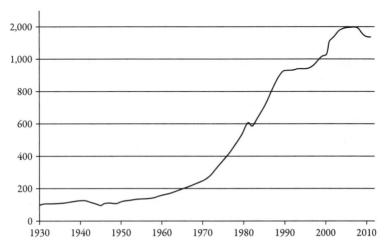

FIGURE 3.7 Legal Services Employment in Thousands

the legal services industry added a large number of both employees and lawyers between 1970 and 1990 and again in the early 2000s, and average compensation rose regardless.

No single cause drove the growth. Factors included the overall growth in the United States economy; increasing legal complexity throughout the period; and the success of bar associations in restricting entry into the profession, which limited the supply of lawyers through the mid-1980s.

The period of strong revenue and income growth between 1950 and the mid-1980s is notable because virtually all lawyers—small firm, solo practitioners, government, and big firm—saw their incomes rise. Because of the Depression, World War II, and the new barriers to entry, there was a limited supply of American lawyers. At the same time, the U.S. economy led the world in manufacturing (in no small part due to the destruction of manufacturing capacity in Europe and Asia) and grew steadily. Limited supply and increased demand floated the profession for thirty years of broad growth.

B.   The Late 1950s and 1960s— The Golden Age of Big Law

Lawyers slowly drifted from solo practice into smaller partnerships and larger law firms. In 1960, about 64 percent of American lawyers were in solo practice; by 1991 the number had shrunk to 45 percent.[9] In 2005, it was down to 37 percent.[10] In the late 1960s, solo practitioners headed 122,000 out of 143,000 American law firms.[11]

Part of the change came from the boom in Big Law. The firms that followed the Cravath system described in chapter 2 truly began to flower. Marc Galanter and Thomas Palay consider the late 1950s and early 1960s the "golden age" for big law firms.[12] Ironically, this period was marked by rampant discrimination against women, African Americans, LGBT persons, and non-Protestant religious groups—certainly not "golden" for most.[13] That term refers to how these firms operated as businesses, not to their personnel decisions.

Law firms grew larger (although still small by today's standards), and profits grew steadily as well.[14] Competition was at a low ebb: lawyers rarely left one firm for another, and many clients were happy to stay with a single law firm in a single city. Lateral hiring was rare. The great bulk of law firm associates and partners were hired directly out of law school or a clerkship and stayed at the firm into partnership, or left to work at smaller firms or as in-house counsel. Associate salaries were generally set at an equivalent "going rate." In New York, the managing partners of the largest firms met annually to agree on these rates.[15] Leverage was very low in comparison to today, but it was high historically. In New York, there were roughly two associates for every partner. Outside of New York it was closer to 1 or 1.5 associates per partner.[16]

"Golden age" firms were much less profitable than today's firms. Even the largest law firms had revenues well under $10 million.[17] Partners were likewise compensated on a modified "lockstep" basis, where tenure in the firm was a determining factor with small adjustments for business generation.[18] The exact calculation is unknown, however, as partner compensation was a taboo topic and largely unknown even within the firms themselves.[19]

Associates were likewise paid well, but hardly the current king's ransom. In Atlanta in 1960 the largest firms paid $300 a month, $3,600 a year[20]—just $27,527 in 2012 dollars. My colleague Glenn Reynolds tells the following anecdote about his father, Charles Reynolds. Charles Reynolds joined the religion faculty of the University of Tennessee as an Assistant Professor in 1969, with a starting salary of $10,800 ($66,705 in 2012 dollars). Just the year before Cravath had unilaterally raised the starting salaries for incoming associates from $10,500 to $15,000.[21] Some firms inside and outside New York tried to hold steady at $10,500, which means that the starting salary for a religion professor at a state university in Knoxville, Tennessee, was more than the starting salary for associates at some major American law firms in 1969. Reynolds does note, however, that the long-term earnings trajectory was considerably less favorable.

Relationships with clients were enduring.[22] Hourly billing was unusual, and many regular clients were billed monthly "for services rendered" with no additional information on the invoice.[23]

The golden age of law firms was a remarkably happy time for American lawyers. While no one would return to the restrictive hiring practices, many contemporary lawyers would gladly sign up for a less competitive, more collaborative environment, solving problems for long-term clients. As we shall see, the tournament of lawyers and natural competitiveness managed to turn the golden age on its head. Big-firm lawyers earned more money, but at a very high cost.

C. 1990–2008—Big Law Explodes, Other Private Lawyers Lose Ground

From 1960 to 1990, the American legal profession experienced a period of almost uninterrupted growth. From 1990 to 2004, there were three recessions for lawyers and the overall growth was slower, under 2 percent per year.

Matt Leichter has created Figure 3.8, which establishes that the current slowdown for lawyers has actually been brewing for a while. Compare the growth in overall GDP with the legal sector's contribution to GDP.[24] The line that trends downward after 2005 (measured by the right axis) shows that, adjusted for inflation, the legal sector has basically shrunk back to its size in 1988. The rising line (measured by the left axis) shows the comparative growth of the economy overall. Taking prices into account the legal profession is just slightly behind where it was in the late 1980s.

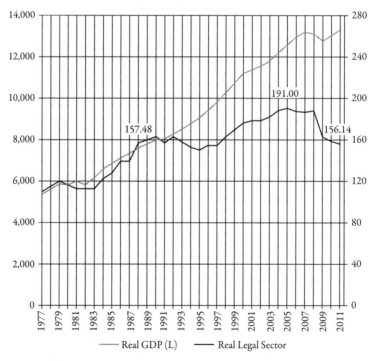

FIGURE 3.8 GDP & Legal Sector Value Added (Billions 2005 $)

All lawyers shared in the growth period from 1960 through the 1980s. The contraction has fallen almost exclusively on small-firm and solo practitioners. As demonstrated below, Big Law exploded between the 1980s and 2008, so almost all of the shrinkage has been felt by small firms and solo practitioners. Many small firms and solo practitioners experienced shrinking real incomes over this period. The average income of a solo practitioner in the United States in 2004 (*before* the recent legal recession) was less than $46,000—about a 30 percent decline, in real dollars, compared to the previous generation.[25] The recession hardly helped: in 2010 the average solo practitioner earned $46,500, a 34 percent decline from 1988.

Despite the slower growth for law as a whole, corporate law firms experienced significant growth in size, earnings, and per partner profits. In 2012, *The American Lawyer* celebrated the twenty-fifth anniversary of the "*Am Law 100*," its annual list of the 100 largest American law firms by revenue.[26] The accompanying growth figures across those twenty-five years are staggering.[27] Revenue increased tenfold: in 1986, the *Am Law 100* collectively had $7 billion in total gross revenue, by 2011, $71 billion. Firm size more than tripled: the *Am Law 100* employed 25,994 lawyers in 1986 and 86,272 lawyers in 2011. Profits per partner, the most treasured measure of firm success, more than quadrupled. The average profits per partner were $324,500 in 1986 (11.3 times the average American's compensation), and only one law firm averaged more than $1 million per partner. By 2011, the average profits per partner were $1.4 million (more than 23 times the average American's compensation), and there were sixty-eight law firms with average profits per partner above a million dollars. Eight firms from the original *Am Law 100* topped 1,000 percent growth in revenues and 500 percent growth in profits per partner over this period.

On at least one measure, the success trickled up. The percentage of American lawyers who work at a big firm rose: in 2011, more than 7 percent of American lawyers worked at an *Am Law 100* firm; it had been under 4 percent in 1986.[28] In 2008, 43 percent of law school graduates that entered the private practice of law started at a firm of 100 lawyers or more, a high-water mark. In 1982 only 15.6 percent did. As a preview of the post-2008 market, this percentage collapsed to 27.7 percent in 2011, the lowest share of law graduates to start at firms of 100 or more lawyers since 1995.[29]

The growth has not been evenly distributed; the biggest firms have gotten even bigger. The *National Law Journal* (NLJ) has published a list of the largest American law firms by head count since 1978. In 2012, it expanded from a top 250 to 350.[30] The 251st largest American law firm in 2012, Post & Schell, had 160 lawyers. In 1978, Post & Schell would have been the 28th largest law firm in America. The 350th largest American law firm, Freeborn & Peters, which had 112 lawyers, would have been the 60th largest law firm. All told, 139,511 lawyers worked at NLJ 350 law firms, with a strong plurality working at the top 50. Using the ABA's count of licensed lawyers, in 2011 more than 11 percent of licensed American lawyers worked at an NLJ 350 law firm.

The growth has accelerated in the top 50. In 2002, the top 50 law firms were 97 percent larger than the next 50 largest firms. In 2012, the gap grew to 123 percent. The growth at the top is not solely in size: the revenue gap has grown as well. In 1986, the revenue difference between the first and the hundredth firm was $191 million. In 2011 that gap had grown tenfold, to $1.97 billion.[31]

Compensation has skyrocketed. In 1986, Cravath, Swain & Moore raised their starting associate salary from $53,000 to $65,000.[32] Between 1997 and 2007, the median starting salary at the nation's largest firms doubled from $80,000 to $160,000,[33] and it has basically stayed at $160,000 since.[34]

D.   Two Professions

In 1976, John Heinz and Edward Laumann conducted a groundbreaking study of the Chicago Bar Association and came to the then surprising conclusion that there were essentially two separate legal professions: lawyers who represent individuals and made a decent living and lawyers who represent corporations and earned much more.[35] Law in America has always been stratified,[36] but the growth of Big Law and the stagnant incomes of the rest of the profession have made the chasm quite marked.

Heinz and his co-authors repeated the Chicago survey in 1995.[37] The distance between the two segments of the bar grew dramatically, with tremendous growth in the incomes and numbers of corporate lawyers, while lawyers in small firms, government, and public-interest practice constituted a declining proportion of the profession and had lower incomes.[38] Many of the lawyers in the second group experienced a loss in real income over the period.[39]

The recent changes in the salary distribution charts for new law graduates, from a rough bell curve to a bimodal distribution, show the trend quite crisply. The National Association for Law Placement (NALP) chart (Figure 3.9) shows the reported salaries for law graduates working full-time as lawyers in 1996.[40] It includes 18,501 reported salaries. In 1996 there were 39,271 JDs awarded by 178 ABA-accredited law schools,[41] so the NALP figures likely overstate the earnings of law graduates, because more than half of the salaries of 1996 law graduates are not reflected in the graph, and more highly paid law firm workers are likelier to report their salaries to NALP.[42]

The 1996 graph (Figure 3.9) shows some smallish humps on the right side of the graph, but it at least approximates a bell curve: the highest point on the graph (representing the greatest percentage of starting salaries) is relatively close to the median salary, while the higher side

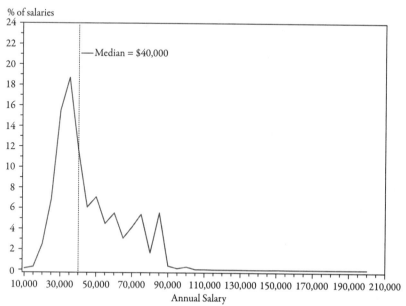

Note: Graph is based on 18,501 salaries. For clarity, salaries above $200,000 are excluded from the graph, but not the percentage calculations shown on the y axis.

FIGURE 3.9 Distribution of Full-Time Salaries—Class of 1996

of the graph tends to cluster around a few humps. There are not two distinct professions here.

In 1996 a good deal of new lawyers in fact earned the median salary. Likewise, the higher, big-firm salaries are close enough to the median that a law graduate would not be shocked at the difference between her possible expectations of law firm life and the reality of government or small-firm employment. Moreover, law school was much less expensive, and thus a better deal for the students, in 1996.

Ten years later, the 2006 graph (Figure 3.10) shows a significant change and a more pronounced gulf between Big Law and the rest of the profession. Again, the numbers overstate corporate law employment. In 2006, 191 ABA-accredited law schools awarded 42,673 JDs,[43] and the NALP graph is based on 22,665 salaries, which is a little more than half of the graduates. The graph shows two rough salary groupings, but given the skew of the NALP data the left-hand peak should be larger and should also probably skew lower.[44]

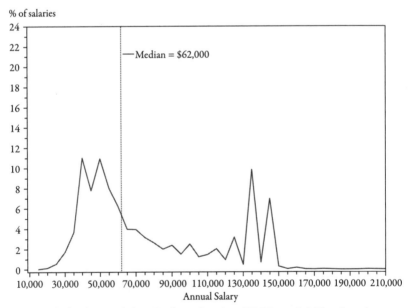

Note: Graph is based on 22,884 salaries. For clarity, salaries above $200,000 are excluded from the graph, but not the percentage calculations shown on the y axis.

FIGURE 3.10 Distribution of Full-Time Salaries—Class of 2006

Few graduates are employed at the median level, and the gap between the Big Law humps and everyone else is extremely pronounced. A student who hoped to work at a big law firm and ends up in a small firm will be disappointed indeed.

The 2011 graph (Figure 3.11) shows an even larger gap, with a sharp peak at $160,000 and everybody else between $35,000 and $65,000.[45] In 2011, there were 18,630 reported salaries,[46] and 200 ABA-accredited schools granted 44,495 new JDs,[47] so the graph does not include well over 50 percent of law graduates' starting salaries. Figure 3.11 thus greatly understates the size of the left-hand hump. The 2012 and 2013 salary distributions look almost identical to the 2011 one.[48]

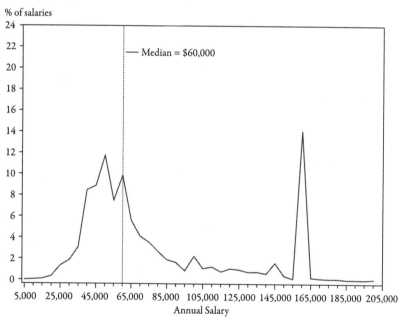

Note: Graph is based on 18,630 salaries. For clarity, salaries above $200,000 are excluded from the graph, but not the percentage calculations shown on the y axis.

FIGURE 3.11 Distribution of Full-Time Salaries—Class of 2011

The recent salary distributions show a very unusual profession. Salaries in most professions resemble a bell curve, with the height of the curve near the mean/median salary. The law graduate market resembled a bell curve as recently as 1996.[49] Since 2000, however, starting lawyer salaries have divided into two very separate groups. The great bulk of new law graduates (and of practicing lawyers) work in the left hump. Inflation-adjusted wages for these lawyers have either held steady or declined over the last forty years,[50] with wages for solo practitioners seeing a 34 percent decline in real dollars over that period.[51]

When the trend reached its apex in the mid-2000s, commentators argued that the bimodal distribution indicated an unhealthy and irrational profession and that it was unsustainable.[52] A simple thought experiment demonstrates the strangeness of the bimodal salary distribution. What are the odds that the last person hired at $160,000 is worth twice as much to her employer as the first person denied that opportunity?

As a counterpoint, consider the starting salaries for business school graduates. In 2009, *BusinessWeek* published graphs for starting salaries for the top thirty business schools, and each of them resembled a bell curve with the peak near the median salary.[53] Likewise, economists Clifford Winston and Vikram Maheshri recently studied contemporary lawyer hourly rates for criminal work, divorce, and estate planning, and their results (Figure 3.12) show classic bell curves.[54]

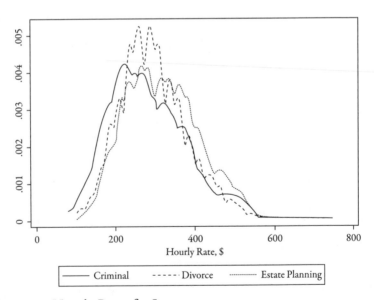

FIGURE 3.12 Hourly Rates for Lawyers

The rates quoted in these three areas tell us much about the non–Big Law private practice of law, because Big Law does not handle most of the business in criminal, divorce, or estate planning. In these areas, the rates charged fall out into a rough bell curve, which presumably represents the highest-demand lawyers commanding higher rates and the bulk of the lawyers in the middle. By comparison, the double-hump graphs show two very distinct professions that are virtually unrelated to each other in salary and earnings.

The trend is also borne out in the IRS data on lawyer earnings. Every year since 1967, the IRS has published the average income for two broad categories of lawyers: sole proprietors and members of a partnership. These two categories are rough proxies for the two legal professions. The partnership measure is actually a slightly depressed measure of Big Law because it includes small partnerships in small communities and does not include alternative business structures like LLCs. Nevertheless, the income gap between these two categories is quite notable.

In 1967, the average income for a solo practitioner was $10,850, and for a law partner, it was $25,280. Adjusted to 2013 dollars, a solo practitioner earned $74,806 and a partner earned $174,295.[55] A law partner earned roughly 2.3 times more than a solo practitioner.

By 1988, a solo practitioner earned $38,393 and a partner earned $98,765. Adjusted for inflation, solo practitioners earned $74,735, a small loss in buying power over a twenty-one-year period. Partners earned an inflation-adjusted salary of $192,254. The gap had widened slightly—partners now earned 2.6 times what solo practitioners did—but the incomes of both groups stayed relatively steady.

In 2010, solo practitioners earned $46,560 and partners earned $354,018. Adjusted for inflation solo practitioners earned $49,741; partners earned $378,210. Partners earned 7.6 times what solo practitioners earned, even after an earnings downturn through the Great Recession. Solo practitioners saw their buying power shrink by over 34 percent from 1988 to 2010.

Figure 3.13 shows how markedly the two lines have receded from each other since the late 1980s.

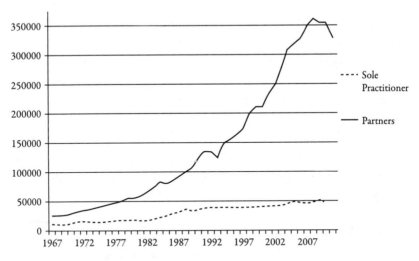

FIGURE 3.13 IRS Income Data

Solo practitioners have lost ground since 2005, but have not faced the declines that law partners have between 2008 and 2011. Partner income declined from an all-time high of $360,794 in 2008 to $327,937 in 2011, almost a 16 percent decrease in real earnings.

Paul Campos compared three different surveys of Alabama lawyers by the Alabama Bar Association from 1985, 1997, and 2009, an analysis that quite markedly demonstrates the decline.[56] The figures below are inflation adjusted to 2009:

17% of Alabama attorneys were making at least $200,000 in 1985 in 2009 dollars, while 8.7% of Alabama attorneys were making $200,000 in 2009.

54% of Alabama attorneys were making at least $100,000 per year in 1985 in 2009 dollars, as compared to 28% in 2009.

In 1997, 76% of Alabama attorneys were making at least $67,000 per year in 2009 dollars. In 2009 approximately 49% were making at least $67,000.

In 1997, 40% of Alabama attorneys were making at least $134,000 per year in 2009 dollars. In 2009 20% of Alabama attorneys were making at least that much.

Perhaps most significantly, 23% of Alabama attorneys were making *less than $25,000* in 2009, and 37% were making less than $50,000.

There are several remarkable statistics here. The decline in income between 1985 and 2009 is stunning. There are still lawyers that make a good living, but it is a much smaller percentage of the profession. Moreover, almost a quarter of the lawyers surveyed, who had practiced for an average of 15–20 years, earned less than $25,000.

That last statistic also tells you everything you need to know about why lawyer oversupply has not solved the access to justice problem. Roughly one-quarter of the lawyers surveyed in Alabama in 2010 are earning less practicing law than they could as a manager at McDonald's, yet access to justice remains an acute problem in Alabama, as it is in every other state. This is because it is impossible to lower the hourly or per transaction fees low enough on individualized, bespoke services to meet the unmet need at an affordable price. Before these lawyers lower their prices further they will leave the practice altogether.

E.   2008 to the Present: Big Law's Comeuppance

The market for all lawyers has taken a beating since 2008. The Bureau of Labor Statistics showed very slow growth in employment in legal services from 2005–7, with an actual loss of total employment in 2008–10. The Census Bureau count of law firm employment, which roughly tracks total Big Law employment, showed a loss of 20,000 jobs between 2004 and 2008, after years of growth.[57]

New law graduates have been the hardest hit. Only 85 percent of the class of 2011 was employed by July 2012, which is the worst percentage since the early 1990s. Even these bleak numbers did not tell the whole story, as the percentage employed in full-time legal work fell to 65 percent, the lowest percentage on record. Likewise, the number of law graduates entering the private practice of law has collapsed, falling below 50 percent in 2011 for the first time since 1975.

The percentage of those entering the private practice of law in a firm (of any size) hit a high-water mark of 64 percent in 1988 and was still 55 percent in 2009. The distribution of employment by firm size, however, changed. Historically small firms (2–10 lawyers) hired more lawyers than large firms (100+ lawyers). The trend reversed in 1998, and large-firm hiring dominated until 2010. The absolute number of law graduates beginning their careers in law firms of 250 or more lawyers has collapsed from 6,100 in 2007 to 3,500 in 2011.[58] The numbers recovered slightly in 2012 and 2013, but are still well below the last few decades.[59]

Even NALP's 2011 estimate that 65 percent of graduates were employed in jobs that required a JD may be inflated. The *Wall Street Journal* calculated the percentage at 55 percent.[60] Professor Paul Campos crunched the same numbers and concluded that only one in three 2011 graduates have "real legal jobs nine months after graduation."[61]

The worst years for Big Law were 2008–10. The *National Law Journal* estimated that the 250 largest firms shed more than 9,500 lawyers in 2009 and 2010, nearly 8 percent of their total lawyers. Profits per partner fell 4.3 percent in 2008 and were basically flat in 2009 (and then started to creep up again from 2010 to 2014). Firms shed equity partners as well: *Am Law 100* firms cut 0.7 percent of them in 2009 and 0.9 percent in 2010.[62]

Revenue grew at a 9.7 percent clip from 2004 to 2008 and just 0.8 percent from 2008 to 2011. Revenue per lawyer at *Am Law 100* firms actually fell slightly from 2007 to 2009, and it has since ticked up a little. Bill Henderson has graphed revenue per lawyer in Figure 3.14, which demonstrates flat growth since 2008.[63]

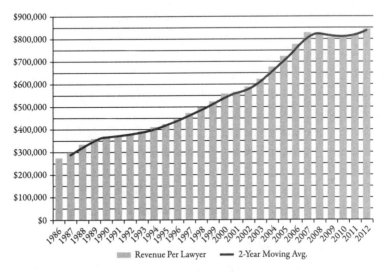

FIGURE 3.14 Average Revenue Per Lawyer (RPL), *Am Law 100*, FY 1986 to 2012

The recent trend is more promising. *Am Law 100*'s issue for 2011 reported small upticks in gross revenues, revenue per lawyer, and profits per partner, and 83 of 100 firms posted revenue growth.[64] The 2012 issue likewise reported modest gains.[65] In 2013 revenues were up, but profits per partner and revenue per lawyer were essentially flat.[66]

The overall revenue trend is a far cry from the boom times.[67] From 2004 to 2008, demand for large-firm services grew at 3.7 percent annually. Growth was –0.04 percent in 2008 to 2012. The lack of demand has meant excess capacity, even with the layoffs and the elimination of partners. From 2001 to 2007, attorney productivity (which measures the productivity of all lawyers, equity partners, income partners, and associates) averaged 1,742 hours per year. In 2009, that number fell to 1,594. Attorney productivity recovered somewhat to 1,641 hours in 2011. Even with less work to bill, realization rates (the percentage of billed hours that are actually paid by clients) have fallen. Realization rates ran in the range of 94 percent pre-recession, but they have fallen as low as 83.5 percent since and have stayed there, as clients have demanded discounts and write-offs.[68]

Even with the downturn, hourly rates have continued to rise despite corporations spending *less* on Big Law. Consider the paradoxical nature of the following graphs from Todd Henderson and Daniel Currell.[69] First, Figure 3.15 shows that average hourly rates in Big Law have continued to rise, even in the teeth of the Great Recession.

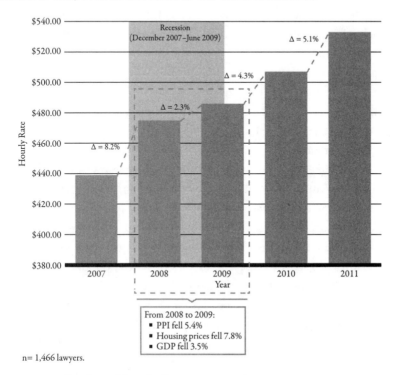

n= 1,466 lawyers.

FIGURE 3.15 Big Law Hourly Rates

Yet, corporations report reducing the amount they are spending on outside counsel. Figure 3.16 shows how corporate counsel answered the question "compared to 2008, our spending on outside counsel in 2009. . . ."

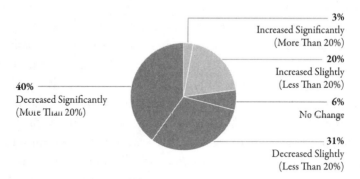

3%
Increased Significantly
(More Than 20%)

20%
Increased Slightly
(Less Than 20%)

6%
No Change

31%
Decreased Slightly
(Less Than 20%)

40%
Decreased Significantly
(More Than 20%)

FIGURE 3.16 "Compared to 2008, our spending on outside counsel in 2009. . . ."

At first glance these data present a contradiction: how can rates rise and overall revenue fall? Part of the explanation is that fewer hours are being billed and fewer of those hours are being realized. Further, "alternative fee arrangements" (i.e., billing by the task, rather than the hour) have become increasingly popular, rising to an estimated 19 percent of law firm revenue in 2013.[70] Billing rates are no longer a useful measure of overall firm health, because those rates are just the sticker price, with significant negotiations occurring in a larger percentage of cases.

Further, Henderson and Currell note that the growth in rates is not evenly distributed: "the billing rates for top performing lawyers have grown at dramatically faster rates than for lower performing lawyers."[71] From 2009 to 2011, partners in the top quartile of large-firm lawyers increased their billing rates by 8 percent and top-quartile associates increased their rates by 18 percent. By comparison, the bottom-quartile partners' billing rates rose only 3 percent, and that of their associates only 4 percent.[72] The same effect can be seen in law firm revenues and profits: bigger is better.[73] This trend continued in the 2012 *Am Law 100*; firms 1–50 had much stronger returns than firms 51–100.[74] The *Am Law*

2013 was even starker: the top 20 firms had banner years and everyone else backslid.[75]

The Great Recession brought a relatively abrupt end to sixty-odd years of exponential and largely uninterrupted growth for Big Law. At every level, Big Law is facing the same separation between the top and the bottom that has affected the profession as a whole since the 1950s. The most profitable firms grow even more profitable and leave their competitors behind. Fewer lawyers become equity partners, which means that more lawyers work for a (relatively lower) salary at more law firms, and fewer receive a share of the profits. Some law firms are hiring two levels of associates: the traditional group is located in the main firm offices and paid $160,000 to start, and the new group is located in a small city, is paid a much lower salary, and is given no hope of becoming partner.[76]

Big Law is separating itself into clubs of haves and have-nots. The top firms continue to grow in size and revenue, and the rest of Big Law stagnates or shrinks. The irony is that Big Law is now reliving the experience of the rest of the profession since the 1980s, as the top pulls away from the middle and the bottom. Over time, these trends may recreate more of a bell-shaped profession, earnings-wise, as the lower end of Big Law fades to meet the upper end of government and small-firm lawyers.

E. Recession or Fundamental Downshift?

Some have argued that the current downturn in the legal market is cyclical, not structural, and that when the economy gets better, the market will return to "normal." For example, Professors Michael Simkovic and Frank McIntyre recently used census wage data from 1996 to 2011 to argue that a law degree was worth approximately $1,000,000 over a lifetime of earnings.[77] The study was criticized for avoiding two large earnings valleys (the 1992–95 law recession and the earnings of graduating law classes from 2009 to 2012) and for overstating historical earnings in light of changed circumstances.[78]

This book argues that these changes are structural and permanent and points to a number of different trends that have led us to where we are. Even Big Law lawyers concur: large majorities of Big Law managing partners apparently now agree that price competition, commoditized work, and non-hourly billing are all likely to increase, which will continue the squeeze on profitability.[79]

The next chapters turn to describing the four "deaths" that are plaguing the legal profession in 2013: death from above, death from below, death from the state, and death from the side.

4

Death from Above
Big Law Stumbles

IN 2009, THE LATE Larry Ribstein famously and presciently declared "The Death of Big Law."[1] Ribstein argued that Big Law faces low growth, higher leverage, fewer partners, increased lateral movement, and slow hiring from law schools, all of which contribute to a coming "death." Current trends make a sudden death unlikely, but long-term deterioration for all but a few firms at the top now seems inevitable.

Ribstein, along with Glenn Reynolds[2] and Bill Henderson,[3] makes a powerful case that the primary reason for the existence of Big Law is "reputational bonding."[4] Clients seek out large corporate law firms because these firms have presumably done the work to select the most able lawyers for the most complicated work. Clients can thus hire a firm by reputation and trust that their work will be handled appropriately. Because law is a credence good,[5] firm reputation plays an especially powerful role in the corporate legal market.

As information becomes more freely available, corporate clients are increasingly concerned with both the price of legal work and its effectiveness. Consequently, the reputational power of law firms is waning.[6] The behavior of law firms seeking ever-higher profits also contributes. Increasing the associate-to-partner ratio and relying on lateral movement erode firm quality control and eventually firm reputation.

The recent collapse of Dewey & LeBoeuf—discussed in greater detail below—is telling because it shows how shallow reputational bonding really is. If a group of partners in a law firm decide that their book of business is worth more elsewhere, they will likely leave. If the firm seems endangered, a mass exodus is probable. If a tipping point is reached, white-shoe law firms that have existed for one hundred years or longer can collapse almost overnight. The truly alarming part of the Dewey & LeBoeuf collapse was that there was so little to the firm. It was basically a building filled with lawyers. When the lawyers bailed, the firm itself was worth almost nothing. In comparison, consider businesses with significant non-human capital. Apple Computers survived years of losses in the 1990s by floating on cash reserves, real estate, and intellectual property. Less happy examples include General Motors and Kodak, which survived through years of losses before eventually succumbing to bankruptcy.

The waning power of reputational bonding tells part of the story, but corporations have also changed their behavior. Corporations have brought increasing pressure on their legal departments to lower costs and demonstrate value in legal expenditures. This has resulted in increased expenditures on outsourcing, insourcing, virtual law firms, and other non-Big Law ways of handling legal work.

As chapter 3 described, Big Law went on a tremendous run from the end of World War II up to 2008, relentlessly growing in size and outpacing inflation in revenue, profits, and profits per partner. This chapter describes the process of killing (or injuring) the goose that laid the golden egg. It starts with a brief description of the Dewey & LeBoeuf collapse, follows with a description of Big Law's business model, and then argues that squeezing every nickel from that model sowed the seeds for the current struggles. The chapter ends by describing how corporate clients have reacted and some predictions on what sorts of legal work Big Law will be able to retain and what kind of work will be lost. The upshot? The richest will get richer and the rest will fall backward toward the pack.

Why we should care about Big Law? Since at least the 1880s the "upper bar" of corporate lawyers has been the bellwether for the American legal profession. They formed the ABA and set the agenda for the law schools and legal profession we see today. They have served at the highest level of government and have been praised as "lawyer-statesmen." Big Law has been the only portion of the American legal profession that has thrived since the mid-1980s. A true collapse would have dramatic repercussions for the entire profession.

One note of caution. Law professors have been predicting the death of Big Law for years with no actual results. *Clearspire*, a virtual law firm that was supposed to be the future of corporate legal services, closed shop in 2014.[7] American law firms are still the biggest and most profitable in the world. There are some data to suggest that we are in a cyclical downturn, not a restructuring, and the 2013 *Am Law 100* report shows some signs of life.[8] Nevertheless, there is substantial evidence of a fundamental restructuring under way.

A.   Dewey & LeBoeuf—A Case Study

Dewey Ballentine was an old, white-shoe Wall Street firm with a sterling lineage. In 1909, Elihu Root Jr., the son of former Senator Elihu Root, and a few other partners founded the firm. In 1946, the firm built upon its excellent provenance by adding Thomas E. Dewey, the former governor of New York and 1940 Republican nominee for the presidency, as a partner.[9] In the twenty-first century Dewey remained a strong player in mergers and acquisitions, but struggled with expensive pensions, overhead, and partner defections. It sought merger partners to ensure survival, starting in 2006–7 with Orrick, Herrington & Sutcliffe.[10]

Those talks collapsed, but Dewey found a match with LeBoeuf, Lamb, Greene & MacRae in 2007. LeBoeuf was another longstanding New York firm, founded in 1929.[11] LeBoeuf specialized in less lucrative, but steadier, work in the insurance and energy industries.

The merger was announced in August 2007. It created a massive firm: at its peak Dewey & LeBoeuf employed 2,500 people, including 1,400 lawyers, across 26 offices.[12] When the merger occurred, Stephen Davis, the chairman of LeBoeuf, noted that size was the key to law firm success. The partners of the new firm joked that "LeBoeuf married up, and Dewey married rich,"[13] reflecting Dewey's longstanding prestige factor and LeBoeuf's financial stability.

Nonetheless, the firm's desire to grow proved its undoing. It launched a lateral hiring binge, luring partners from other firms with lucrative guaranteed compensation packages. In 2010, in the hope that the legal recession was ending, Dewey & LeBoeuf doubled down on its growth plan with even more aggressive lateral hiring, covering what it hoped were temporary shortfalls with loans. These lateral hires created a massive gap between the highest- and lowest-paid partners and placed enormous strain on an already struggling firm.

In the ensuing bankruptcy proceedings the scope of these deals came to light. For example, former partner Michael Fitzgerald has objected to the Dewey & LeBoeuf bankruptcy plan and claims that Dewey & LeBoeuf owes him nearly $38 million in guaranteed compensation, payable in "fixed monthly and yearly payments of an unspecified amount 'not tied to the profits or losses of the Firm' and payable 'even if Fitzgerald was terminated for any reason other than Cause.'"[14] Even more remarkable than the compensation details is the fact that Fitzgerald joined Dewey & LeBoeuf in early *2011*. In the teeth of a massive slowdown in Big Law and months before the firm would collapse, Dewey & LeBoeuf was aggressively adding partners with large, guaranteed compensation packages.

By October 2011, the firm could not pay its bills and informed its partners that compensation would have to be lowered or deferred. Lawyer defections increased. By April 2012, Dewey & LeBoeuf threw in the towel and publicly encouraged its lawyers to "seek out alternative opportunities."[15] The firm ended up in bankruptcy in May, with ninety employees tasked with winding down the business, and partners facing the prospect of "clawbacks" of past compensation.[16]

In October 2013, *The New Yorker* published a lengthy exposé of the firm's collapse.[17] The financial details were already largely known, but the article published insider accounts and e-mails that showed the depths of the firm's dysfunction. Infighting, jealousy, paranoid plotting, and angry, profane, and radically sub-professional language were apparently common as the firm imploded. The Dewey & LeBoeuf e-mails are also front and center in the charges of criminal fraud leveled against former Chairman Steven Davis and three other members of the firm's management team.[18] Nevertheless, save your tears for the citizens of the Central African Republic, as most of Dewey & LeBoeuf's leaders landed on their feet elsewhere, including Davis's deal to be a legal advisor to the United Arab Emirates.[19]

In retrospect, the odd thing about Dewey & LeBoeuf was just how little there actually was to it. Two firms that had existed for more than eighty years and had earned the trust of huge corporations and investment banks folded in a period of less than six months. There is a great scene in the movie *Braveheart*, in which British King Edward Long-shanks learns that William Wallace has sacked the northern stronghold of York. Longshanks pales and notes that if it could happen in York, it could happen anywhere in England. Anyone working in Big Law like-wise blanched as they read the news. If any firm loses enough of their partners, the whole thing collapses. More pointedly, if a firm is just a collection of high-paid laterals that will leave when compensation dips, slowdowns represent existential crises. Nor is Dewey & LeBoeuf alone. The Howrey law firm, founded in 1956, went bankrupt in 2011 after an almost identical run of over-reach.[20]

In some ways the Dewey & LeBoeuf meltdown is too perfect an ex-ample and proves too much. After all, most *Am Law 100* firms persist in relative health even after 2008. Other mega law firms created through aggressive mergers and lateral hiring, like DLA Piper and Greenberg Traurig, are still in business. Likewise, firms failed before and after Dewey & LeBoeuf, so maybe this story cannot tell us much about the future of Big Law.

Nevertheless, Dewey & LeBoeuf is simply the current state of af-fairs on steroids. Consider the recent wave of layoffs at Weil, Gotshal & Manges (though the firm is in no danger of closing),[21] or the searing *New Republic* article detailing the disintegration of the firm culture of Mayer Brown.[22] Law firms are trading on their existing prestige and reputation to try to wring out what they can now. Short-term think-ing and irresponsible growth is the current strategy for many firms. Firms are willing to mortgage decades of firm culture and reputation in return for growing or maintaining profits per partner and revenue.

B.   A Word on the Big Law Financial Model

From Paul Cravath's time to now the elements of profitability at a law firm have not changed all that much. The least-changing element has been the revenue side: law firm revenue comes almost exclusively from bills paid by their clients. Originally Big Law tended to charge by the matter, rather than by the hour. Bills were monthly and "for services rendered."

In the 1950s and 1960s firms and clients transitioned into itemized bills dominated by hourly charges for legal work. George Shepherd and Morgan Cloud place the blame on expanded discovery, which made litigation more expensive.[23] Regardless of why it occurred, this change shifted much of the risk of complex legal work to the client. With fixed fees the lawyers may have faced a loss if a seemingly simple case grew complicated. Hourly fees shifted this risk to the client.

While fixed-fee arrangements are enjoying a comeback, the hourly bill is still Big Law's bread and butter. This may seem too obvious a point to belabor, but consider just how bespoke law still is: the basic product is the hourly work of individuals sold to individual clients. *McSweeney's* recently ran a spoof article entitled "I am an Artisinal Lawyer," in which the lawyer promised to "painstakingly draft" legal documents like "an 18th-century barrister" using a "feather quill" and "linen and vellum" paper.[24] The spoof was particularly amusing because it is so close to the actuality of corporate law. Law firms do not generally sell what *Legal-Zoom* sells, which is broad templates or commoditized work. Or at least they tell their clients they do not sell such work. Corporate law firms work off of templates for creating deal documents, discovery materials, or litigation materials as much or more than any other type of lawyer.

The obvious counterbalance to revenue is expenses. The biggest expense of any American law firm is the salaries of the lawyers. Expenses like office overhead (rent, travel, etc.) and non-lawyer salaries also count. Revenue above expenses forms the profit that goes to the equity partners.

There are three other concepts that are critical to understanding profitability. The first is *utilization*. This measures the amount of work that can be billed given the number of lawyers at the firm, and asks how close to 100 percent capacity the firm is at any given time. It is rarely possible to hit 100 percent (that would mean every lawyer in the firm, from the senior partner to the junior trusts and estates associate, was billing every minute of the day), but the closer to 100 percent the better for the equity partners. Because salaries are a fixed cost, more utilization brings additional profit without adding any other costs (other than the frequently ignored human cost of working too many hours).

The second is *realization*. Realization is the difference between the hours billed by the lawyers in the firm and the amount paid by the clients. Some clients simply default on their bills and others will argue over certain charges and refuse to pay. The gap between the bills that go out the door and the payments that come in is the realization rate. Again, the closer to 100 percent the better for the equity partners, because low realization rates are even worse than low utilization. Some of the lawyer hours that go unpaid could have been spent on other matters that might have been realized.

Last, there is *leverage*. Leverage measures the ratio between the number of salaried lawyers (traditionally associates) and equity partners. A partner I worked with at a Big Law firm once told me "no one ever got rich working by the hour." He was making the point that though he made money when he billed out his own work, he made much more when he billed out the work of multiple associates at a rate far higher than our salaries.

In theory, assuming sufficient work, the optimal law firm will have high utilization rates, will realize all of its bills, and will expand leverage indefinitely. The higher the leverage, the more profit for equity partners, as there are more salaried lawyers creating spillover value. As we shall see below, there are disadvantages to pushing too hard on any of these three factors.

C.   How to Relentlessly Increase Profits?

Because Big Law has billed hourly since the 1970s, there are limited routes to increased profitability, especially since costs rose throughout this period. There was stiff competition for top law school talent, which firms saw as the key product they were selling, so salaries kept jumping up. Cravath unilaterally raised its starting salary to $15,000 in 1968 and from $53,000 to $65,000 in 1986.[25] Simpson Thatcher unilaterally bumped starting salaries from $145,000 to $160,000 in 2007.[26]

How to offset the higher costs in salary? Equity partners could personally bill more hours at higher rates—and they have done that over time—but remember, "no one ever got rich working by the hour." So Big Law has turned to a number of other strategies.

Law firms have greatly increased leverage by shrinking the number of equity partners and raising the number of associates. Law firms have tightened the partner side of the equation in four ways. Fewer lawyers become equity partners. Lower-performing equity partners are asked to leave or are terminated. Firms have gone so far as to eliminate entire practice areas deemed to be insufficiently profitable, like trusts and estates.[27] Many firms have added a non-equity partner track, basically creating a permanent associate class.[28] These moves shrink the leverage equation's denominator.

At the same time, firms have increased the number of associates. Even after the associate attrition of 2008–9, leverage rates have continued to rise. In Galanter and Palay's *Tournament of Lawyers* the authors reported with some surprise that between 1960 and 1985 leverage increased from a ratio of 1.15 associates to partners to 1.45.[29] The *highest* leverage rate in 1985 was 2.86 at Weil, Gotshal. Of 51 firms listed, only 5 had rates above 2.[30]

In 2012, 38 of the *Am Law 100* firms had leverage rates above 4 to 1. Four firms had rates above 7 to 1, with Edwards Wildman Palmer leading the way at 10.7 to 1. Only 3 firms out of 100 remained below the 1985 average of 1.45.[31] Bill Henderson's *From Big Law to Lean Law* offers a great graphic (Figure 4.1) showing the relentless growth in leverage, peaking near 4.5 in 2011.[32]

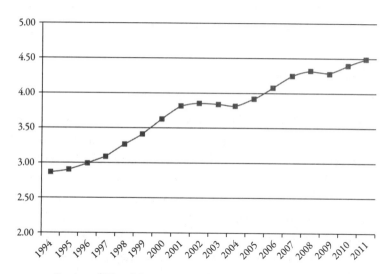

FIGURE 4.1 Ratio of Total Lawyers to Equity Partners (Leverage), *Am Law 100*, FY 1994–2011

In addition to adding to the number of non-equity lawyers, firms have looked to boost utilization, by raising the billable hours target for associates, with the biggest growth in expectations at the largest law firms.[33] Partners are also expected to bill more.[34]

Firms have tried to pass along as many of their expenses as possible to clients, often at a profit.[35] Charges for legal research, copying, word processing, etc. have been transferred from law firms to clients over the years, although post-2008 clients have been far less willing to pay.[36]

Law firms have also attempted to slash overhead and non-lawyer salaries, with staff terminations and pay cuts common since 2008.[37]

Firms have continuously and relentlessly raised their billing rates, even in the teeth of the 2008 recession. Some of that has been offset by client discounts or fixed-fee work, but a big part of the story of Big Law's growth through 2008 was clients accepting continually higher rates.

Many law firms have looked to the lateral market to bring in partners with a significant "book of business" (i.e., rainmakers). Mergers have also been popular, as a hedge against lateral defections. Lateral partner moves increased by 10 percent between 2007 and 2011, while promotion to equity partner fell by 21 percent over the same period. The longer-term trend is even more striking: lateral partner movement in the *Am Law 200* rose from 1,998 in 2001 to 3,012 in 2011. Lateral movement by associates grew even more, increasing by 61 percent between 2009 and 2010 and another 63 percent the next year.[38]

Bill Henderson has demonstrated a significant change in the nature of partner lateral movement: from 2000 to 2008 the bulk of lateral moves were upward: a partner left a less profitable firm to join a more profitable one. Since 2009 that trend has turned on its head, with lateral moves increasingly from higher to lower profitability, presumably because less profitable partners are being shed and forced down the food chain.[39]

Henderson thinks firms are pursuing a "too big to fail" approach through mergers and laterals, theoretically protecting themselves against the increasingly likely event that some partners will leave to greener pastures.[40] An uptick in firm mergers is more evidence of this strategy.[41] Nevertheless, the lateral market has hardly proven a panacea, with 40 percent of a survey of large firms reporting that their lateral moves were break-even or unsuccessful.[42] In a different survey, 96 percent of law firm managing partners expected to grow their firm through lateral partner hiring in the next two years, while only 28 percent related that lateral hiring had been a highly effective strategy in the past.[43] In Bill Henderson and Chris Zorn's comprehensive study of lateral moves since 2000 there was no statistical relationship between aggressive lateral hiring and profits. To the contrary, the most profitable firms have the lowest rates of lateral hiring.[44]

D.   Time to Pay the Piper—How Is Dewey & LeBoeuf Like Oedipus Rex?

Taken together, this series of profit-maximizing strategies have proven to be very destructive to law firms and, since 2008, largely ineffective. Consider how closely Big Law's dilemma resembles a Greek tragedy. When Big Law looks around and asks, "Who destroyed our beautiful city?" the answer is "We did." In classical tragedy the hero is undone by his own best qualities, and there is some element of that in Big Law. It has taken enormous energy and creativity to grow Big Law exponentially at the same time as raising revenues and profits. Nevertheless, the growth has diluted many of the things that made Big Law valuable in the first place: some firms have sold their souls for growth.

E.   What Is It Exactly That Big Law Sells?

Start with the question of what Big Law actually sells to their clients. In the narrow sense, the question is quite obvious: it sells complex legal work. The harder question is why they sell it in the form they do. Presumably, if it were cheaper and more profitable to operate as a solo practitioner or a small firm, then Big Law's lawyers would do so. As noted above, large law firms are expensive propositions. The cost side of the equation—staff salaries, rent, and other expenses—is quite high, cutting into the profits of the equity partners. The structure itself must offer concomitant benefits.

Remember that the heart of Big Law is "reputational bonding."[45] Law firms select and train the best lawyers, and clients can choose those lawyers by firm reputation, rather than attempting to sort individual lawyers based on some other criteria. Thus, rather than standing alone, a lawyer can join up with other lawyers of similar caliber and sell the entire firm to a client.

The "credence good" aspect of legal work seems to make the most sense when an individual is selecting a lawyer, but not necessarily for a corporation. Why would a corporate legal department be forced to rely on something as amorphous as firm reputation in selecting a lawyer? This is especially so in 2013 when the Internet, information sharing among corporate legal departments, and even relatively complex statistical models meant to gather law firm "value" make it much easier for corporations to sort lawyers. In a recent *Wall Street Journal* article a series of general counsels expressed doubts about the viability of hiring a law firm on reputation rather than individual lawyers at different law firms.[46]

The answer transcends sorting; law firms offer significant CYA capacities. Just as "no one ever got fired for buying IBM," a corporate legal department can generally hire a big law firm and if things go south, at least they chose a firm with a strong reputation.

The sheer scale of large law firms also creates the capacity to handle very large or very rushed transactions or litigation matters. From the corporation's point of view there is no need to have an internal legal department capable of dealing with "peak load." When bigger or more serious cases arise, a large law firm can handle it.

From the equity/billing partner's point of view, the firm serves as a vehicle for leveraging her expertise and value. Rather than just selling her time, the equity partner gets to tie her services to the work of other, presumably less valuable lawyers, as well as costs like copying or legal research. As Todd Henderson and Daniel Currell note, this means that the true billing rates of elite lawyers are thus much higher than the actual rate paid per hour: the client is paying that lawyer's hourly rate, plus everything that comes along with it.[47]

Reputation and quality are the two key ingredients. The nature of the growth in Big Law, however, undercuts these two pillars. Bill Henderson and Larry Ribstein argue that Big Law is essentially short selling its reputational capital for near-term profits.

While leverage raises profits per partner, it clearly undercuts the training function of big law firms. Hiring the best was only a small portion of the success of the Cravath model. Law firm training, as partners teach associates to practice law in the "Cravath way," played a key role as well. When there are more than four associates for every partner the training function is hampered (or nonexistent).

Moreover, the hours/utilization crunch has meant that every year partners and associates press to spend more of their time on billable matters. This means that training must either occur while the client pays, or the lawyers must sacrifice precious time to an unbillable matter.

Nor are clients blind to this very problem. Clients have begun to reject paying high rates for inexperienced associates.[48] This rejection strikes at the heart of the Big Law model, which pays top dollar for talent, and then trains that talent on the job, all the while billing out the work to clients. If clients refuse to pay for that work, then leverage, realization, and utilization all take a profitability hit.

Law firms have reacted to this by increasing their lateral hiring of associates and partners. But this dilutes the firm culture. The Cravath system explicitly avoided hiring laterals, because those lawyers would not be trained in the Cravath way. The same problem exists today. Lawyers brought in as laterals are less likely to buy into a firm's internal culture or style of lawyering and are much likelier to see themselves as a portable book of business than an integral part of an ongoing concern. It is a rational perspective. In a time of lateral churn, mandated partner departures, and a radical tightening in the number of equity partners, why would any associate or partner assume working for a firm is a long-term commitment?

If there is any lesson to be learned from Dewey & LeBoeuf, it is that attracting and over-paying significant numbers of laterals does not make your firm more profitable or stable. To the contrary, the lawyers coming in have likely left their old firm in large part because they hope to make more money at the new firm. It may sometimes be for a better cultural fit, but the nature of the lateral market means that the new lawyers are likely to be at the firm for the money as much or more than because of a fit with the firm itself.

The trend of growing through lateral partner hires or mergers is like burning the furniture to heat one's apartment. Each lateral move makes the next lateral move more likely, and makes every lawyer in the firm increasingly concerned with her own portability. In firms with high lateral churn, it is extremely difficult to create a firm-first culture—many of the partners have come from the outside, for more money and sometimes for guaranteed payments. The partners that have come up through the firm are naturally jealous and worried that the laterals are making more or are not carrying their weight. These partners also see that lower-performing partners are asked to leave, again incentivizing business growth above all else.

Big Law has long been seen as a misery-creating structure, but there is something especially insidious about the lateral and merger trend. Dan Gilbert and Jane Ebert's study of happiness levels suggests the debilitating effects of lawyers continuously considering whether they should leave or stay.[49] Gilbert and Ebert ran a study where they gave undergraduate photography students free prints. One group of students were told they could return their prints later for a different choice and one group was told they had a one-time-only choice. The students with the choice to return the print are eventually less satisfied with their print than the students with the one-time choice of a print. Similarly, lawyers who work in the shadow of a potential lateral move are likely to be less satisfied with their work, because they are facing a daily question of whether they are happy with their firm or would be happier and better paid elsewhere. Barry Schwartz's research into how humans struggle when offered too many choices similarly predicts unhappiness from this circumstance.[50]

Size also means limited monitoring. When a law firm has hundreds or thousands of lawyers in offices that span continents it is very difficult for the firm to maintain a consistent firm culture or quality control.

Leverage, the reliance on lateral partner hiring, and firms asking partners to leave if they are insufficiently profitable also corrode the classic law firm tournament of lawyers.[51] In the Cravath model, law firms hire outstanding young lawyers as associates who then compete over a period of years (six or eight or ten) to become a partner. The cream rises to the top, partnership-wise, and all of the associates are encouraged to work hard as competitors.

When leverage is relatively low, the possibility of making partner is meant to motivate the associates to work hard and compete against each other for the prize of partnership. In current Big Law the odds of any associate becoming a partner have shrunk substantially, to the point where large numbers of associates are unlikely to be captivated by the tournament. Widespread lateral hiring also discourages associates. And of course the prize itself has become less attractive: equity partners earn more money now, but they also work much harder and face at least the same amount of pressure as partners as they did as associates.

Because so few associates become equity partners there is great pressure on the traditional "up or out" aspect of the tournament. Some law firms have balked at losing excellent senior lawyers and have thus created a non-equity partnership track, which is typically a sort of permanent salaried associate rank. These salaried employees are likewise no longer motivated by the tournament, and may in fact be embittered by it.

I worked for two years in Big Law and never once considered continuing on to compete for partnership. I found the work interesting and liked my colleagues. Nevertheless, the road to partnership was unimaginably long, the odds too slim, and the payoff too little.

Nor am I unusual. Big Law has been hiring women and men at roughly equal rates for years, but still has relatively few female partners.[52] One explanation is that the tournament as currently constructed requires complete attention to work, at the cost of family or children, and many women (and men) are not willing to make the necessary sacrifices. *Above the Law* published a particularly heartbreaking departure memo of a female Big Law associate.[53] In the memo the associate described her average day in minute detail as she tried to balance her family and career. Her day started at 4 a.m. with her baby crying and hit bottom when she fell asleep in front of her laptop from 9:45 to 11:30 p.m. before grinding out a little more work before bed at 1:30 a.m. The schedule is so grim it is a wonder she made it more than a few weeks.

One Big Law puzzle is why firms have bent so many aspects of the Cravath model, but have stayed firm on high starting salaries and the basic terms and conditions of work. Since the 1960s law firms have generally chosen not to compete on starting salary, instead bunching together on a single, relatively high number. Nor do firms do much to differentiate themselves on the nature or structure of the work, despite evidence that associates are unhappy and that some promising lawyers leave regardless of the salary.

Thus, the quest for profits has brought us to a point where there are fewer owners (equity partners) at the top of larger firms, and the firms are spread across more offices and frequently staffed by lawyers who cut their teeth in other firms. The process is continuing, so perhaps it has not reached a critical juncture yet, but continuous expansion and growth of leverage cannot coexist forever with high-quality work, firm reputation, or firm culture.

The cruel irony? These strategies are not even very successful in the law firm profits-per-partner rat race. Firms that pursue the more traditional Cravath model of few laterals and lockstep compensation tend to cluster at the top of the profits-per-partner rankings.[54] A recent *New York Times* article pointed to Cravath, Debevoise & Plimpton, and Cleary, Gottlieb as examples of extraordinarily successful firms that have lockstep compensation.[55] Each of these firms rank highly in profits per partner—in the 2012 *Am Law 100* Cravath was fifth, Cleary seventh, and Debevoise twenty-first.[56] Likewise, the top firm in profits per partner, Wachtell, works largely in lockstep,[57] as does Davis Polk.[58]

The *Times* noted that lockstep compensation builds firm culture:

> A shared sense of purpose is something you hear repeatedly when discussing the cultures of Cravath, Cleary, and Debevoise. Listen to Michael W. Blair, the presiding partner at Debevoise, and one could think he presides over a utopian socialist community. He throws around phrases like "one for all and all for one" and "we're the one-firm firm." He highlights Debevoise's genteel culture—its teamwork, camaraderie, and decency. The lock-step system, he said, reinforces that culture. The idea is to attract and motivate partners with a shared set of values who want to dedicate their life to the firm, and not just look for the next big thing themselves. "The only way a partner does better is if the firm does better," Mr. Blair said. "Individual success doesn't mean very much here; we're all incented for collective success."[59]

In 2011 Bernie Nussbaum, a longtime partner at Wachtell and former White House counsel and Watergate prosecutor, came to speak at the University of Tennessee. I had the pleasure of having lunch with him, and he expressed similar sentiments about lockstep compensation. He noted that at Wachtell everyone works hard and makes a lot of money, so the young partners do not begrudge the higher payments to the older partners, at least partially because they expect to be an older partner themselves someday. With that goal in mind the young lawyers work hard to build the firm as a whole because that is the key to their future compensation.

There is a chicken and egg problem here: maybe it is easier to be lockstep when everyone makes a lot of money. Nevertheless, it should give the rest of Big Law pause to note that many of the most successful firms have stayed close to their roots and some of the firms that have pursued the modern strategies of growth through laterals and guaranteed payments have collapsed in spectacular fashion.

F.   The Inevitable Result of Continually Raising Rates

Big Law has raised profits and revenue by continuously raising their hourly rates and their charges for various costs like word processing, copying, and legal research. This strategy has a significant downside.

Large corporations (Big Law's bread and butter) have lots of different types of legal work, from litigation to real estate transactions to intellectual property to mergers and acquisitions. In the early years of Big Law, corporations would often have a single law firm do all, or the great majority, of their legal work. For some firms and clients this relationship lasted well into the 1970s. There were always matters that were too small for a large law firm, but generally speaking clients and firms worked together. Like the gentleman's agreements that kept lateral movement of lawyers rare, law firms did not try very hard to poach other clients.

Over time legal work got much more expensive, and corporations reacted in a number of ways, many of which would eventually prove detrimental to the Big Law model. Many corporations stopped using a single firm as outside counsel, and began to divide their legal spend, shopping around and pitting firms against each other to save money.

The wave of mergers and acquisitions that began in the 1980s also meant that longstanding clients were bought or merged, frequently ending long law firm relationships. This destabilized the old model and created a more competitive atmosphere in Big Law. Firms became quite open about "cross-selling," "client development," and even outright poaching.

For a while profits continued to rise, but competition tends to lead to discounting and price discrimination, and post-2008 it clearly has. Despite rising sticker prices (hourly rates) the total amount corporations are spending on Big Law is down and the use of alternative fee arrangements (read: discounts) is rising steadily.

Consider Chester Paul Beach, Associate General Counsel of United Technologies Corporation (UTC), a public company with a market capitalization of approximately $70 billion. UTC has reduced external legal costs from about thirty-three basis points (0.33 percent) of revenue to twenty-two basis points (0.22 percent) over a ten-year period with "no loss in quality of representation." UTC is "passionate about killing the hourly rate" and is "trying to actively destroy the current model."[60]

Comcast has likewise slashed its outside legal expenditures and is insisting on alternative billing.[61]

Similarly, corporate clients are objecting to a whole raft of previously billable items. Clients have started refusing to allow first- or second-year associates to staff their matters. UTC, for example, does not allow first- and second-year associates on projects without "special permission" because they "are worthless."[62] Clients are also objecting to copying costs, legal research fees, and word processing.[63]

Corporate legal departments have begun to band together, share information, and bring concentrated pressure on Big Law. The Association of Corporate Counsel has launched a "Value Challenge . . . an initiative to reconnect the value and the cost of legal services" and lists "in-house value champions" and their strategies for holding down costs.[64]

The billing issues are small potatoes in comparison to the growth of in-house legal departments.[65] Objections to bills and alternative fees just mean less money for the same volume of work. The structural change in corporate counsel means the disappearance of some work altogether. Corporate law departments have grown larger and more powerful. The general counsel, and not outside counsel, is now the main source of legal counsel and advice to corporate leadership, and is in charge of divvying up the work.[66] The Association of Corporate Counsel's 2011 census showed growth of in-house legal departments through the recession, as well as indicating "that in-house counsel are turning less frequently to outside counsel to handle their legal matters and they are handling more work in-house."[67]

The *Harvard Business Review* noted the change in the nature and stature of in-house counsel. These offices no longer are staffed by former Big Law generalists, but by a bevy of high-quality specialists, headed up by a general counsel who is involved at all levels of corporate decision-making. The *Harvard Business Review*'s upshot? Larger and better in-house counsel's offices mean "a smaller total legal spend (inside plus outside) for the company."[68]

In another change, in-house legal departments have begun to hire directly out of law school, rather than after a stretch in Big Law.[69] Consider the NALP hiring data. In 1992, 59 percent of law graduates started at a law firm and 8.9 percent started in business. Twenty years later the law firm percentage had fallen to 49.5 percent (an all-time low) and the business percentage jumped to 18.1 percent.[70] Some of those graduates are working in non-JD-required jobs, but some are working directly as in-house counsel.

The advantage to hiring and training in-house lawyers fresh from law school is that they are trained from the beginning into the corporate counsel mindset. Law firm "training emphasis is on putting out fires, whereas in-house counsel focus on preventing them."[71] Note that corporate counsel's offices are thus adopting a modified "Cravath model," at the same time that law firms are abandoning hiring new lawyers.

More importantly, one of the great legacies of building in-house legal departments from former Big Law lawyers is a natural affinity for Big Law. In essence, corporate law departments have been hiring hammers, and to a hammer most problems look like nails. When facing a project or a case too large to handle in-house, a former Big Law lawyer naturally assumes Big Law is the solution. Lawyers trained in-house or non-lawyers that control legal budgets are much more likely to consider insourcing, alternative law firms, outsourcing, or computerization.

In-house counsel is, in fact, using a bevy of lower-cost options to replace some of the work that Big Law used to handle. The most famous of these are the virtual law firms. *Axiom* is a prime example.[72] *Axiom* was started by a former Big Law lawyer and offers corporate clients access to over 1,000 former Big Law associates across three continents. *Axiom* claims $130 million in revenues and 35 percent annual growth.[73] A 2013 influx of venture capital suggests a company valuation of roughly $500 million.[74] *Axiom* is able to charge clients less by focusing on process innovation and radically low fixed costs, skipping Big Law's large staffs and expensive offices. The *Axiom* lawyers also do not face the partnership rat race or the hourly billing requirements of Big Law.[75] *Valorem* runs on a similar model, a collection of trial lawyers committed to task billing and efficiencies in corporate litigation.[76]

Axiom is a close cousin to Big Law. It is a different structure for highly qualified U.S. lawyers, providing soup-to-nuts representation to corporations. Outsourcing is a different matter. *Pangea3* is a fast-growing "legal process outsourcing" (LPO) firm that employees English-speaking and common-law-trained lawyers in India to do legal work such as document review or due diligence that used to be done in the United States[77] *Pangea3* claims to have grown 40–60 percent a year since its founding in 2004, and currently employees 850 lawyers.[78] *Pangea3* was successful enough to be purchased by the legal information giant Thomson Reuters in 2010.[79] As of yet, LPO work has passed muster under state prohibitions of the unauthorized practice of law (UPL) because the LPO provider works under a licensed lawyer, who is ultimately responsible for the work.[80]

Outsourcing is still a second cousin to Big Law: it is paying humans to do legal work. Computerized LPO vendors are offering a completely different version of the product: routine and large-scale discovery and due diligence work, which has heretofore been done by imperfect humans, is instead done by powerful computers. Both *The Atlantic* and *the Wall Street Journal* have highlighted the advantages in accuracy and cost of using computers to do large-scale discovery work.[81] The computer programmers who set up the systems claim that they are radically cheaper *and* more accurate than humans.[82]

Anyone who worked in Big Law in the 1990s or early 2000s has a story of a massive litigation or due diligence project gone mad: rotating teams of young associates poring over hundreds of boxes of documents in a warehouse, all the while billing their time to befuddled corporate clients. Even at the time it seemed like a crazy and horrible misuse of human capital, let alone a massive waste of money for clients. When something cannot go on forever, it won't, and these sorts of tasks are not coming back to Big Law anytime soon.

Outsourcing and computerization presume that legal work can be broken into constituent parts, and that not everything needs to be done by a highly paid human in the United States. Legal work has been divvied up into a production chain, and right now these companies are focusing on the lowest-hanging fruit: work that hardly seems worth $200–500 an hour. Todd Henderson and Daniel Currell liken the head of this supply chain to a prime contractor, and wonder whether lawyers can stay on top.[83] A similarly critical question is *which* lawyer will sit in the driver's seat. If corporate counsel wrests the wheel away from Big Law, firms will be reduced to being part of a supply chain and relegated to much less lucrative and powerful work.

Has outsourcing and computerization had an effect? Bill Henderson looked at the census data for "Law Office Employment" and compared it to what the Census Bureau calls "All Other Legal Services."[84] Law Office employment has actually shrunk since 1998, while "all other legal services" have grown 8.5 percent annually and 140 percent over the entire period.

The workers in the "other legal services" category are much cheaper. The average job in a law office pays $80,000. The average "other legal services" job pays $46,000. There are still many, many more employees in law offices than in "other legal services" (1,172,748 versus 23,504), but the trend in favor of non-lawyers is clear.

G.   Why Did Law Firms Push So Hard on Profitability?

To a certain extent the question of "why?" is sort of silly. Law firms wring every last dollar out of their model because they can and because that is how markets work. Nevertheless, there is a willful and self-destructive bent to the continuous focus on growth and profits above firm culture and client relationships. Big Law is filled with smart and hardworking strategic thinkers, and yet they have run their own businesses in an increasingly shortsighted manner.

From 1950 into the 1980s Big Law grew steadily and slowly, and the growth generally matched that of the profession as a whole. From the 1980s and onward, however, Big Law boomed, with an unsustainable competition for growth, profits per partner, increased leverage, lateral hiring, and squeezing more out of corporate legal departments.

Some of the motivation was greed, part of it was just the natural inclination for success to breed excess, but a portion of the changes stem from envy. A watershed year was 1986. September 1986 saw the launch of the television series *L.A. Law* on NBC,[85] and 1986 was the first year of the *Am Law 100*.[86] The *Am Law 100* and *L.A. Law* had a very simple message: Big Law was a (very successful) vehicle for making money.

L.A. Law was a groundbreaking legal drama/soap opera, set at a fictional Big Law firm in Los Angeles. The lawyers were good-looking, drove expensive cars, wore fancy suits, and worked in beautiful offices on gripping cases. But most of all, the partners were rich—very, very rich. The first scene of the pilot features fictional super-lawyer Arnie Becker behind the wheel in a Porsche with a "litig8r" license plate. *L.A. Law* (and its progeny like *Allie McBeal* or *The Good Wife*) was a powerful draw into the profession and the new arrivals expected to live the life of Arnie Becker, or at least earn a similar amount.

The irony, of course, was just how dissimilar the office was from a real law firm. The fictional McKenzie, Brackman law firm seemed to have more partners than associates, and it appeared as though the total number of lawyers was ten to fifteen. They met *every day* as a firm to discuss their current business. Criminal defense and divorce law seemed more important than corporate litigation or mergers and acquisitions. In the pilot one of the associates complained about having to bill *1,600* hours a year. Anyone who watched the show and then went to law school expecting to work at McKenzie, Brackman would be surprised indeed when they arrived in the actuality of Big Law.

The launch of the *Am Law 100*, *The American Lawyer*'s list of the 100 most profitable law firms in America, similarly revolutionized how Big Law partners saw themselves and their business. The *Am Law 100* allowed partners at the biggest law firms in the United States to compare size, overall revenues, and their profits per partner for the first time. The original Big Law model was opaque on salaries and profits *within* any individual law firm: comparisons across law firms were out of the question.[87] The *Am Law 100* forced transparency.

The information proved transformational. The year 2012 marked the twenty-fifth anniversary of the *Am Law 100*.[88] As part of the anniversary, *The American Lawyer* interviewed founder Steve Brill about the effect of the *Am Law 100*.[89] In a particularly telling anecdote, Brill says that after it launched he immediately got a call from a partner at O'Melveney in Los Angeles, who complained that partners at Gibson Dunn made more than those at O'Melveney. The revealing quote: "until this magazine came out my wife thought that I made a lot of money, now she sees that I make $30,000 less [than a partner at Gibson Dunn] and she thinks I'm a failure." Brill candidly admits the "bad side" of the rankings: "it made people who were very happy and making a very good living . . . dissatisfied [and] aggrieved."[90]

Humans are inherently comparative, and much of human happiness is derived from our perception of our relative stature among our peer group.[91] Lawyers are an especially comparative and competitive group, so the rankings were like fuel for the fire.

The competition and comparisons extended beyond the legal field. Partners in Big Law could not help but notice that investment bankers seemed to earn more money for less work. Nothing makes a rich person more miserable than working with the ultra-rich. Likewise, many lawyers working in small and medium-sized firms felt the comparative sting of Big Law. In short, the perceived inequities in the system left many more unhappy than happy.

Consider the happiness research on Olympic medalists: bronze medal winners are happier than silver medalists. This is because bronze medal winners compare themselves to the non-medalists, whom they defeated, whereas silver medalists compare themselves to the gold medalist.[92] Competitors who look upward for comparison points are naturally less happy, and the *Am Law 100* created a lot of silver medalists. Nancy Levit and Douglas Linder's *The Happy Lawyer* has an outstanding review of the painful and negative consequences of upward comparisons for lawyers.[93]

H.   Upshot—What Work Will Stay, What Work Will Go

In 2010 Larry Ribstein famously declared "the Death of Big Law,"[94] and yet while growth has stalled, Big Law is still very much with us. In fact, at the top of the food chain things are looking rosier than ever. How can this be, in light of the overall trends described above?

The answer lies in an understanding of the type of work that Big Law will be able to keep for the foreseeable future and the type of work that is getting squeezed out. Dan Currell is an executive director with the Corporate Executive Board, and he spends much of his time surveying corporate general counsels.

He describes corporate legal work as falling into roughly two categories. In one category there is the run-of-the-mill legal work. This is the legal department's traditional budget, which, like any other unit in a corporation, must continuously justify its benefits and cut costs where necessary. It is here that Big Law is losing out. Corporations are bucking up against bills, demanding alternative fee arrangements, bringing some of this work in-house, and looking into outsourcing and computerization. As corporate counsel reimagines its role and disaggregates and parcels out work in the most efficient manner, Big Law's role and remuneration will naturally be reduced.

There is a second category of corporate legal work. This work is complicated and extremely important to the corporation. Think of large mergers or acquisitions, complicated bankruptcies, high-level tax work, or litigation that might threaten huge damages or the loss of a major profit center. These matters are colloquially called "bet-the-company" legal work. In these sorts of cases corporations are much less likely to nickel-and-dime Big Law. The goal is to get the best possible outcome and cost is secondary to quality.

Consider the recent Apple versus Samsung patent litigation. Court documents showed that partners working on the case billed as much as $800 an hour. Expert estimates of the total cost of litigation run from tens of millions to as much as $500 million.[95] Yet, the same experts agreed that it was money well spent. The case was so critical to both companies that cost was the least of their concerns. In these situations the costs of the legal work are dwarfed by the potential business impact, and for companies like Samsung or Apple even hundreds of millions of legal fees is a small amount in comparison to other line item expenditures.

There is a subset of "bet-the-company" cases where litigation functions as a consumption good. In most economic models we assume that corporations or individuals pursue litigation for economic gains: they assume that the costs of litigation will be offset by some future monetary gain. This, however, does not describe much actual human behavior in litigation. This is because sometimes litigation or other legal work is a "consumption good," which means the client is paying for it because it pleases her, not because it makes economic sense. This behavior is remarkably common, even among corporations. Sometimes it is worth the money to drag someone into court or to seek justice, regardless of whether it makes financial sense. Game theorists have demonstrated that humans will punish others for what they consider to be antisocial or unfair behavior, even when it proves costly to the punisher.[96] Fortunately for lawyers, human irrationality is not on the wane, so this type of legal work will remain lucrative.

This also explains the twin features of Big Law pricing: hourly rates are rising at the same time as overall legal spending shrinks and alternative fee arrangements are more common. Increasingly, hourly billing is for cases that corporations do not want to dicker over. This clarifies why the top firms in the *Am Law 100* are separating from the rest: those firms are able to capture more of the highest-end work and get paid accordingly.

The good news for Big Law is that the world is a complicated place, packed with complex law. When it is worth it to do so, corporations will pay a great deal of money to navigate that world, probably even more than they are paying right now, as evidenced by rising hourly rates for the best lawyers.

The bad news for Big Law is that outside of these "bet-the-company" cases corporations are increasingly willing to try cheaper providers. In particular, tasks that seem simple or routine, like document review or due diligence, will continue to be stripped from Big Law. Over time any work that can be routinized and commoditized will be, and over time that work will either be done much more cheaply by Big Law or, more likely, will drift to other providers.

Why will Big Law lose that work? Because if Big Law leveraged their expertise to create low-cost alternatives to their own products they would cannibalize their own businesses, as clients abandoned expensive hourly work for cheap commodity work. This is a regular feature of information-age disruptive innovations. Newspapers refused to create something similar to *Craigslist* (even though they could have), because it would have destroyed their lucrative business in classified ads. This did not stay the reaper, however. Law firms can slow their day of reckoning by convincing corporations not to trust LPO or computerization options, but this is likely a delay, not a reprieve.

These circumstances will exacerbate the winner-take-all nature of the current legal market. Many lawyers who would have made a tremendous living in the Big Law of the 1990s or 2000s will be pushed back toward the rest of the profession, while the firms that are able to continue to draw the high-end work will grow wealthier. As chapter 10 argues, it is also consistent with the broader information-age trend toward winner-take-all markets. When computers and outsourcing replace U.S. workers, a narrower slice of people earn a lot of money and many of the workers who made a good living lose what they have.

I. Is Legal Work More Like an Earthquake or the Weather?

It is also worth asking what type of legal work computers are good at. One of the biggest stories of the information age is the power of computers to crunch massive amounts of data. The algorithms and models that underlie predictive models and search engines can be as complex as humans can imagine and can also analyze data sets of virtually unlimited size.[97]

Nevertheless, as Nate Silver's *The Signal and the Noise* points out, computers and algorithms are only as good as the human understanding underlying the models.[98] The differences between predicting the weather and earthquakes demonstrate this phenomenon. Jokes about weathermen aside, Silver argues that weather forecasting is relatively accurate in the near term and has greatly improved.[99] The combination of better human understanding of what causes the weather and better data gathering has led to more accurate forecasting.

This is only true in the near term, however.[100] One way to measure the success or failure of weather prediction is to compare it to the simplest possible model: a combination of what the weather was like yesterday and what the weather has historically been like on any given day. Within a range of one to three days, current computer models are much better than the rough estimation. At longer periods of time it is roughly equal, and past a week the modern computer models are actually worse than the rough estimate. This is because the weather is extraordinarily complex, and as we try to stretch our predictions this complexity becomes harder to understand and predict.

In comparison, earthquake modeling has not progressed much beyond the simplest model, which uses past earthquakes to calculate the rough odds of an earthquake of any given magnitude occurring in any given locality.[101] The problem with the simple model, however, is that it can only tell us the likelihood of an earthquake happening at any given time. It offers almost no information about when that time might be. So if there is a one thousand to one shot of a major earthquake occurring, that does not mean that one will occur every thousand years. To the contrary, there could be two in twenty years or none in three thousand years.

Over the years there have been attempts to create more complex models that claimed they could predict when an earthquake would actually occur. Unfortunately, these methods have been unsuccessful, many of them performing worse than simple chance.[102] Silver argues that the difference between the weather and earthquakes is that we have a much better handle on the mechanisms that drive the weather, as well as better data. Weather and earthquakes are both extremely complex, but one occurs above the ground and one below, and we do not have sufficient data about earthquakes to create a useful predictive model.

Is legal work more like the weather or an earthquake? Like both of those phenomena, legal work at the Big Law level is quite complicated, frequently involving overlapping statutes, cases, regulations, and customs from different countries. The good news for Big Law is that the interaction of this complexity also relies upon lots of individual humans (politicians, regulators, judges, juries, opposing parties, other corporations, etc.) and computers have a hard time predicting human behavior at the micro level.

Consider the difference in the success of computer programs that play chess and answer *Jeopardy!* questions to those that play poker. Computers have conquered chess and *Jeopardy!*, but poker requires much more of an understanding of and an ability to predict human behavior. This is why it has taken computer programmers longer to conquer poker and why the best players can (for now) still beat the best machines (at least in "no limit" Texas Holdem, the most popular poker game).[103] Current artificicoal intelligence is good enough to beat all but the very best poker players, though.[104]

Human defeat came faster in chess and in *Jeopardy!* IBM's Deep Blue defeated chess grandmaster Garry Kasparov and IBM's Watson defeated *Jeopardy!* champions, but not by imitating human cognition. To the contrary, Deep Blue and Watson triumphed by doing what computers do—performing an avalanche of calculations on a mass of data very quickly—exceptionally well.

Chess is a complicated game, but it has clear boundaries: a set number of squares and pieces and rules for how and where each piece can move.[105] Nevertheless, because of the number of possible moves and the length of the game there are too many possible moves and outcomes for even the most powerful current computer to consider *every* move.[106] Likewise, it is very hard to program a computer to think strategically like a human being.

Deep Blue circumvented these problems with a mix of chess strategy and brute computing power. In order to determine the best move Deep Blue considered many more moves than any human could and also consulted a database filled with the results of hundreds of thousands of chess games played by grandmasters, and could thus choose a move that had been most likely to be successful in the past. Thus a human plays not only a computer, but also the ghosts of grandmasters past. Deep Blue did not defeat chess masters via superior strategy or tactics; it won by performing so many calculations so quickly on such a mass of data that humans were eventually outmatched.

The TV game show *Jeopardy!* presented a much messier problem for computers. It requires an understanding of puns, natural language, and nuance. Watson followed the Deep Blue playbook for defeating humans. It loaded up more data than most humans could memorize and then used a computer capable of completing 200 million searches in a second to analyze each *Jeopardy!* answer to find the suitable response. Watson worked from about a terabyte of searchable text, including the entirety of Wikipedia, a complete dictionary, a complete thesaurus, the Bible, the Internet Movie Database, and other documents. For each *Jeopardy!* answer Watson searched its database using different algorithms and came to an expected best answer. When Watson was sure enough of an answer (the probability that its answer was correct was high enough) it rang in and answered.

Both Deep Blue and Watson triumphed not by beating humans at their own game, but by doing what computers do well (calculations and searches through large datasets) very fast. In law the question is not whether a computer can accurately imitate the way humans think. Rather, it is whether brute computing power and speed can allow computers to reach appropriate answers through different routes. In particular, much legal work consists of analyzing legal arguments and predicting future outcomes like the range of results from an ongoing litigation. Insurance companies already use their vast reservoir of data to set settlement amounts, to determine legal strategies, and to choose which cases to litigate and how. *Lex Machina*, a "legal analytics" consultancy, claims to do the same for IP litigation.[107] Much of the raw data of legal work (briefs, SEC filings, even oral arguments) are publicly available and thus possibly available for a predictive computer dataset. Peter Thiel recently invested in *Judicata*, a high-tech law company that hopes to "map the legal genome" with high-level computerized analysis of case law.[108]

Further, computers do not necessarily need to be better than humans to replace humans. Once data are gathered, software is written, and processes are created, computers are much cheaper than humans. The computer programs that now handle document review claim to be at least as accurate as humans. But even if they were less accurate, if they are 10 percent of the price or lower, computers do not need to be better, they just need to be acceptable.

The bad news for lawyers is twofold. First, lots of legal work is relatively rote. As noted above, computers and outsourcing will swallow this work. Second, even relatively simple computer models of legal prediction can be pretty powerful. For example, an insurance company with sufficient data can use a computer to determine the likely number of auto accidents, the likely number of lawsuits generated from those accidents, the average settlements necessary for those lawsuits, and the likely results for those cases that proceed to trial.[109] Like the simple weather report, this method will miss some of the subtleties a more complex model or an experienced lawyer might find, but the simple model would also not be subject to any biases or preconceived notions. Of course, a computer model does not necessarily have to be better than humans (although they frequently are), because humans are so much more expensive.

Still, much of the legal work done by Big Law is complex and unusual enough that there will be insufficient data for a computer to predict or apply the law. In these situations statistical models face two dangers. One is a problem that is "out of sample," meaning this instance is sufficiently different from previous incidences that relying on the past could result in grave errors.[110] The other is "over-fitting," which is trying to explain every past incidence with a very complex model, rather than looking at the general thrust of the data.[111]

It is also worth remembering that legal complexity is also fluid and growing, as new laws, regulations, and precedents join existing law every day. Technology has itself accelerated this process. Court opinions, statutes, and regulations are all longer than they once were and are now more readily available for analysis, citation, and cross-referencing. Technology has also greatly increased the incidence of cross-border legal problems and interactions between the laws of multiple states on the same transactions. All of this complexity is good news for lawyers. In some ways the future of the legal services market depends on a race between human-created complexity and computer-driven analysis.

Nevertheless, as data collection and analysis get better, at least some legal work that is now considered complex and unpredictable will become easier to predict. Even in complex areas, a mix of statistical analysis and human ingenuity is likely to triumph over humans alone, suggesting that Big Law should be working harder on computerization and data analysis. The upshot of the "Moneyball" era in baseball, when the Oakland A's used statistical analysis to find bargain baseball players,[112] was *not* the elimination of human scouting. The upshot was that the best organizations used human scouts *and* machines to make decisions.[113] The *New York Times* recently reported on a Hollywood script consultant who uses a data-driven algorithm to advise on script rewrites.[114] Savvy lawyers will combine their expertise with data and number crunching to improve performance.

Routine work will continue to slowly drift away from Big Law. Complex representations that involve the interactions of multiple humans and the law will remain the province of highly paid humans (working in concert with computers) for the foreseeable future. That category of work will likely continue to grow more expensive and lucrative over time. Unfortunately, that category of work seems likely to continue to shrink as corporate clients grow more comfortable with computers, insourcing, and outsourcing, and as those replacements for expensive Big Law lawyers improve.

In sum, the lifeblood of Big Law, corporate legal work, is becoming harder to get, and over time fewer lawyers will reap the benefits of that work. Death from above.

5

LegalZoom and Death from Below

CHAPTER 3 LAID OUT a pretty grim reality for small-firm and solo law-yers: adjusted for inflation their earnings have been falling since the 1980s. The causes of this decline are explored more fully in chapters 6 and 7. This chapter argues that, sadly, the bad news is just beginning for this segment of the profession. Computerization has come to the legal services market and solo practitioners and small-firm lawyers are on the front lines. Big Law should not rest easy, however, as the history of disruptive innovations tells us that it may be next.

Lawyers are not alone in this challenge. From the industrial revolution forward, one industry after another has transitioned from individual humans selling individual wares—whether shoes, wagons, legal advice, or account-ing advice—to mass production. Manufactured goods endured the transi-tion first, as shoemakers, dressmakers, and blacksmiths gave way to factories.

The industrial age did not destroy knowledge jobs. Those workers prospered in a bigger, more complex economy. The information revolu-tion and globalization have begun to bring knowledge occupations to heel. For example, small-town accountants who made their living serving individuals and small businesses have seen demand for their services rap-idly decline because of tax preparation and accounting software. When computers replace humans the services become much, much cheaper, and the human providers face lower demand and make a lot less money.

Most solo and small-firm practitioners operate in a manner that would be familiar to their counterparts from 1960 and even 1880. They individually represent small businesses and individuals on a mix of different matters involving business litigation, contract drafting, divorces, criminal charges, or incorporation. These jobs have been made easier by computers and forms, and specialization is more common now even at the small-firm level, but as a general rule these lawyers still make a living offering one-on-one services to individual clients.[1] While the last forty years have not been kind to these lawyers, they are about to see an even greater disruption as computerization becomes more prevalent.

A.   Disruptive Technologies—The Christensen Model

Clayton Christensen's book *The Innovator's Dilemma* presents a model for disruptive technologies that readily applies to lawyers facing a burgeoning online threat.[2] Christensen tackles a puzzling question: How is it that forward-thinking and market-leading companies fail to address disruptive innovations before it is too late? Christensen does not blame shortsighted management. It is often rational in the short term for market-leading companies to ignore disruptive technologies.

Christensen argues that disruptive technologies bring death from below: the competitors start by focusing on a segment of the market that is more low margin, frequently offering a worse product to these customers at much cheaper prices. The producers at the top of the market who are providing the more high-margin goods are at first unconcerned. Why would they worry about losing the low end of the market when they are dominating the higher-margin work? Initially this strategy actually *improves* profitability, as market leaders abandon low-margin work to focus on the most profitable areas. Further, the high-end producers do not want to compete with the low-end producers. The disruptive product is worse, cheaper, and lower margin, so competing in the low-margin market might cannibalize more profitable sales.

But the producers in the lower end of the market eventually master the low-margin work and gradually work their way up the chain to compete for the higher-margin work. Thus, what appears to be the best short-term strategy turns out to be disastrous in the long term.

Christensen offers multiple examples, but the steel industry is particularly evocative.[3] Up through the 1970s, massive integrated steel companies made most of the world's steel. But in the 1960s, a new technology arrived. "Mini mills" could melt scrap metal in comparably tiny electric furnaces to create steel. Mini mills made steel 20 percent more cheaply than large, integrated mills. But, because they worked from scrap, the quality was at first much poorer than the steel from the integrated mills, so the integrated mills continued to dominate the market.

The mini mills competed at first by focusing on rebar. Rebar is short for "reinforcing bar" and is a round steel rod used in reinforced concrete construction. Because rebar is typically covered over in concrete it has few specifications, so it was the easiest product for the mini mills to make. Not coincidentally, rebar was also the very bottom, lowest-margin portion of the steel market. The integrated mills were happy to abandon the rebar market to the mini mills because it was a low-margin, dog-eat-dog market. In fact, when the integrated mills abandoned rebar, their gross-margin profitability actually improved, because they left a lower-margin market to focus on higher-margin ones.

Nevertheless, as the mini mills mastered rebar production and survived a price war at the low end of the market, they eventually moved on to the next tier of the market, angle iron and thicker bars and rods. This segment of the market was higher margin than rebar, but still less profitable than structural or sheet steel, so again the integrated mills ceded this portion of the market to focus on the higher-margin work. Over time the mini mills kept climbing the ladder and they have now driven many integrated mills out of business.

The problem with disruptive technologies is that a rational supplier at the top of the market will have no incentive to compete with them, or pay attention to them at all. Why? Christensen notes three reasons:

First, disruptive products are simpler and cheaper; they generally promise lower margins, not greater profits. Second, disruptive technologies typically are first commercialized in emerging or insignificant markets. And third, leading firms' most profitable customers generally don't want, and indeed initially can't use, products based on disruptive technologies. By and large, a disruptive technology is initially embraced by the least profitable customers in a market. Hence, most companies with a practiced discipline of listening to their best customers and identifying new products that promise greater profitability and growth are rarely able to build a case for investing in disruptive technologies until it is too late.[4]

Bill Henderson has applied Christensen's work to the legal market, focusing on how outsourcing, computerization, and alternative-delivery law firms like *Axiom* may become disruptive to Big Law. Henderson includes a chart (Figure 5.1) to show how these innovations might affect Big Law.[5]

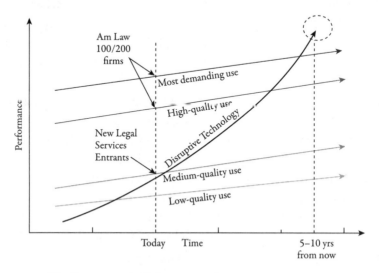

FIGURE 5.1 The Innovator's Dilemma in Law

Henderson focuses on the top of the market and at firms like *Axiom* and *Valorem* that are alternatives to Big Law, but not total replacements of Big Law. Small-firm and solo practitioners are much closer to the rebar market, however, a dog-eat-dog area where providers are battling each other for low-margin work. And it is these lawyers who are starting to feel the bite of disruption.

B. *LegalZoom* **and Interactive Legal Forms**

LegalZoom and *Rocket Lawyer*, among others,[6] have already begun to encroach upon, and may eventually cripple, the business of solo and small-firm practitioners. This chapter focuses on *LegalZoom* as an instructive and well-known example of this phenomenon, but others will also be briefly discussed.

Brian Liu and Brian Lee, two refugee lawyers from Big Law, and Edward Hartman, an Internet entrepreneur, launched *LegalZoom.com* in 2001.[7] Lee and Liu cold-called former O.J. Simpson defense lawyer Robert Shapiro and convinced him to join the company as a spokesman.[8] *LegalZoom*'s mission is:

> to set new standards for convenience and service in an industry not typically known for great customer care. We believe it should be easy for anyone to create a last will, incorporate a business, trademark a name or take care of other common legal matters. For us, the goal is not simply to provide a smart, cost-effective alternative—it's to make sure everyone gets the legal protection they need.[9]

As predicted by Christensen, initially lawyers and bar associations paid little attention to the provision of legal services via the Internet. At first Internet law consisted of chat boards offering very general advice and sites like *LegalZoom* selling various legal forms. The forms themselves were not very sophisticated and were very inexpensive.[10] From 2001 until the late 2000s, *LegalZoom* (and other sites) went about building their businesses and improving their forms and software with little notice or attention from the organized bar.

Given that every state in the union has rules or law against the unauthorized practice of law (UPL), this initial acquiescence is rather puzzling. One answer is that bar associations and judges feared legislative uprisings if they overreached. The Texas Bar Association had early success in barring a similar, off-line program called "Quicken Family Lawyer" as UPL, only to be briskly overruled by the Texas legislature.[11] In some states the prosecution and definition of UPL fall under state supreme court "inherent authority," so the legislature's ability to overturn an aggressive UPL court decision might be limited.[12]

Likewise, in the early 2000s the ABA sought to create a model definition of the practice of law, likely as a precursor to increased UPL enforcement.[13] The Department of Justice and the Federal Trade Commission quickly sent the ABA a comment letter objecting to the proposed definition as overbroad and anti-competitive.[14] Given that the ABA settled an antitrust investigation over its accreditation of law schools in 1995,[15] this letter was a shot across the bow on UPL. Bar associations may have thought that pressing their case against *LegalZoom* might make the situation worse.

LegalZoom and other online forms providers also present a strange UPL case.[16] State bars have long allowed the publication of "forms books" despite the UPL strictures, but have generally drawn the line at the provision of advice along with forms.[17] *LegalZoom* sells both blank forms for customers to print out and fill in themselves, which courts have found to be virtually identical to a formbook,[18] and interactive forms, where the customers answer questions and *LegalZoom* builds out the forms.[19] The latter, hybrid program has puzzled state bars and seems to straddle the UPL line.

Christensen's work explains why lawyers were initially unconcerned with *LegalZoom*. At first *LegalZoom* was not really competing with private lawyers. *LegalZoom* is the classic Christensen disruptive technology—it started by servicing the lowest-margin part of the market and has gradually inched its way up.

American lawyers currently do very little paid work for the poor and the middle class. Gillian Hadfield has done a comprehensive review of the legal needs of ordinary Americans and found the provision of services in comparison to the unmet need "startlingly low."[20] Part of this is because even relatively inexpensive lawyers charge quite a bit by the hour or transaction, and even for straightforward work those hours add up. Given the ever-growing expense of undergraduate and law school educations, more lawyers compete over more remunerative work and eschew the lower end of the market. When the *average* income of a solo practitioner is around $46,500, a lawyer does not have to fall too far below average before she would consider quitting law before cutting her rates further. Regardless of the reasons, solo and small-firm practitioners spend a great deal of time explaining to potential customers that they cannot afford legal services.

In 2001, when *LegalZoom* started out, anyone willing to incorporate their company or write their will on the Internet was very unlikely to be able to afford a lawyer anyway. *LegalZoom* thus was not in direct competition with lawyers, it was merely soaking up a portion of the market lawyers had long since unilaterally abandoned.

The first wave of clients *LegalZoom* grabbed were no loss at all. Clients who could not afford a "real lawyer" and would settle for a form that might not even be particularly suited to their jurisdiction were hardly worth losing any sleep over. *LegalZoom* made no attempt, nor could it because of UPL, to snatch any in-court litigation. This meant that large swaths of small-firm practice (contested divorces, child custody, small commercial lawsuits, criminal defense, etc.) remained unreachable.

Over time, however, *LegalZoom* has climbed the ladder and lawyers and bar associations have started to notice. Estate planning lawyers noticed first. Three recent articles by wills and estates practitioners are sharply critical of *LegalZoom* for UPL and seem quite concerned about the threat to their business and of course an alleged threat to the public.[21] These lawyers have reasons for concern. A colleague recently decided to update his will. He called the lawyer who had written the first will ten years ago and was so stunned by the cost that he built a new will on *LegalZoom* for roughly 1/10th the price.

LegalZoom has faced increased UPL scrutiny as well. A lawyer in Missouri filed a class action suit against *LegalZoom* for UPL in 2011.[22] The case was settled before trial when *LegalZoom* agreed to a small payment and some unspecified changes in its business practices. The CEO of *LegalZoom* stated that they settled the suit "with little change in [the] business, agreeing mainly to pay lawyers' fees"[23] and *LegalZoom* operates almost exactly the same in Missouri as it does in other states.[24]

The Washington state attorney general investigated *LegalZoom* for UPL in 2010. *LegalZoom* settled by paying $20,000 in costs and agreeing not to violate Washington law, while continuing to operate in the state with no changes in its business practices.[25]

In 2014 *LegalZoom* had its first outright victory. The South Carolina Supreme Court held that *LegalZoom*'s interactive forms were substantially similar to forms offered by the Court itself, and thus not UPL at all.

LegalZoom has taken a more proactive stance in North Carolina.[26] The story begins in 2003, when the state bar notified *LegalZoom* it was opening a UPL inquiry into the company's online legal documents.[27] *LegalZoom* responded that it did not provide legal services and the bar dropped the matter.[28]

In 2007, the bar opened a second inquiry over *LegalZoom* forming corporations in North Carolina. *LegalZoom* replied that its business model was the same as 2003 and that it still did not offer legal services. This time the bar issued a "Letter of Caution" ordering *LegalZoom* to "cease and desist" from offering online incorporation documents in North Carolina.[29] *LegalZoom* objected to the findings in the letter, and continued to operate unchanged in North Carolina, with no further legal repercussions.[30]

In 2010, the bar rejected *LegalZoom*'s attempt to register its prepaid legal services plan staffed by North Carolina lawyers, because *Legal-Zoom*'s online forms still violated state UPL restrictions. *LegalZoom* sued the state bar in 2011, pressing for a court ruling that it does not violate UPL. So far *LegalZoom* has survived a motion to dismiss, but the district court has not ruled on the central UPL issue.[31]

In addition to its new, more muscular legal strategy, *LegalZoom* has adopted two powerful non-litigation approaches. First, it has simply ignored the threat of UPL, getting bigger and more prevalent all the time. This is actually its most powerful tool. The larger, older, and more common *LegalZoom* gets, the less likely a court will find UPL and the more likely that a legislature might attempt to overrule an adverse decision. If *LegalZoom* does eventually go public, it will create an additional group of interested parties in any UPL lawsuit: shareholders.

Second, *LegalZoom* has started offering a network of local attorneys to field calls from its customers. *LegalZoom*'s attempt to register this program in North Carolina precipitated the suit described above. *Forbes* described the initiative as "effectively trying to buy off the enemy by setting up a network of local attorneys."[32] These *LegalZoom* lawyers should fear being bought off too cheaply, however. When computers commoditize knowledge work that work inevitably becomes much cheaper.

Regardless of the UPL wrangling, *LegalZoom* has drawn substantial venture capital, announcing most recently that the European private equity firm Permira would buy a controlling stake in the company for more than $200 million.[33] According to *Forbes*, *LegalZoom* matches the venture capital checklist: it is a "disruptive model in a huge, decentralized business" and it "targets the high-volume, low-cost business of providing basic consumer and business documents."[34] Steven Harrick of Institutional Venture Partners described *LegalZoom*'s appeal as follows: "The vast majority of the industry is still practicing law the old-fashioned way and overcharging customers."[35]

LegalZoom filed an S-1 form with the SEC in advance of a presumed initial public offering (IPO).[36] With *LegalZoom*'s sale to Permira the IPO is now shelved, although the S-1 form still contains the first widely available public data about *LegalZoom*, and as one might expect pre-IPO, it tells a rosy tale of growing revenues and future profits. The overview:

> We developed our easy-to-use, online legal platform to make the law more accessible to small businesses and consumers. Our scalable technology platform enables the efficient creation of personalized legal documents, automates our supply chain and fulfillment workflow management, and provides customer analytics to help us improve our services. For small businesses and consumers who want legal advice, we offer subscription legal plans that connect our customers with experienced attorneys who participate in our legal plan network.
>
> We have served approximately two million customers over the last 10 years. In 2011, nine out of ten of the approximately 34,000 customers who responded to a survey we provided said they would recommend LegalZoom to their friends and family. Our customers placed approximately 490,000 orders and more than 20 percent of new California limited liability companies were formed using our online legal platform in 2011. We believe the volume of transactions processed through our online legal platform creates a scale advantage that deepens our knowledge and enables us to improve the quality and depth of the services we provide to our customers.[37]

This description should frighten lawyers. *LegalZoom* generated *20 percent* of the new LLC filings in California in 2011. Astounding! *LegalZoom* reports that in 2011 it formed more than 1,500 LLCs and 200 corporations in South Carolina as well, so California is not an outlier.[38]

LegalZoom served nearly a half a million new clients just in 2011. Some of these customers may not have been able to afford a lawyer in the first instance, but drafting LLC forms or incorporating businesses has long been a staple of legal practice. The loss of 20 percent of that business in California is not a promising sign for traditional lawyers. *LegalZoom* (and its competitors) seem unlikely to stall at only 20 percent of that business.

The uptake of innovative technologies frequently follows an S-shaped curve, where adoption rises slowly at first, followed by a sharp increase and then a leveling off. In Figure 5.2, consumers adopting the technology are shown in the bell curve, and market share is shown in the S curve.

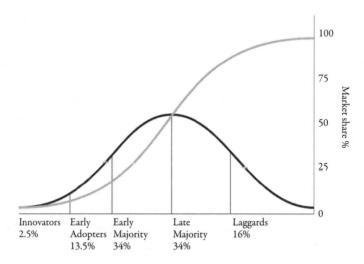

FIGURE 5.2 The S Curve for Adoption of Technology

The 20 percent of LLC filers in California are likely early adopters, cutting a path for wider market acceptance.

Revenue is growing as well. Revenue was $103 million in 2009, $120 million in 2010, $156 million in 2011, rising to almost $47 million in the first three months of 2012. The firm turned a modest profit in 2011 and again in the first quarter of 2012. *LegalZoom* projects even more growth, explicitly targeting the $97 billion that small businesses and consumers spent on legal services in 2011.

LegalZoom first scheduled its IPO for August 2011, and then rescheduled due to "market conditions."[39] Reportedly *LegalZoom* hoped to raise up to $96 billion on $8 to $10 a share, but faced a likelier price of $6 to $8 a share, reducing the company's potential valuation by up to a third.[40] The end result was a private equity sale.

Some lawyers have crowed about the rescheduling of *LegalZoom*'s IPO, arguing that it shows that traditional legal services are stiffer competition than originally thought.[41] The irony is that the *LegalZoom* IPO was hurt by stiff competition from other online forms providers and the possibility that *free* online forms might eventually drive *LegalZoom* out of business, or at least significantly lower their growth potential.[42] In short, the concern about *LegalZoom* is not the existing providers—small-firm and solo practitioners—but rather cheaper or free online forms.

For example, the Legal Services Corporation has started a website of publicly available free legal forms,[43] and some state court systems have as well.[44] These sites do not provide all of the forms that *LegalZoom* sells, but they do overlap to a degree that might worry potential *LegalZoom* investors. Similarly, *Google* owns *Rocket Lawyer*, which is one of *Legal-Zoom*'s primary competitors. *Rocket Lawyer* actually had more unique visitors than *LegalZoom* in October 2012 (being owned by *Google* has its perks), and has been aggressively pricing its forms, even advertising some as "free."[45] In what is probably not a promising sign, *LegalZoom* reacted by suing *Rocket Lawyer* for deceptive and unfair business practices.[46]

LegalZoom also faces competition from websites that offer lawyer review or consultation, along with interactive forms. Richard Granat was a pioneer in the field with his fixed-fee divorces in Maryland at *md-familylawyer.com*.[47] *SmartLegalForms* offers legal forms and legal advice by a lawyer in a package deal, with an explicit dig at *LegalZoom*, calling *LegalZoom* a more expensive "non-lawyer document preparation service" and "the old way" of Internet law.[48]

There are thus legitimate concerns about the future profitability of *Legal-Zoom*. Regardless of the IPO cancellation or the correct valuation of *Legal-Zoom*, it is apparent that the company is currently worth quite a substantial amount of money. The caliber of venture capital involved speaks volumes.

It is likely that *LegalZoom* and its competitors will grow in prevalence and as a source of competition for traditional lawyers. It is also unlikely that *LegalZoom*'s problems—a price war on forms or the rise of free forms—will do much to assist current lawyers. *LegalZoom* is already much cheaper than traditional lawyers, so if the price of online forms collapses (and swamps *LegalZoom*) that will hardly help.

The greater worry for lawyers is that *LegalZoom* and its competitors may eventually be cheaper *and* better. Right now lawyers are reaping the benefits of using interactive computer forms themselves, but *Legal-Zoom* may eventually do a volume of business that will allow them to surpass the quality of individualized work. As *LegalZoom* puts it: "The high volume of transactions we handle and feedback we receive from customers and government agencies give us a scale advantage that deepens our knowledge and enables us to further develop additional services to address our customers' needs and refine our business processes."[49]

LegalZoom may be able to use its volume business to rapidly adopt new elements in its forms that have been approved by the courts or have proven especially effective. If *LegalZoom* can efficiently discern what is working best nationwide, it could stay ahead of the curve in a way that an individual lawyer probably cannot. It could even affect the course of the law by bringing certain types of will codicils or LLC provisions to the fore.

Right now *LegalZoom* is automating legal processes: it is using a machine to approximate the human process. Richard Susskind notes that often new technologies do more than automate, sometimes they *innovate,* "which means they allow us to perform tasks that previously were not possible (or even imaginable)."[50] Over time *LegalZoom* and its competitors may shift from automation to innovation.

Traditional lawyers have tried three responses to the threat of *LegalZoom.* First, if you can't beat 'em, join 'em. *LegalZoom* and *Rocket Lawyer* and other online providers are starting to sell legal services and advice by flesh-and-blood lawyers through subscription or fixed-price models.[51] The lawyers that participate in these services may be more likely to survive the storm, but as individualized services get commoditized, packaged, and sold over the Web, incomes will shrink.

Second, some lawyers are occupying a middle space. Many small-firm and solo practitioner's offices are now essentially a front for online forms providers. For example, the National Law Foundation offers "fully editable forms" to lawyers for "as low as $19," covering virtually every type of legal drafting.[52] State bar associations are creating online databases of interactive forms for use by their members, with an explicit eye toward "competition from web-based companies like *LegalZoom* and Rocket Lawyer."[53]

DirectLaw is among the websites that helps lawyers set up virtual law offices.[54] Virtual law offices promise to make current legal practice easier and more affordable by creating a virtual space to interact with clients and to allow clients to work on forms online for later review by the lawyer. They also help lawyers and clients to shift legal work within time and space (i.e., from any computer and at any time).

There is also the physical space created by *LegalForce* in Palo Alto. *LegalForce* is the brainchild of Raj Abhyanker, a lawyer and engineer who started *Trademarkia,* a website that allowed users to search for trademarks and, not coincidentally, to apply for trademarks.[55] *Trademarkia* is now the biggest source of trademark applications in the world. But *LegalForce*, rather than opting to remain online only, has opened a bricks-and-mortar store in Palo Alto that looks like a high-design Starbucks. Customers can buy books, meet with a (non-lawyer) legal concierge, and if they want to pay a flat fee, meet with a lawyer. It is a sign of the roil in the market when Internet entrepreneurs are starting up physical spaces to meet with lawyers at the same time as regular lawyers are trying to build virtual law practices.

Lawyers occupying this middle space will profit short term, as they charge the same or slightly less for their services, while gaining the benefits of technology. Unless these lawyers are adding value, however, this is a very short-term model. As customers figure out that they can eliminate the middleman—here the human lawyer—this business may eventually dry up.

Lastly, small-firm and solo practitioners will still lay claim to two traditional areas of legal services where UPL has traditionally blocked outside competition: legal advice and in-court litigation. Even these areas are not as safe as they appear.

C.   Online Legal Advice

Legal advice is under some pressure from online providers. First, there is the truly free provision of advice in online communities like *MetaTalk*.[56] The acronyms "IANAL" ("I am not a lawyer") and "IAALBNYL" ("I am a lawyer, but not your lawyer")[57] are common introductions to question-and-answer sessions on legal matters. The advice is general and informal, but it is permanent, searchable, and available to the public.

Other websites attempt to leverage free legal advice into business for the answering lawyers. *Avvo* is a website that serves as an attorney evaluation service and offers free legal advice. Users post questions and attorneys answer them publicly. *Avvo* works like "Ask.com" or other crowdsourcing Q&A sites. The answers are stored, browsable, and searchable. *Avvo* also has listings of lawyers, with a controversial (at least among lower-ranked lawyers), multi-factor rating system. *Avvo* makes money through advertising on the site and selling "Avvo pro," a subscription service for lawyers to track their *Avvo* profile.[58] Thus, *Avvo* leverages its ratings and traffic to draw lawyers into giving free advice with the hope of gaining paid work. *Avvo* draws traffic/potential clients to the site with free advice or ratings.

LawPivot offers more formal and confidential free legal advice. Lawyers answer specific and detailed questions for free, again with an eye toward generating business.[59] *Rocket Lawyer* recently acquired *Law-Pivot*. *Rocket Lawyer* has kept *LawPivot* as a freestanding business, but also plans to adopt the Q&A method on its own site. Richard Granat, CEO of *DirectLaw*, a website that helps lawyers to set up virtual law offices, counsels lawyers to answer questions on *Avvo* or *LawPivot* to raise their online profile and draw business.[60]

LegalZoom and *Rocket Lawyer* are just two of the many websites that are seeking to intermediate between consumers and inexpensive legal advice, taking a cut and lowering the overall price. Even if UPL enforcement suddenly sprang to life against online legal advice, these Internet suppliers would still drive the price of legal advice down.

Like the provision of forms by *LegalZoom*, much current online provision of legal advice is hardly a threat to lawyers. Much of the advice now given for free online was given for free at cocktail parties in years past, with a similar "this is not legal advice" disclaimer. But, like *LegalZoom*'s forms business, the advice business is a serious matter, and *Avvo*, *LegalZoom*, and *Rocket Lawyer* are explicitly targeting small-firm and solo practitioners. As the technology improves, the competitive pressures on traditional lawyers will grow ever stiffer.

D.   In-Court Litigation

In-court litigation, however, will remain a bulwark. In-court representation of clients is the easiest area of UPL for the judiciary to police and it is the area least likely to be attacked by political opponents or lawyer competitors. Since the turn of the nineteenth century American judges have insisted that only lawyers may represent clients in their courts. Appearing *pro se* (without a lawyer) is always allowed and is constitutionally protected in some circumstances.[61] But many American courts have been relatively hostile to *pro se* representation, expecting *pro se* litigants to handle the case the way a lawyer would: with timely objections, correct phrasing of questions, limited argument in opening statements, and so forth.[62] There may be some bend on this issue in *pro se* courts (courts where a majority of cases have no lawyers) like child support or housing court, but in cases where lawyers make their bread and butter, *pro se* representation is likely to remain dicey.

Even in courts with large *pro se* dockets lawyers have managed to suppress some reforms. For example, the Tennessee Supreme Court recently led a statewide effort to address a growing crisis for poor people seeking a divorce.[63] Many of the more aggressive reforms, notably form pleading designed for more complicated *pro se* divorces, were dead on arrival. The divorce bar was not going to stand for any changes that threatened their grip on middle- and upper-income divorces. Nevertheless, as chapter 11 describes, the overall trend is positive, as the ABA's list of resources for *pro se* litigants in all fifty states alone establishes.[64]

To a cynical observer, the plight of *pro se* litigants, and the continuing complexity of American court procedures and evidentiary rules, are just advertising for lawyers. All a potential client has to do is watch five minutes of a confused and struggling *pro se* litigant before deciding to spend the money to hire a lawyer. American courts have operated on this basis since at least the turn of the twentieth century, so change seems unlikely to come briskly, regardless of technology.

In-court litigation is also the sole route to a truly enforceable judgment. Even as mediation and arbitration grow more popular, a litigant that wishes to enforce a judgment through a property or income lien must use a government-run court, and lawyers and judges are, and will likely stay, the gatekeepers to that power. The importance of this power should not be underestimated, because it makes all private dispute resolution second best.

Small-firm and solo practitioners will thus still be able to count on litigation work. Moreover, like the "bet-the-company" cases that will continue to float Big Law, small-firm and solo practitioners have a hardcore class of work that technology will not replace anytime soon and where ability to pay is more of an issue than willingness to pay. Child-custody cases, criminal defense, some divorces, complicated partnership agreements, and tax work are all examples of this type of work. When a middle-class person decides to write a will or a power of attorney she is likely to think hard about using an online provider rather than paying 2–10 times the price for an actual lawyer. This is especially so if the online provider is thought to be of acceptable quality.

But, when a middle-class person is arrested for DUI and faces a manda-tory jail sentence, seizure of her car, and the loss of her license for a year, the question is not whether she should hire a lawyer; it is how much she can afford to pay. Similarly, a client will pay quite a bit to a lawyer to win a bitter child-custody fight.

Some small-firm and solo practitioner litigation work is also a "con-sumption good," purchased for pleasure rather than for economic rea-sons. Nasty divorce cases frequently cost *much* more than the amount the spouses are fighting over. Nevertheless, the litigants pay the fees because the case has become about more than money, and fighting it provides more pleasure (by way of spite) than settling it.

Nevertheless, the number of trials is in a free fall, and every year there is less in-court work to be done. If lawyers (Big Law or small firm) lose the parts of the litigation process that do not occur in court—and they are already losing chunks of the discovery process to legal process outsourcing—keeping the in-court work will be cold comfort indeed.

And litigation itself may not immune from computerization. Online dispute resolution (ODR) has been gaining traction, and court delays and overcrowding make it a more attractive option. Some ODR websites are quite simple. For example, *Cybersettle* is a platform for settlement through a computerized system of double-blind offers and demands.[65]

Other ODR systems aim to reproduce the more substantive process of mediating disputes on the merits, rather than just exchanging set-tlement offers. Colin Rule directed the *eBay* and *PayPal* ODR systems from 2003 to 2011.[66] *EBay* and *PayPal* are natural sites for ODR. They have lots of low-dollar transactions that occur across state and even international lines, making litigation cost prohibitive or simply impos-sible. The *eBay* process proved exceptionally successful, handling up to sixty million disputes a year, and settling approximately 90 percent of them with no human input on the company side.

Colin Rule and others licensed the *eBay* software and launched *Mo-dria,* an ODR system for hire.[67] *Modria* sells a "Fairness Engine" that attempts substantive as well as financial settlement of disputes. It starts with a "diagnosis module" that gathers relevant information. A "ne-gotiation module" summarizes areas of agreement and disagreement and makes suggestions for solving the issue. If these do not result in settlement, a "mediation module" with a neutral third party begins and the final step is arbitration.[68] *Modria* claims that the "vast majority" of claims are settled in the first two steps without a human ever becoming involved.[69] Nor does *Modria* see itself only as a small-claims alternative for e-business: it is targeting bigger-ticket disagreements, as well as complicated issues like patent disputes.[70]

Modria regularly notes the expense of in-court litigation and court backlogs as selling points for its services.[71] *Modria*'s roots are in disputes that few lawyers ever handled—small e-commerce disputes—but its potential is much, much larger. Like *LegalZoom*, *Modria* is backed by fairly serious venture capital.[72]

Online divorce mediation is a particularly hot area. *Modria* and *LawMediaLabs* have created *DivorceMediationResources.com*,[73] an online program meant to change contested divorces into uncontested divorces, in other words to change divorces from work for lawyers to work for online retailers. *Wevorce* is a similar site that uses an online "legal architect," rather than dueling lawyers, to design the parameters of a divorce settlement.[74] *Wevorce* was recently featured in a *New York Times Magazine* article and has drawn high-end venture capital.[75] As litigation becomes slower and more expensive, alternatives are natural and likely.

E.   Today Small Firms, Tomorrow the World

Christensen's work also suggests that Big Law may want to more closely examine what *LegalZoom* and other online law sites are doing in the low end of the market. As these websites improve and master the low-margin work, these entrepreneurs will inevitably target the higher-margin work. Bill Henderson tells a great story about Larry Ribstein presenting his *Death of Big Law* paper to a roomful of baffled and disbelieving managing partners. Their reaction to the proposed threat of *LegalZoom* has been similar: online form-makers could never replace the high-end services they provide.

Is it unimaginable that *LegalZoom* could use its experience in drafting LLC and incorporation documents to begin stealing IPO or other higher-end work? Many Big Law deals work off of similar templates. Mitu Gulati and Robert E. Scott have written a book called *The Three and a Half Minute Transaction* that details exactly how much boilerplate goes into some Big Law work.[76] Gulati and Scott did a massive study of sovereign debt contracts, tracking the appearance of the "pari passu" clause, a clause that had appeared in sovereign debt contracts for so long that its provenance and meaning had become obscured. In the 2000s it rose from obscurity to a new, controversial, and unforeseen meaning in a Brussels court. Nevertheless, Gulati and Scott found that the clause continued to be included without change or clarification in most sovereign debt contracts after the decision. Gulati and Scott argue that the continued use of the clause is explained by herd behavior, even among elite law firms, and the fact that complicated financial instruments like bond contracts largely consist of unexamined boilerplate.[77] Given the relative standardization of much transactional work, Big Law should certainly look beyond their near-term competitors (in-house counsel and alternative law firms) and consider the disruptive possibilities of interactive forms.

The same is true of replacements for litigation. Arbitration has already grown tremendously in popularity, but most arbitration is really "court-light" and still involves lawyers. Mediation or non-lawyer dispute resolution should be of greater concern to Big Law. As *Modria* and other ODR providers improve, corporations may choose to eschew expensive litigation or even arbitration in favor of computerized dispute resolution.

F. The Upshot

Technological changes often come more slowly than we think. Some technological innovations that seem likely to succeed now will never get off the ground. Conversely, successful innovations bring unforeseen, profound, and transformative changes.

Competition from machines has finally arrived for lawyers. These changes mean that the slowdown in the legal market is not recessionary, but structural, ongoing, and likely to accelerate. The venture capital backing *LegalZoom*, *Modria*, *Avvo*, and *Rocket Lawyer* tells you volumes about the potential for online disruption of traditional legal services. As *LegalZoom* and others begin to perfect their services, they will expand into other areas of legal work, until lawyers offer only true bespoke services: cases where the work is complicated, is relatively unusual, and has important consequences.

Just as was the case for Big Law, a concentrated chunk of bespoke legal work will remain. This will consist of the small-firm versions of "bet-the-company" work—child-custody battles or contract battles that could sink a small business. Likewise, because of the structure of American courts and UPL protections, most profitable in-court work will likely remain the province of lawyers or confused and overmatched *pro se* litigants for the foreseeable future. Outside of court, it seems likely that any work that can be routinized or rationalized will be swallowed up. Death from below.

6

Death from the State

Tort Reform, Judicial Hostility, and Budget Cuts

THIS IS A BOOK about the American market for legal services; it is not about substantive law. Nevertheless, substantive law and policy decisions by federal, state, and local governments have a profound effect on the market for lawyers. Changes in law and government policy have negatively affected the market for lawyers since the 1980s, after a long period during which expansion in the reach of law tended to be more favorable. Some readers will cheer these changes as long overdue and others will decry them, but this chapter is descriptive, not normative. Regardless of one's opinion about the expansion of the tort and products liability law through the 1980s or the subsequent rollback, these changes have had a substantial effect on the economics of legal practice, with expansion creating work and raising earnings, and contraction doing the opposite.

A preliminary note on two ways the state has been particularly helpful to lawyers: first, recall the discussion of advantageous lawyer regulation in chapters 2 and 3. The various barriers to entry, especially the ban on the unauthorized practice of law, have floated lawyers for years. While the Winston, Crandall, and Maheshri estimate that entry regulation boosted lawyer earnings by $64 billion in 2004 is probably overstated,[1] there is little doubt the regulations have been quite helpful.

Second, as discussed in chapter 13, there has been continued growth in legal complexity in America. This is a less-direct subsidy to the legal profession, but a much more powerful one. Gillian Hadfield has vividly described our "law-thick world" and how it drives demand for legal services. Law governs an ever-increasing share of our economy and our lives, seeking to control and guide human behavior. For now a lawyer is the obvious guide through the complexity.

A. Broad Strokes

Post–World War II, American law grew larger and more complex, and reached more areas of our lives. I teach torts and products liability and these areas expanded pretty consistently from World War II forward. There were new causes of action, reaching broader types of injuries, and allowing different categories and larger amounts of damages.

The same process occurred across multiple areas of the law, including the law of the workplace, environmental law, constitutional law, and others. The expansion was driven by courts and by legislatures and by regulatory agencies and occurred at every level of government: local, state, and federal. For better or for worse, America came to rely on law and the courts to handle an expanded list of societal issues.

All of this expansion meant more (and better-paid) work for lawyers. This period of expansion, not coincidentally, corresponded to a growth in the number and earnings of American lawyers. Part of the growth detailed in chapter 3 from 1950 to 1980 is explainable by America's expanding economy, but part of it was American law's growing ambit.

Since the 1980s there has been a rollback. The most obvious example is the tort reform movement, but there are a number of governmental and court trends that have made practicing law in America less lucrative over the last thirty years.

B. Tort Reform

Tort reform advocates have successfully attacked the American civil litigation system on all levels. They have persuaded state and federal legislatures to pass restrictive legislation, changed the approach of American courts, and most importantly altered American (and juror) attitudes toward lawyers and lawsuits. Tort reform has been a legal movement at one level, but more importantly it has been a public relations effort.[2] The importance of public persuasion is evinced by the movement's reliance on anecdotes, from the McDonald's coffee spill litigation to stories of the disappearing seesaw.[3]

The first wave of tort reform came in the 1970s and focused on medical malpractice. Many state legislatures capped damages for pain and suffering, shortened statutes of limitations, eliminated the collateral source rule,[4] and limited plaintiff's lawyer's fees.[5] Common law courts had previously handled medical malpractice and most other American torts, so the legislative incursion was a significant change.

In 1986, the Department of Justice published a report claiming that the tort system and large damage awards were causing rising insurance rates and a "current crisis in insurance availability and affordability."[6] The report recommended a menu of familiar tort reforms, including caps on non-economic damages, elimination of the collateral source rule and joint and several liability, and limitations on contingency fees.

Between 1985 and 1988, forty-eight state legislatures responded with some sort of legislation.[7] Thirty states limited joint and several liability, twenty-five capped punitive damages, twenty-three placed a cap on damages for pain and suffering, and twelve limited contingency fees.[8] At the same time some states moved to restrict products liability suits by adopting statutes of repose or "useful life statutes" that limited manufacturer liability to a set period of time (usually ten to twelve years) after manufacture, regardless of when the injury occurred.[9]

State governments continued to expand tort reform through the present, with more states adopting the reforms listed above. Some have placed hard caps on all damages (not just pain and suffering) or eliminated punitive damages altogether.[10] If you are curious about your own state, the American Tort Reform Association's (ATRA) website has a map of the fifty states, with each state's tort reform efforts listed by statute name and date.[11] Every state is represented and every state has enacted some combination of the reforms listed above.

At the low end of the legal market, state and federal fee caps have been particularly devastating. Federal law limits the legal fees plaintiffs can pay in Federal Tort Claims Act cases, Social Security disability cases, False Claims Act cases, and veterans' benefits disputes,[12] and state laws have limited recoveries in tort cases and workers' compensation cases. Small-firm lawyers and solo practitioners who make their living securing government benefits for their clients have long been among the poorest lawyers in America. Fee caps on benefits cases have forced these lawyers to leave the practice, earn less, or handle a greater volume of cases. Consider a 2011 Florida lawsuit challenging statutory fee caps for workers, compensation. The lawyers involved claimed that the fee caps resulted in an effective hourly rate of $6.84 for their work.[13]

1. *Securities Fraud and Class Actions*

For much of the 1980s and 1990s, large-scale class action and securities regulation lawsuits were among the most lucrative plaintiff's-side work in America. A series of legislative and judicial changes made these cases harder to bring, harder to win, and less lucrative. These changes have devastated the plaintiff's bar and meant less work for the defense bar

For example, the Private Securities Law Reform Act of 1995 (PSLRA)[14] and the Securities Litigation Uniform Standards Act of 1998 (SLUSA)[15] placed limits on shareholder securities-fraud lawsuits. The PSLRA heightened pleading standards, stayed discovery pending a motion to dismiss, added new sanctions for "frivolous" suits, and changed the rules for selecting and compensating lead plaintiffs.[16] It also replaced joint and several liability with proportionate liability, capped damages, and created a safe harbor for certain forward-looking statements.

When plaintiff's lawyers reacted by abandoning federal court for friendlier state courts, Congress passed SLUSA to drag them back to Federal Court and the strictures of the PSLRA. The dismissal rate for securities-fraud class actions roughly doubled after the PSLRA[17] and a number of securities litigation firms went out of business or moved on to less lucrative work.[18] Similar to Big Law, a small number of the biggest (and presumably best) plaintiff's-side firms survived,[19] but the overall market was devastated, with fewer lawyers and smaller earnings.

The Class Action Fairness Act of 2005 (CAFA)[20] made similar changes to class action work. CAFA capped some attorney fees, required governmental notice before settlements, and removed most class actions from state courts.[21] Court decisions have raised pleading standards for plaintiffs and made it harder to certify a class.[22] These changes have splintered a number of cases that formerly would have been handled through class actions into individualized, multidistrict litigations.[23] Beth Burch has noted that lucrative large class action cases that used to "yield substantial plaintiffs' attorneys' fees" have been replaced by "smaller classes and nonclass aggregation" that require greater expenses in administration and advertising to find clients, and result in smaller awards.[24] These changes have led to fewer lawyers pursuing these cases for smaller payouts.

The Supreme Court has also made it much easier for corporations to sidestep class actions altogether. In *AT&T Mobility v. Concepcion*[25] the Court upheld a class action waiver in AT&T's customer service agreement, which required customers to arbitrate all disputes.[26] The California Supreme Court had found such clauses unconscionable and unenforceable.[27] The Supreme Court disagreed and held that the Federal Arbitration Act preempted state law protection of class actions.[28] In *American Express Co. v. Italian Colors Restaurant*, the Court extended *Concepcion* to class action waivers where the amount at issue is less than the cost of arbitration.[29]

If you have wondered what is in the twenty-page "terms of use" you agreed to for *iTunes* or your mobile phone, now you have some idea. Post-*Concepcion* these waivers have become even more pervasive, so individualized arbitration is becoming the rule and class actions are becoming an ever-dwindling exception.

2. *The Upshot*

By the mid-1990s, national groups like the U.S. Chamber of Commerce and ATRA realized "that the greatest return on investment is at the state level" and moved to change state laws and affect state supreme court elections.[30] The campaign has been so successful that a 2007 cover story in *BusinessWeek* crowed about "How Business Trounced the Trial Lawyers."[31]

While tort reform has been most obvious in its statutory form, it has been at least as effective in its effect on potential jurors and on the judiciary itself. There is a raucous and open scholarly debate about whether there is, or ever has been, an American "litigation crisis."[32] What is not disputed, however, is that the American people are convinced there is and was. This has resulted in more hostile juries and judges. Since the 1980s judges have been less likely to expand the law and more likely to dismiss individual cases before trial.[33] Even the cases that have gone to juries have been worth less, because many juries suspect that plaintiff's lawyers and plaintiffs themselves are greedy weasels profiting from a broken system.[34]

The irony is that plaintiff's lawyers are at least partially responsible for the success of tort reform. Like the partners in Big Law, successful plaintiff's lawyers pushed the envelope in terms of overall damages, their share of those damages, and the types of cases they brought. It is true that tort reform proponents have focused on a few, outlier cases to build their argument through anecdote. Nevertheless, there were plaintiff's lawyers that brought and argued each of those outlier cases. Lester Brickman's *Lawyer Barons* is somewhat heavy-handed, but it is a 545-page, data-driven book assaulting the greed and overreach of plaintiff's lawyers.[35]

C.   Lawyer Advertising and Fee Schedules

Between 1975 and 1980, the Supreme Court dismantled a great deal of anti-competitive bar regulation. In 1975, the Supreme Court banned mandatory bar fee schedules.[36] These schedules were extremely common and locked in a set rate for simple legal matters like divorces or incorporation. Two years later the Court struck down most limitations on lawyer advertising.[37] Some bans on in-person solicitation were also held unconstitutional in 1978.[38]

Taken together these rulings greatly increased competition at the low end of the market. There were no longer floors on what a lawyer could charge, and lawyers were free to advertise these lower prices. Prices fell for most routine legal services after these rulings.[39]

Attorney advertising has had an additional effect, however. Over time attorney advertising has become largely the province of the plaintiff's bar.[40] These ads have often been extremely shrill or in bad taste,[41] adding to the public and judicial perception that the tort system is broken and in need of reform.

D.   Tort Reform and Advertising Lead to Settlement Mills

Tort reform has had a devastating effect upon the earnings of plaintiff's-side lawyers.[42] First, and unsurprisingly, damages caps mean that tort defendants—mostly insurance companies—pay out less on an aggregate basis and on a per-case basis.[43] These changes have had a negative effect on individual case values and on earnings.[44] In one survey of Texas plaintiff's lawyers on the effects of tort reform, 90 percent reported negative effects on their business, 84 percent reported smaller settlements, 88 percent reported higher costs per case, and 60 percent reported that cases took longer to complete.[45] Plaintiff's lawyers have responded by changing the mix of their cases, limiting their representation to cases with bigger damages and surer recoveries, or leaving the practice altogether.[46]

Tort reform has had a lesser, but still negative, effect on the solo practitioners and small firms that handle the occasional personal injury case. This is because the caps on damages and heightened requirements for expert reports have made the work much harder to dabble in successfully. Like the securities regulation experience, the lawyers who have survived post-tort reform still make a good, although more modest, living. The middle group of dabblers or less-able lawyers, however, has largely been eliminated.

The defense bar has also been affected because tort reform has suppressed both the number of personal injury lawsuits and the value of these lawsuits.[47] Many more personal injury lawsuits are being settled for a lesser amount, since the damages caps work as a ceiling and set the parameters for negotiation. Defense lawyers are only necessary for cases that present uncertain damages. Because tort reform largely removes the high-end uncertainty on damages, personal injury cases have grown more routinized and less lucrative, hurting plaintiff's lawyers, but also affecting the defense side as well.[48]

In 2006, Herbert Kritzer wrote an article entitled *The Commodification of Insurance Defense Practice*,[49] which discussed a trend that has only accelerated since. Insurance companies can settle an increasing number of cases without ever involving a lawyer. The cases that do not settle can be litigated interchangeably by inside or outside counsel at very suppressed hourly rates. Insurance companies handle so many similar cases that they produce highly detailed litigation manuals and give local counsel limited discretion.[50] Pre-tort reform insurance companies and defendants feared uncertainty in verdicts, and would litigate more cases and pay more for defense counsel to avoid a catastrophic verdict.[51] Post-tort reform those cases are vanishingly few. This takes some cases from Big Law and pushes them down to lower-priced insurance defense firms (damages caps change tort claims from potential "bet-the-company" cases to capped potential liabilities) and also takes cases from insurance defense firms and gives them to insurance adjusters. At each level less is spent and lawyers of all stripes earn less.

One sign of the financial straits for lawyers engaged in tort law is the rise of the settlement mill. Just as swarms of jellyfish are an unhealthy sign in the ocean,[52] the replacement of more traditional plaintiff's-side firms with settlement mills is a sure sign of death from the state. Nora Freeman Engstrom has done the most comprehensive work on settlement mills to date and her work should be required reading for anyone attempting to understand what is happening to the plaintiff's bar in the wake of tort reform.[53]

She notes ten hallmark features of the settlement mills (in comparison to more traditional plaintiff's-side practice):

> Settlement mills necessarily (1) are high-volume personal injury practices that (2) engage in aggressive advertising from which they obtain a high proportion of their clients, (3) epitomize "entrepreneurial legal practices," and (4) take few—if any—cases to trial. In addition, settlement mills generally (5) charge tiered contingency fees; (6) do not engage in rigorous case screening and thus primarily represent victims with low-dollar claims; (7) do not prioritize meaningful attorney-client interaction; (8) incentivize settlements via mandatory quotas or by offering negotiators awards or fee-based compensation; (9) resolve cases quickly, usually within two-to-eight months of the accident; and (10) rarely file lawsuits.[54]

Note the distinction with a traditional plaintiff's-side firm. Traditional plaintiff's-side lawyers carry heavy caseloads, frequently as many as seventy open files at a time. But traditional plaintiff's attorneys are pikers in comparison to the settlement mill counterpart: settlement mill attorneys carry upward of two hundred to three hundred.[55] Some plaintiff's-side lawyers advertise, but the heart of their business remains referrals and word of mouth.[56] Settlement mills rely wholly on a blizzard of advertising.[57] Most importantly, settlement mills almost never file cases, let alone go to trial. They exist solely to settle cases with insurance companies, often at a relative discount.[58]

Settlement mills are successful by running a volume business and by settling their cases as quickly as possible. Engstrom notes that the settlement mills thus operate as a kind of *de facto* no-fault system. Most of their clients receive something from the insurance companies, even if that amount is less than the client might receive if litigation were filed and prosecuted by a more traditional lawyer.

The open question is why the insurance companies pay when there is almost no threat of litigation. The simple answer is that insurers like settlement mills, because insurance companies value a quick settlement, certainty, and predictability above even wringing out the best possible deal on every case:[59]

> Thus, though settlement mills lack the proverbial stick of trial, they do have appetizing carrots: Pay up, and you will likely pay less on the largest and theoretically costliest claims, close files without delay, settle for predictable sums, and save on attorney's fees and costs. Though some settlement mills cannot credibly threaten to take a claim to court, they do have another threat to levy: If you refuse to tender a reasonable offer, a conventional attorney might take the case.

Engstrom notes the most worrisome aspect of the settlement mills: to a certain extent these lawyers work primarily for the insurance companies, not the three hundred or so clients they represent at a time. Their job is to get the best, quickest settlement possible and then sell it to the client, not necessarily to represent the client's interests to the fullest.[60] Engstrom estimates that clients with small claims are actually better off with settlement mills, but larger claims get short shrift.

Settlement mills are a natural response to tort reform. As the value of each individual claim shrinks, some lawyers respond by handling the maximum volume of cases regardless of their individual merits, with the goal of just getting a small settlement on a lot of cases rather than working a portfolio of cases through litigation and hoping for larger returns on a portion of those cases.

Settlement mills eat into traditional legal work in two important ways. First, they soak up some meritorious claims with large damages from more traditional plaintiff's-side firms. Given that the number of these cases is already shrinking under tort reform, the loss is not insubstantial. Second, settlement mills eat into defense-side work as well because they allow insurance adjusters to settle a great number of claims without ever engaging their inside or outside counsel (which litigation inevitably does).

Settlement mills are another example of the elimination of the law-yer middle class. The best and most successful plaintiff's-side firms have survived tort reform, albeit earning less. Other plaintiff's firms have transitioned out of law and into advertising and mass settlement. The great middle group of lawyers that made a living on these cases has largely been squeezed out.

D.   Supreme Court Hostility to Litigation

The tort reform discussion above focused on legislative enactments, but the judiciary has played a substantial role in curtailing litigation, to the detriment of lawyer earnings. This section focuses on how the U.S. Supreme Court has accepted many of the arguments of the tort reformers as true and how the Court has curtailed some types of liti-gation as a result.

The attitude of the Court matters because it does more than decide individual cases of federal and constitutional law; the Court sets the tone and agenda for America's judiciary. This was true under the War-ren Court of the 1960s and its aftermath in the 1970s. Those Courts led a tremendous expansion in the ambit of law and promoted litiga-tion and courts as the solution to multiple societal and constitutional problems.

The current Court has also proven influential in its more recent roll-back. There are multiple examples of the Court evincing a desire to limit litigation and accepting the basic tenets of the tort reform advo-cates, but I will present three: tightening pleading standards, judicial due process review of punitive damages, and hostility to the granting of statutory attorney fees.

Two recent decisions—*Bell Atlantic Corp. v. Twombly*[61] and *Ash-croft v. Iqbal*[62]—are the most recent and obvious examples of tighten-ing pleading standards, but these decisions are emblematic of a larger trend.[63] In these cases the Court held that Rule 8 of the Federal Rules of Civil Procedure (FRCP) requires plaintiffs to present a "plausible" claim for relief in the complaint.[64] The text of Rule 8 requires only a "short and plain" statement of facts and claims, and has done so since that Rule's inception,[65] so these decisions marked a significant tighten-ing in pleading standards.[66]

In both of these cases the Court seemed to be reacting, at least in part, to the tort reform narrative of frivolous lawsuits choking the courts. In *Twombly* the Court worried about "largely groundless" claims and "costly and expensive discovery," and argued that dismissal is often necessary "at the point of minimum expenditure of time and money by the parties and the court."[67] Likewise, in *Iqbal* the Court discussed "discovery abuse" and emphasized the need to weed deficient cases out early.[68]

Commentators have argued vociferously that these cases display a naked hostility to litigation. Arthur Miller said the cases were "motivated in significant part by a desire to develop a stronger role for motions to dismiss to filter out a hypothesized excess of meritless litigation, to deter allegedly abusive practices, and to contain costs."[69] Elizabeth Schneider thinks the cases stem from "widespread and general hostility to litigation."[70] Tort reform advocates happily agreed. Washington Legal Foundation lawyer Richard Samp said the Court "is sort of fed up with excesses in the tort system" and *Iqbal* and *Twombly* show they are "looking for ways to try to eliminate frivolous lawsuits."[71]

The actual effectiveness of *Iqbal* and *Twombly* is open to debate,[72] but it certainly encapsulates a judicial attitude of distrust of litigation and distaste for lengthy and expensive discovery. This attitude has trickled down in state and federal courts and has contributed to the ever-shrinking number of trials. Courts on all levels are looking to dispose of cases early and without trials. If *Iqbal* and *Twombly* cause more cases to be dismissed before discovery—where as much as 90 percent of the expense of litigation is generated[73]—the loss to litigators paid by the hour (mostly defense lawyers) will be notable.

The Supreme Court has also held that the Due Process Clause of the Constitution bans certain punitive damage awards. In *BMW v. Gore* the Court announced a three-part test for the constitutionality of a punitive damages award: the reprehensibility of the defendant's conduct, the ratio between the punitive damages award and compensatory damages, and comparable civil or criminal sanctions for similar conduct.[74] In *State Farm v. Campbell* the Court suggested that "single digit multipliers" between punitive and compensatory damages are "more likely to comport with due process."[75]

The Supreme Court's punitive damages jurisprudence shows the power and effectiveness of the tort reform movement. As with any other aspect of the tort system there is and was a heated empirical battle about whether punitive damages were unpredictable or too large or too prevalent.[76] Nevertheless, the Court's language and holdings clearly establish which version of the debate they preferred. Justice O'Connor noted the unfortunate "trend toward multimillion dollar" punitive damages awards and that "punitive damages [were] skyrocketing."[77] The Court explicitly worried about "punitive damages that 'run wild'"[78] and has decried "the stark unpredictability of punitive awards."[79]

These judicial decisions are of a piece with tort reform generally. They have lowered the total amount of damages awarded and placed a ceiling on the largest amount any individual case might be worth. These decisions bite into plaintiff's lawyer recoveries, but also decrease the use of defense counsel. Because of the multiplier limit, defendants can pretty easily determine the outside limits of their potential liability for punitive damages, encouraging quicker and lower settlements and less litigation. Ironically, the cases most likely to proceed to trial in the past, cases with horrible facts and potentially huge damage amounts, are now the least likely. An insurance company can quickly offer the maximum recovery under either the applicable award cap or under the insurance policy, leaving little upside to continued litigation.

The Supreme Court has also shown a marked hostility to fee-shifting statutes. There are hundreds of federal and state statutes that allow successful plaintiffs to collect attorney's fees.[80] Fee-shifting statutes are part of the American system of encouraging "private attorneys general" to enforce legal rights. When Congress (or a state legislature) is concerned that private individuals might have a hard time finding a lawyer to vindicate a legal right, Congress adds a prevailing party fee-shifting provision.[81]

For the last forty years, the Supreme Court has continuously read these statutes as narrowly as possible, granting fees in a shrinking group of cases. In 1975, in *Alyeska Pipeline Service Co. v. Wilderness Society*, the Supreme Court held that federal courts could not grant attorney's fees without an explicit statutory mandate, overruling a grant of fees in a successful environmental lawsuit.[82] Congress briskly responded in 1976, passing Section 1988, which granted attorney's fees in a bevy of federal civil rights actions.[83]

Nevertheless, the Court has remained hostile, refusing fees for time spent in administrative proceedings,[84] for cases where plaintiffs win only "nominal damages,"[85] for expert witness costs,[86] or for cases that settle without an explicit consent judgment granting fees.[87] Jeffrey Brand argues that these results arise from the Court's "deeply held view that public interest lawyers should be expected to act on a higher moral plane" and "the assumption that public interest litigation is not part and parcel of ordinary practice, but is more in the nature of charity or volunteer work."[88] Deborah Weissman thinks they reflect a continuing and "deepening hostility" to fee shifting.[89]

Regardless of the wisdom of these decisions, they have had a tightening effect on plaintiff's lawyers who handle discrimination or constitutional litigation. Likewise, shrinking the number of those cases impinges on the work of defending those cases.

E.   Shrinking Budgets for Lawyers for the Poor

The 1960s saw the growth of two new areas of employment for American lawyers: a new wave of defense lawyers for the indigent following *Gideon v. Arizona* and a new wave of civil lawyers for the poor in legal aid societies. The funding for these programs and the earnings of these lawyers, however, have been shrinking or flat since the 1980s.

American civil legal aid societies are more than 130 years old, although the first iterations were privately funded and frequently staffed by volunteers or law students.[90] As part of the War on Poverty in the 1960s, more formal legal services programs received federal grants and began serving the poor. Legal aid programs have proven controversial since and have faced a series of different budget cuts. The most severe were in the 1980s under the Reagan administration, but there were also cuts in the mid-1990s and again in the 2000s. The low point of the Reagan-era funding was a 25 percent reduction in funding in 1982.[91] Despite the size of the past cuts, legal aid societies would do cartwheels to return to the 1982 funding levels. The 2012 legal aid budget saw a 14 percent cut to $348 million and in 2013 it was reduced to $340 million, continuing a long-term trend of shrinkage via one step forward, two steps back.[92] Legal aid's 1982 funding would be more than $785 million in 2012 dollars.

Over the same period of time, funding for indigent defense has suffered similar stagnation or cuts. As far back as the 1970s, there have been reports outlining the relatively limited funding for indigent defense, with caseloads rising and funding flat or shrinking over the years.[93] The recent budget crises in state and local governments have resulted in further and deeper budget cuts.[94]

Consider the federal public defenders program. The budget sequester in fiscal year 2013 caused a 10 percent reduction in funding, and funding and staffing levels have not recovered since.[95] These budget cuts have two different effects. Most directly, there are fewer public defenders to handle more defendants, and those lawyers get paid less to do more work, likely in a worse fashion.

Indirectly, the indigent defense funding crisis is emblematic of the fate of small-firm and solo practitioners nationwide. Because of conflicts of interest or local funding issues, private lawyers actually handle a significant number of indigent defense cases. When they do, they are usually paid according to state statutes. The Spangenberg Group has gathered these statutes for the ABA since 1999, with the last report in 2007.[96] Most states have not increased their pay rates for non-capital felonies much over this period, and the hourly rates and the caps on representations are all relatively low. For example, Tennessee has not raised its hourly rates since 1994. Payments in all non-death penalty cases are $40 an hour for out-of-court work and $50 per hour for in-court work. The fees are capped at $1,000, $2,000, or $3,000, depending on the seriousness of the charges.[97]

These caps raise the real question of how a lawyer would make a living under these statutes. The answer is a high-volume practice and attempts to plea-bargain most or all cases. Still it is difficult to gather enough cases to earn a very good living.

There is an unfortunate trend of discounting the importance of this segment of the market. At least two factors suggest it is quite important. First, note how closely the timing of the expansion of these programs corresponds to the growth in the number and earnings of American lawyers and how the shrinkage in those programs likewise correlates with lower earnings.

Second, consider the importance the ABA places on these programs. The ABA has been an outspoken and passionate supporter of additional funding for both legal aid[98] and public defenders.[99] If you ever wonder about whether a segment of a market matters, look to see if the trade association is lobbying heavily for it.

F.   The Threat of Broader Budget Cuts

As noted above, the budget cuts for lawyers for the poor have been a regular feature of that sector since at least the 1980s. The recent spate of fiscal austerity in state and federal budgets raises two larger concerns.

The first is that state and federal governments may be required to lay off lawyers. The percentage of American lawyers working for the government has remained relatively steady for the last forty years or so, at 11 percent in 1975, in 1995,[100] and again in 2005 (the year of the most recent ABA study).[101] The number of licensed lawyers almost tripled over that same period,[102] so government employment has been an important source of employment. The NALP hiring data similarly shows that the percentage of lawyers starting their careers in the government has fluctuated between 11 and 13 percent over the last twenty years.

These jobs are not as remunerative as jobs in Big Law, but on average they pay more than solo or small-firm practice and provide steadier employment.[103] Budget cuts naturally mean fewer of these jobs, at lower salaries. The federal government has slowed hiring into its honors programs for recent graduates,[104] and state governments have cut budgets and forced lawyer layoffs.[105] Many government positions have been unfilled as older lawyers retire.[106]

There are also steep budget cuts to the judiciary and resulting case delays. At least forty-two states have recently reduced judicial budgets, thirty-four have laid off court employees, and twenty-three have reduced operating hours.[107] California's budget crisis has necessitated particularly deep cuts. Because of the constitutional guarantee of a speedy trial, criminal cases are prioritized and the average wait time for a civil trial has doubled.[108] Economists Nels Pearsall, Bo Shippen, and Roy Weinstein analyzed the national slowdown in case clearance rates (the time it takes courts to settle civil disputes) and estimated that the new delays will cost the U.S. economy approximately $52.2 billion.[109]

From the legal profession's point of view, these delays could not come at a worse time. Delays and inefficiencies may bring short-term comfort in longer cases and higher billings, but they raise the specter of corporations or individuals abandoning court-driven dispute resolution altogether. Remember that in chapter 5, *Modria*'s pitch for online dispute resolution focuses on the lengthy delays, expense, and inefficiency of current court processes and extends an invitation to try something cheaper and quicker. American lawyers have been relying on litigation as a lifeboat. If budget cuts make litigation untenable or too expensive, that boat may spring additional leaks.

G.   The Upshot

American legislatures and courts have generally been much less friendly to the legal profession over the last thirty years or so. Government has limited the number and worth of various tort claims in reaction to a perceived litigation crisis and cut funding for lawyers and courts. At all levels the government has joined in the squeeze on American lawyers. Death from the state.

7

Death from the Side

More Lawyers Fight for Slices of a Smaller Pie

THE LAST CHALLENGE FOR the profession is the longstanding oversupply of law school graduates. Since the mid-1980s law schools have granted more JDs than there are full-time jobs practicing law. This situation has deteriorated considerably since 2008, because the lawyers who lost their jobs during the Great Recession have been added to the ranks of job seekers, creating a substantial bubble of unemployed and under-employed JD-holders. The situation is bad enough that *Above the Law* has created its own "Lost Generation" graphic and meme to describe the current employment situation.[1]

It is important to understand the provenance and depth of the problem, because if one only considers popular accounts of the law market downturn, one might think the problem for lawyers and law schools began in 2008.[2] Instead, the surfeit of law school graduates has existed for thirty years. This lawyer oversupply explains why small-firm and solo practitioner incomes have fallen over that same period. There are more people who want to do that work than the work can support comfortably, so the salaries are continuously driven down.

The oversupply does not affect Big Law, however, because in that market, historically, corporations have been competing over legal talent, so an extra 10,000 lawyers looking for work at the middle and low end of the market does not affect salaries in the high end of the market. As chapters 3 and 4 demonstrate, over the same period of time that law schools have been pumping out too many JDs, Big Law came to resemble its own separate profession, with its own salary scale and hiring. But, even the safe haven of Big Law has started to crumble. The biggest and most successful firms are getting bigger and more successful. The lawyers at the firms that are left behind are being slowly pushed back to the rest of the pack. As a result of the many lawyers exiting Big Law and thirty years of untenably large law school classes, lawyers are facing death from the side.

A.   Oversupply

The ABA Section on Legal Education and Admissions to the Bar has kept detailed statistics on the number of law students at ABA-accredited schools since 1963–4. ABA-accredited schools now grant four times more JDs than they did forty-five years ago. In 1963–4, ABA-accredited law schools granted 9,638 JDs. In 1973–4 that number had risen to 22,342, in 1983–4, it was 36,389, in 1993–4 it was 40,213,[3] and in 2012–13 it hit 46,478. Figure 7.1 shows the growth in the number of JDs awarded over this period.

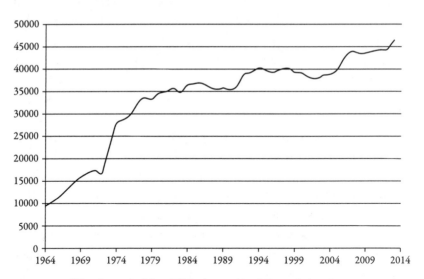

FIGURE 7.1 JDs Awarded by ABA-Accredited Law Schools

Contrary to the current focus on the size of law school classes, the steepest increase occurred in the 1970s, not the 1990s or 2000s. The Class of 1970 had 16,733 JDs and the class of 1980 had 34,590. As chapter 3 showed, over the same period of time the number of licensed lawyers almost doubled, and incomes rose for all lawyers. The growth in law schools outpaced the growth in the number of new jobs for lawyers almost immediately, but at least the growth in the 1970s and the early 1980s was connected to a rising market for all lawyers. By the mid-1980s the oversupply of law graduates began to catch up with the earnings of small-firm and solo practitioners, and the shrinkage in earnings described in chapter 3 began in earnest. Nevertheless, law schools doubled down on their growth, adding another 10,000 graduates a year between 1980 and 2013. Thirty-two new ABA-accredited law schools opened between 1980 and 2012[4] and existing law schools grew larger.[5]

In order to estimate the extent of the oversupply, Marc Gans used the ABA's count of JDs awarded to create a rolling forty-year total of the number of JDs awarded to compare against the number of American lawyers.[6] This count is imperfect because some law graduates may retire before forty years have passed since law school graduation, and because some law graduates fail the bar. Nevertheless, surveys show that lawyers tend to work well beyond the age of 65,[7] and that 95 percent of law graduates eventually pass the bar,[8] so these critiques are less powerful than one might think. Further, the ABA count of law graduates does not include non-ABA-accredited law schools (there are more than forty in California[9] and a smattering elsewhere in the country), which may mean the number is actually too low.

Comparing the number of JDs to the number of American lawyers is not as easy as it sounds, however, as there are actually at least three respectable numbers one could use to count lawyers. This book mainly uses the ABA count, because it counts every person licensed to practice law in America,[10] and is thus the fullest possible count of the number of lawyers. Nevertheless, there are licensed law graduates who do not actually practice law, so that number is likely high.

A second count comes from the Census Bureau's annual Current Population Survey (CPS). The CPS asks individuals to state their occupations and then tallies the responses.[11] The number who respond "lawyer" makes up the CPS count. Since 1990, the CPS count has run lower than the ABA count, likely reflecting that there were individuals licensed to practice law who do not self-describe as a "lawyer" for their occupation. Because there have been more law graduates than law jobs over this period, the CPS count is probably more accurate than the ABA count.

The last count is the Bureau of Labor Statistics' (BLS) biannual Occupational Outlook Handbook (OOH), which generates its head count of

American lawyers by considering a number of different BLS and Census statistics and business surveys.[12] This has been the lowest count of the number of American lawyers since 1978. A legal market pessimist may want to use these lowest numbers because the OOH does not include anyone capable of working as a lawyer but not presently working as a lawyer (which the ABA does), nor does it count anyone who simply says she is a lawyer (as the CPS does), but rather it uses a broader group of more disinterested statistics to estimate actual lawyer employment.

The numbers are quite divergent. In 2010 the forty-year count of ABA-accredited JDs was 1,412,007. The ABA counted 1,203,097 licensed lawyers,[13] CPS estimated the number of lawyers at 1,080,000,[14] and the OOH clocked in at a shockingly low 728,200.[15] Again, if one believes the OOH numbers, there are almost 500,000 licensed lawyers who are not currently working as lawyers. Even if the CPS numbers are right, there are 120,000 licensed individuals who do not self-identify as lawyers. The gaps in these counts alone speak volumes about the state of the profession.

Regardless of the count you choose, however, the number of law graduates has greatly outstripped the number of lawyers for years. Marc Gans created the graph shown in Figure 7.2, with "40-Year Model" standing for the forty-year sum of law graduates.[16]

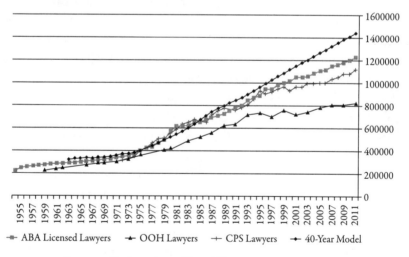

FIGURE 7.2 Lawyer Estimations Over Time

The mid-1980s is the first time that the forty-year sum passes the ABA and CPS count for good. That period is likely when law school oversupply began. Not coincidentally, it also marks the decline period for the earnings of small-firm and solo practitioners.

If it is true that there has been an oversupply of law graduates for almost thirty years, a new puzzle arises: Where have all of those law school graduates gone? The answer can be found in the NALP (National Association of Legal Professionals) data. The graduates have been unable to find work as a lawyer, so they have moved to jobs where a JD is preferred, but not required, or to non-law jobs altogether. Marc Gans separated the NALP data out into full-time jobs (where he could) and then removed graduates starting their own practice, those in JD-preferred jobs, those who were unemployed, and those in non-JD jobs to create a "True Employment Percentage" for law school graduates. Table 7.1 shows the results and Figure 7.3 (displayed on p. 126) graphs the percentage of law graduates unable to find full-time work requiring a JD. One could quibble with his methodology—the decision to exclude graduates who hang out a shingle is questionable, for example—but the gap between the True Employment Percentage and NALP-reported employment (which includes part-time and full-time employment and any job from law firm associate to Starbucks barista as employment) is large enough to overcome any nitpicking:[17]

TABLE 7.1 True Employment Percentage

YEAR	True Employment Percentage	NALP reported employment[1]	Gap
2012	61.6%	86.8%	25.20%
2011	56.0%	87.90%	31.90%
2010	58.4%	87.6%	29.20%
2009	61.4%	88.3%	26.90%
2008	68.1%	89.9%	21.80%
2007	71.5%	91.9%	20.40%
2006	69.8%	90.7%	20.90%
2005	67.9%	89.6%	21.70%
2004	67.3%	88.9%	21.60%
2003	68.2%	88.9%	20.70%
2002	69.2%	89.0%	19.80%
2001	69.9%	90.0%	20.10%

continued

TABLE 7.1 *continued*

YEAR	True Employment Percentage	NALP reported employment[1]	Gap
2000	73.4%	91.5%	18.10%
1999	70.7%	90.3%	19.60%
1998	68.6%	89.9%	21.30%
1997	66.5%	89.4%	22.90%
1996	62.5%	87.4%	24.90%
1995	61.4%	86.7%	25.30%
1994	60.1%	84.7%	24.60%
1993	57.7%	83.4%	25.70%
1992	62.2%	83.5%	21.30%
1991	68.2%	85.9%	17.70%
1990	76.7%	88.4%	11.70%
1989	78.5%		
1988	80.4%		
1987	79.1%		
1986	75.3%		
1985	74.1%		

[1]This percentage was only reported through 1990, but other NALP data allowed Gans to calculate the true employment percentage through 1985. *See* Gans, *Not a New Problem,* at 25–7.

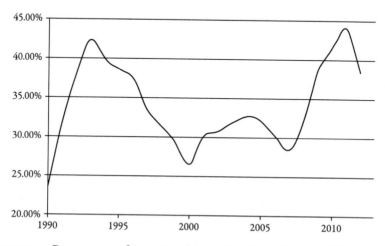

FIGURE 7.3 Percentage of Law Graduates Unable to Find Full-Time Work as a Lawyer

These data are remarkable on several fronts. Most importantly, they well establish that law graduates have had a hard time making it as lawyers for years. The trend was the worst in the mid-1990s and again in the 2010s, but in every year since 2010 more than 20 percent of all law graduates have been unable to get full-time work as a lawyer.

The data also show the relative uselessness of NALP's reported employment percentage number (the number used in the *U.S. News* ranking, although with a new weighting in favor of law jobs for the 2014 rankings).[18] When NALP and law schools ask graduates for their employment status, if they are working at all, NALP reports them as employed. This is why NALP's 2010 top-line number suggests that eight out of ten law graduates were employed, when almost half of the class of 2010 could not get a job that required a JD.

The NALP first-job numbers do not tell the whole story, though. NALP's *After the JD* survey shows that seven years after law school graduation "business—not practicing" is a significant growth area for the survey respondents.[19]

The data establishing an outflow from the legal profession by unemployed and under-employed JD-holders also explain another puzzle, which is why lawyer unemployment has remained relatively low, even now in the teeth of the Great Recession. Lawyer unemployment was 1.5 percent in 2011 (against a national rate of 9.6 percent), rising to a still very low 2.1 percent in 2013.[20] The outflux of JD-holders means that few stay in the profession if they are unemployed for long. Likewise, lawyers are likely to be under-employed, limping along as solo practitioners or part-time contract workers, rather than unemployed.

But maybe the outflow is good news? Law schools have always suggested that there are lots of uses for a JD besides being a lawyer. For example, Hastings Law School's career office has a guide to "Careers Outside of Legal Practice" that highlights the applicability of the "analytical and advocacy skills honed during law school" to "many other careers."[21] Maybe these graduates are actually thrilled with their current employment status regardless of not being a lawyer.

Two data points suggest otherwise. First, law graduates in non-law jobs are much more likely to be looking for other work than law graduates in jobs requiring a JD. In the NALP surveys those with JD-required jobs are three times less likely than those in JD-preferred or non-JD jobs to be looking for other work.[22] Likewise, the *After the JD* survey found that "the least satisfied [law graduates] are in business but are not practicing law."[23] The most satisfied lawyers worked as inside counsel in business.[24]

Second, NALP itself has offered some examples of the types of non-JD work law graduates reported doing, including: "carpentry and remodeling, driving school, flight attendant, landscape design, law exam proctor, middle school Spanish teacher, minister, muffler business, plumber, and teacher at nursing school."[25] These are fine and enjoyable occupations, but do not seem likely to benefit enough from a law school education to justify the expense and lost time of a JD.

Regardless of where the non-lawyers go, current lawyers face a flood of new entrants every year into what is already a very competitive market. Between 2004 and 2008 (*before* the Great Recession and the recent crash in legal markets) OOH estimated that the number of Americans employed as lawyers grew by only 1 percent, from 735,000 to 760,000.[26] Over the same period that only 25,000 new lawyer jobs were created (academic years 2003–8), ABA-accredited law schools graduated roughly 208,000 JDs, almost 28 percent of the number of existing lawyers.[27] In light of the post-2008 recession and including retirements and deaths, OOH estimates that there will be approximately 73,600 new lawyer jobs between now and 2020.[28] Law schools seem likely to continue to graduate more than 35,000 new JDs a year, meaning that 300,000 or so law graduates may be fighting over 74,000 jobs. Even if law schools cut back to 30,000 JDs a year (which would likely require some law schools to close and would entail drastic cuts in class size for those that remained open) 240,000 JDs would seek those 74,000 jobs.

Using older and more generous state-level BLS data, blogger Matt Leichter has broken out the oversupply of law school graduates to new lawyer jobs on a state-by-state basis.[29] He has the ratio listed in a chart and a very depressing interactive map. Massachusetts "leads" with more than five law graduates for every opening and the national average is almost two graduates for every one law job.

The pressure of these excess graduates will be felt especially in the part of the market that is already the most saturated and competitive:

small-firm and solo practice. This is because law graduates facing a particularly poor legal market are increasingly opting for hanging up a shingle. In 2009, 2010, and 2011, more than 1,000 law graduates each year reported entering solo practice, a 30 percent increase over the typical yield from 1998–2008, and more than any period dating back to 1993.[30] Law schools are likewise trying to convince law graduates to "go rural" and open solo or small-firm practices in small towns.[31]

B.   Add in the Newly Unemployed

Similarly, Big Law has shed quite a number of lawyer jobs over the last few years. The 2010 *National Law Journal* survey of the 250 biggest American law firms reported "the biggest two-year drop" in law firm employment in the survey's thirty-three-year history.[32] Law firms shed 5,259 lawyers in 2009 and another 1,402 in 2010, mostly associates.[33] Some of these lawyers joined corporations, some left the profession, and some found work in academia or government, but many of them joined smaller firms or started solo practices. *Corporate Counsel Magazine* has noted the trend of Big Law refugees starting small firms,[34] and Carolyn Elefant, a well-known blogger on solo practice at *myshingle.com*, has been describing an accelerating "Big Law to Small Law trend."[35] A former Big Law associate turned solo that noticed the trend is now selling the *Lawyer 2.0* software package, aimed at easing the transition into small-firm practice.[36] The *After the JD* survey shows a significant shift of lawyers out of other practice settings and into solo practice—71 percent of the solo practitioners surveyed started their practice in a different setting.[37]

As chapter 3 demonstrated, these intrepid souls will meet stiff competition and shrinking earnings. Even with these new additions, the IRS data suggests that there were 28,000 fewer solo practitioners in 2009 than in 2007, as solo practitioners moved up to small firms or moved out of the market altogether.

Displaced Big Law lawyers and new graduates mean increased competition for the lawyers already practicing in these areas, as additional hungry mouths squabble over the work that remains. When more people compete over less work the cost of that work goes down for consumers and wages also decline. Death from the side.

Part II

LAW SCHOOLS

8

A Brief History of American Law Schools

THE HISTORY OF AMERICAN law schools runs parallel to the American legal profession. These two spheres have existed in symbiosis since the turn of the twentieth century. When the profession experienced boom times, law schools followed along. When the profession suffered in the Depression, many law schools closed. As soon as graduation from an ABA-accredited law school became a prerequisite to bar admission, most unaccredited law schools either sought accreditation or closed. A boom period followed World War II, with more ABA-accredited law schools teaching bigger classes of students for higher tuition. The boom made sense until the 1980s, as the entire profession grew exponentially. Nevertheless, law schools continued to expand class sizes and raise tuition as professional opportunities waned for the majority of their graduates. That trend appears to be at an end or at least a stall currently, as chapter 10 describes.

A. 1870–1940—The Birth and Entrenchment of the Elite Model

In the first half of the nineteenth century the vast majority of American lawyers entered practice through apprenticeship. There were very few law schools. In 1840, there were only nine university-affiliated law schools in America, with a total of 345 students. Law schools opened and closed regularly throughout this period.[1]

The second half of the nineteenth century saw the rise of the American law school. Law schools became dominant because of interlocking intellectual, professional, and economic trends from 1850 to 1940. As an intellectual matter, reformers attempted to rationalize the study of law in a scientific manner.[2] Thus, when the University of Georgia founded its law school in 1858, it did so to teach law "not as a collection of arbitrary rules, but as a connected logical system."[3]

Christopher Columbus Langdell, Dean of the Harvard Law School, created the educational model for these efforts: the "case method," the same basic pedagogical approach still used in first-year law school curricula today.[4] In addition to the case method, Harvard designed several other key features of American law schools: minimum academic standards for admission, a graded and sequential curriculum, minimum academic standards for continuation in the program, a full-time career track for the faculty, and an expanded law library.[5]

As a professional matter, bar associations reformed and rose to prominence during this period with the explicit aim of reprofessionalizing lawyers. The elite lawyers who formed the ABA found university-based legal education more attractive because it employed the allegedly scientific case method.[6] Throughout this period law professors and bar associations derided apprenticeship as non-scientific and poor training for the new, more professional practice of law.[7] As early as 1879, the ABA proclaimed "[t]here is little if any dispute now as to the relative merits of education by means of law schools, and that to be got by mere practical training or apprenticeship as an attorney's clerk. Without disparagement of mere practical advantages, the verdict of the best informed is in favor of the schools."[8]

University law schools were also elite and exclusive and there was a conspicuous element of anti-Semitism, nativism, and classism to these bar efforts.[9] A law school that imitated Harvard and required full-time study and undergraduate education beforehand would naturally be more expensive in time and money, and thus much more likely to keep "undesirables" out of the practice than proprietary night law schools or even apprenticeship.

Economically, rapid industrialization and urbanization created a large demand for lawyers, and apprenticeships could not meet this demand. The profession tripled in size between 1860 and 1900.[10] It would have been physically impossible for all of these new lawyers to sit as apprentices with existing lawyers. The decline of legal apprenticeships was also part of a broader trend. Industrialization, immigration, rationalization, and a population boom made apprenticeships largely obsolete in all American professions.[11]

Despite the collapse of apprenticeship, the elite law school model did not become the sole gateway to the profession until well into the twentieth century. Alongside the new "elite" law schools there was an explosion of "proprietary" law schools, taught largely by part-time adjuncts (judges or practicing lawyers) and frequently operated as night schools.[12] These law schools grew exponentially from 1890 to 1930 and posed a powerful threat to the elite model:

> From 1890 to 1930, the number of law schools tripled, and the number of law students increased more than eightfold. Most of the new law schools were for-profit night schools; in 1928, two-thirds of law students studied part-time, up from one-third in 1889. Many of the new schools offered cheap courses of study of fewer than three years. Most of the new students were from large cities, and many were immigrants.[13]

In 1920, there were approximately 20,992 students in 143 American law schools. By 1929, that number had swollen to 43,876 in 178 schools, with much of the growth in proprietary schools.[14]

Unsurprisingly, the elite bar was not pleased with the volume of new entrants. Bar associations and regulators tarred these schools as diploma mills.[15] These critiques sometimes verged into classism and racism, as night schools often required no educational prerequisites and tended to educate immigrants, Jews, and the working class.[16] There was also raw protectionism, as the elite bar sought to protect itself against a flood of new competitors.[17]

The triumph of the elite model came in fits and starts. In 1900, thirty-two charter law schools formed the American Association of Law Schools (AALS) in Saratoga Springs, N.Y.,[18] where the ABA met biannually and had been founded twenty-two years earlier.[19] The first AALS President was Professor James Bradley Thayer of Harvard Law School. The goal was "the improvement of the legal profession through legal education."[20] It was the first organization to establish quality standards for American law schools, with four founding requirements: (1) law students had to have completed high school; (2) a law school education must last at least two years of thirty weeks per year; (3) competency examinations for graduation; and (4) convenient access to a law library.[21] The length of the required legal education was quickly expanded to three years and AALS membership temporarily shrank.[22] The AALS struggled to convince proprietary law schools to close or adopt the elite model. In 1919, only 48 of the 120 American law schools were members of the AALS.[23]

Thus, ABA accreditation was born. The first round of ABA accreditation started with 31 accredited schools in 1923 and reached 71 by 1929.[24] Accreditation was voluntary and, at first, not a requirement for sitting for the bar.[25] Over time, the ABA, AALS, and other bar associations convinced legislatures and courts to adopt a series of entry barriers. By the 1920s, some period of law school study and a written bar examination became standard state requirements for becoming a lawyer, but still the proprietary schools loomed as a threat.[26] During the Depression the elite model triumphed:

> By the end of the 1930s, most states began to require some years of college in advance of law school, most states required graduation from an ABA-accredited law school (instead of apprenticeship [or graduation from an unaccredited school]), a set number of years (usually three) of law school, a formal character and fitness test, the elimination of the diploma privilege, and a harder, written bar exam run by a central authority under the unified bar or the state supreme court.[27]

Nevertheless, it took a while before most lawyers fit the current model of graduation from college and an ABA-accredited law school. For example, in 1876 there were more lawyers in America than college graduates.[28] Figure 8.1 (displayed on p. 137) shows the number of years spent in undergraduate, law school, or "reading the law," for every Supreme Court Justice from John Jay through Elena Kagan.[29] The chart makes clear that the dominance of the current model (even at the most elite level of the profession) is a relatively recent phenomenon. The first year that every Supreme Court Justice on a single Court had spent four years in undergraduate education and three years in law school was 1986. Likewise, completing law school did not become more prevalent than reading the law until the turn of the twentieth century.

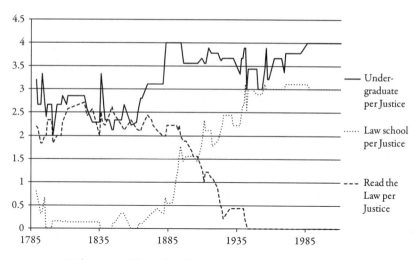

FIGURE 8.1 Education Years Per Justice

The timing of the various changes is also telling. Consider the growth period for law schools between 1880 and 1930. As the demand for lawyers increased, the number of law schools tracked upward. The replacement of apprenticeships with law schools was a pro-competitive move at first, as law schools popped up to meet demand from students who wanted to enter the profession, and as there was a strong market for legal work.

When the economy soured in the Depression and demand for legal work fell, the profession briskly increased barriers to entry. This tightening limited competition and made existing licenses more valuable, since existing practitioners did not have to pass the heightened entry standards. In most states ABA-accredited law schools captured a significant market—anyone who wanted to practice law in the United States. In case you doubt the extraordinary advantage granted to ABA-accredited schools by states requiring ABA accreditation, consider this statistic: seventy law schools went out of business between 1930 and 1950, and sixty-nine of them were unaccredited.[30]

B. 1950–2007—Boom Times Again

By 1940, the number of law students had fallen to 30,830 at 180 law schools (78 ABA-accredited) from a high-water mark of 44,341 students in 1927.[31] As chapter 3 demonstrated, 1950 through the mid-1980s was a period of substantial growth in the earnings and number of lawyers. Law school growth followed along. From the 1980s forward, small-firm and solo practitioner earnings stagnated or actually lost ground against inflation. Law school expansion continued heedlessly, with growth in the number of law students, the number of law schools, the number of ABA-accredited law schools, tuition charged, and the size and re-muneration of law faculties. If anything, the growth in law schools accelerated during the down period. Law schools doubled down on size and expense just when a law school degree became less valuable and the number of jobs available requiring a JD shrunk in comparison to the number of law graduates.

In 1953, there were 34,423 law students at 167 American law schools (126 ABA-accredited). Thirty years later in 1983, there were 127,195 law students at 173 ABA-accredited law schools.[32] In 2011–12, there were 146,288 law students at 201 ABA-accredited law schools.[33] In 2011, ABA-accredited law schools graduated 44,495 JDs; that number was 9,638 in 1963.[34]

Figure 8.2 shows the growth in total ABA-accredited enrollment since 1963–64.

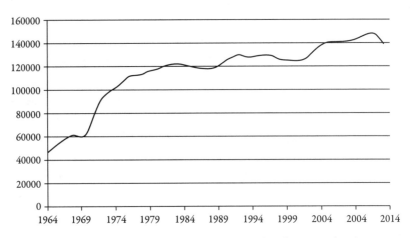

FIGURE 8.2 Total JD Enrollment, ABA-Accredited Law Schools

The growth was most rapid during the true boom years and was almost flat between 1984 (121,201) and 2001 (125,173). As chapter 7 dem-onstrated, law schools were still graduating more JDs than the market for lawyers could absorb, but at least law schools were not expand-ing. Law schools grew six times faster from 2001 to 2011 than they did between 1984 and 2001.[35] As discussed in chapter 9, the number of JD enrollees has fallen markedly since 2011.

There was an even bigger boom in law school faculties. In 1947, there were 992 full-time law professors. By 1985–6, there were 4,881, and another 1,652 deans and law librarians, for a total of 6,533.[36] In 2012–13, the total number of full-time administrators, law librarians, skills-training faculty, and teaching faculty had grown to 27,082.[37] Student-faculty ratios shrank greatly over this period as well.[38] Teaching loads went down, and salaries went up.[39]

In order to pay for this additional staff, there has been a steep increase in tuition. Between 1985 and 2009, law school tuition rose 820 percent for in-state residents at public institutions and 375 percent at private institutions.[40] According to ABA statistics, the average tuition for an in-state student at a public school in 1985 was $2,006.[41] In 2012, it was $23,214. Out-of-state tuition at public schools averaged $4,724 in 1985 and $36,202 in 2012. Private school tuition rose from an average of $7,526 to $40,634. These increases in tuition occurred at the same time as the market for lawyers peaked and fell backward. Law schools became much more expensive exactly as a legal education became less valuable.

Higher tuition means more debt. In just the last eleven years the average amount of law school debt rose from $46,499 to $84,600 at public schools and from $70,147 to a whopping $122,158 at private law schools, as shown in Figure 8.3.[42]

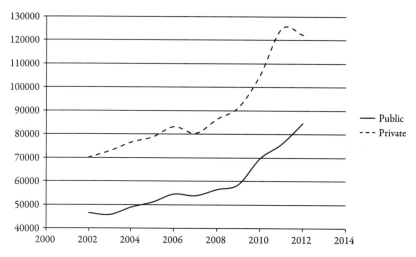

FIGURE 8.3 Average Law School Debt

The cost of undergraduate education has likewise risen much faster than inflation;[43] so law school debt is just a portion of total law student indebtedness.[44] For example, the New America Education Policy Program examined the federal data on law graduate indebtedness from 2012. Their dataset included all law students who borrowed money to pay for law school and counted their entire indebtedness, including undergraduate, living expenses, and so forth. In 2012 the 50th percentile law graduate borrower had $140,616 in debt and the 75th percentile $193,823.[45] Please do not let your eyes glaze over when reading the last figure. A full 25% of law students that borrowed money to attend law school finished with a debt load of $193,000 or more.

Student debt is worse at private schools and is often inversely related to quality. Table 8.1 (displayed on pp. 141–42) lists the top fifteen law schools for student loan debt for 2013 law graduates.[46] The list includes the U.S. News rank[47] for the school, the percentage of graduates who leave with debt, the bar passage rate, and the employment rate. The list is pretty shocking for the relative quality of the schools, the value of the degrees, and the total indebtedness.

Nine of the top-15 law schools for indebtedness are in U.S. News's tier two, meaning that they are not ranked among the top-150 law schools in America. The employment percentages for nine months after graduation are as low as Whittier's 23.6 percent and bar passage rates include Thomas Jefferson's 36.6 percent. In the current market for lawyer jobs, these tuition and debt load figures are unconscionable.

Even the decent schools on this list offer questionable value. American, Loyola Marymount, and Catholic—all well-considered law schools—have bar passage rates of 82.5 percent and below, and placement rates of 47.8 percent, 46.9 percent, and 66.7 percent respectively. At the higher end, only 71.1 percent of the graduates of Georgetown, the 14th-ranked school in America, were employed in JD or JD-preferred jobs nine months after graduation in 2013. Only N.Y.U. and Northwestern appear to be relatively sure bets on this list.

The top law schools led the tuition run-up. The mean tuition at a top-14 law school has risen from $39,513 to $49,551 in just the seven years from 2004 to 2011.[48] Paul Campos adjusted Harvard's tuition to 2011 dollars to show just how much faster tuition has grown than inflation. Since 1971, "Harvard's tuition has more than quadrupled in

TABLE 8.1 The Top Fifteen Law Schools for Student Loan Debt for 2013 Law Graduates

LAW SCHOOL	Average Debt	Percentage of Graduates with Debt	Tuition	U.S. News Rank	Bar Passage Rate	Employment Percentage Nine Months after Graduation[1]
Thomas Jefferson School of Law	$168,800	98%	$42,000	2T[2]	36.6% CA	32.2%
California Western School of Law	$167,867	89%	$43,700	2T	78.6% CA	42.1%
Phoenix School of Law	$162,627	97%	$39,533	2T	67.3% AZ	55%
Northwestern University	$156,791	82%	$53,468	12	93.9% IL	84.7%
New York Law School	$154,647	83%	$49,225	2T	80.3% NY	47.0%
American University (Washington)	$152,659	77%	$46,794	56	76.8% NY	47.8%
New York University	$149,336	81%	$51,150	6	95.5% NY	93.8%
Southwestern Law School	$147,976	79%	$43,850	2T	60.7% CA	52.3%
Georgetown University	$146,169	78%	$48,835	14	92.6% NY	71.1%
Whittier College	$143,536	92%	$40,310	2T	55.4% CA	23.6%

continued

TABLE 8.1 *continued*

LAW SCHOOL	Average Debt	Percentage of Graduates with Debt	Tuition	U.S. News Rank	Bar Passage Rate	Employment Percentage Nine Months after Graduation[1]
Florida Coastal School of Law	$143,111	92%	$39,370	2T	76% FL	41%
John Marshall Law School	$142,587	87%	$41,305	2T	83.3% IL	56.1%
Atlanta's John Marshall Law School	$142,515	92%	$34,800[3]	2T	73.0% GA	51.5%
Catholic University of America (Columbus)	$142,115	85%	$43,080	80	77.6% MD	66.7%
Loyola Marymount University	$141,936	78%	$44,230	68	82.5% CA	46.9%

[1]This counts JD-required and JD-advantage jobs, so it counts more jobs than the "True Employment Percentage" described in chapter 7.

[2]*U.S. News and World Report* ranks the top 150 law schools and then lumps the remaining 46 into a "second tier." 2T thus means it is among the lowest-ranked schools.

[3]John Marshall Atlanta unhelpfully lists their tuition as $1,200 per credit hour. *See* John Marshall Law School, *FAQs*, http://www.johnmarshall.edu/futurestudent/admissions-aid/faqs/ (last visited March 28, 2013). Eighty-eight hours are required to graduate, so $34,800 is an estimate of a year's tuition.

real, inflation-adjusted terms, and has nearly doubled in just the past 20 years":

HARVARD LAW SCHOOL TUITION (in 2011 dollars):

1971: $12,386

1981: $15,862

1991: $27,207

2001: $35,817

2012: $50,880[49]

Tuition at other top schools has grown similarly.

This meteoric rise in tuition occurred at very wealthy institutions. Yale Law School's endowment was $984 million in 2012.[50] In 2008, Harvard Law School's endowment was more than $1.7 billion.[51] Stanford Law School's endowment is estimated to be somewhere between $600 and 700 million.[52] In a 2012 speech at Stanford Law School, Paul Campos jokingly suggested that the law school cut its tuition by 30 percent, to $33,000, roughly its inflation-adjusted tuition in 2004.[53] The suggestion was met by guffaws, but it only involved a modest cut to the tuition levels of 2004, eight short years before Campos's speech, by one of the richest educational institutions on the planet. The tuition spikes for the top schools are especially disappointing because these schools set student expectations for what law school costs and give cover to all law schools.

Ironically, even attending one of these schools does not guarantee a top job in this legal economy. Derek Muller broke down the employment data used by *U.S. News* for the 2014 rankings and found that even elite institutions are having a hard time placing all of their graduates in elite placements (which he defines as a job at a law firm with one hundred or more lawyers or a federal clerkship).[54] Admittedly, this list leaves out public interest or other government work, but the percentages below suggest that some or many of the graduates of top law schools will be earning less than they planned when they borrowed upward of $150,000. Here are the top ten percentages:

1. Stanford University 72.9 percent
2. Columbia University 69.5 percent
3. University of Pennsylvania 67.1 percent
4. Yale University 66.4 percent
5. Harvard University 65.0 percent
6. Northwestern University 61.4 percent
7. Duke University 56.1 percent
8. University of Chicago 54.2 percent
9. New York University 54.1 percent
10. University of California–Berkeley 51.3 percent

The percentages for graduates of the rest of the law schools in America are much lower.

C. How and Why Did It Happen?

What made it possible to continuously grow the size, number, and tuition of law schools? Start with the students, the demand side of the equation. There has been a misunderstanding of exactly what lawyers do and what they earn. The perception problem is partially based upon popular culture. Starting with the television series *L.A. Law* and John Grisham's book *The Firm,* and continuing through television series like *Boston Legal* and *The Good Wife,* there is a sense that most lawyers work in fancy law firms, with good-looking people, doing extremely interesting work and earning a king's ransom. Even the president of the ABA has noted that law school applicants raised on television lawyers are frequently confused about the nature of, and remuneration for, the practice of law.[55]

The growth only made sense if law schools and applicants thought that law school was training students to work in Big Law, where earnings rose tremendously over the last thirty years. Figure 8.4 (displayed on p. 145) shows the bimodal salary distribution for 2006 starting salaries reported to NALP.

The right-hand side of the graph in Figure 8.4 shows the salaries law students thought lawyers made, with six-figure salaries right out of law school. They read news stories about starting salaries of $160,000 and thought that their biggest concern post–law school would be work-life

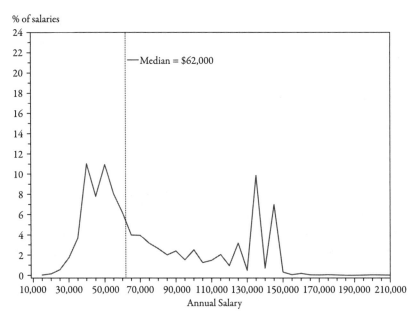

% of salaries

FIGURE 8.4 Distribution of Full-Time Salaries—Class of 2006

balance in a big firm. Law school prices rose to reflect this misunderstanding. How else does it make sense to pay $150,000 in tuition to potentially work in solo practice, where the average salary is $46,500?

As the salary distribution drifted into a bimodal split, the problem grew larger and larger. For the last seven years almost no law graduates have earned the median or mean salary; that number has been in the valley between the two humps. The ever-growing distance between the two humps means that students who hoped/planned to work in Big Law take a mighty tumble in earnings expectations in the likely event that they fail to get a Big Law job. In a typical bell-shaped curve most people bunch in the middle, so expectations are more sensible and there is less of a financial sting to finishing in the bottom 90 percent.

Even if applicants understand that they have to finish in the top 10–20 percent of the class to get the highest-paying jobs, they assume they will finish in the top 10 percent. Some of this is optimism bias,[56] but some of it is actually quite rational. This is because a law student admitted at a top-50 school has likely been very successful in undergraduate education. For example, in 2012 the median GPA for the University of Alabama was 3.83 and was 3.65 for Arizona State.

Even relatively lower-profile schools like Pepperdine (3.63 median) or San Diego (3.50 median) admit students with stellar undergraduate records.[57] It is not surprising that these students would expect to finish law school near the top of their class; that is what they have done their entire educational career. When you tell an undergraduate entering many law schools that she must be in the top 10 percent in law school to get the job she would like (whether it is a job with a law firm or the Sierra Club) she is likely to say, "That's great news! Because I've been in the top 10 percent my whole life!"

Many of these same students went to law school because they were bad at math, so the harsh reality of a mandatory curve and class rankings only dawns on them after first semester, when half of the students learn that they are in the bottom half of the class. At this point, optimism over paying back law school loans with a high-paying job is replaced by the harsh reality of a challenging job search and a relatively modest salary.

Law schools helped create the confusion. Law school employment statistics and average salary information provided to websites and the *U.S. News* were misleading (or in some cases actually false) for years, leading to the lawsuits described more fully in chapter 9.

Further, the great majority of American law professors graduated from an elite law school during a time when most students who wanted jobs in Big Law were able to get them.[58] Most law professors have very limited practice experience, and the practice experience they have was likely in Big Law.[59] So, regardless of where a professor teaches, she probably agreed with the applicants that the world of law practice looks like Big Law. If a professor has any experience as a lawyer, that is where it came from. Law school classes are frequently taught as if the students will all be first-year associates in Big Law someday. Law professors will sometimes give students impassioned advice about not trying to bill eighty hours in a week, work advice that almost none of the students they are speaking to will ever need.

Thus, everyone was confused about what law school is for and where lawyers actually work. The vast majority of American law students will never work in Big Law, so there was a deep disconnect between law school, law students, professors, and the actual legal market.

There were also more potential customers. Many more Americans now enter and complete college. In 1947, 5.4 percent of the adult population was college graduates. By 2003, that number had grown to 27.9 percent.[60]

A significant portion of these graduates majored in the humanities or the social sciences. Often these graduates find law school a natural fit. Earnings for humanities majors tend to run lower than earnings for other college graduates,[61] and they tend to graduate with general skills in analysis, reading, and writing, but few job-ready skills. Many business schools will not accept students directly after finishing college and medical school requires a specific set of undergraduate classes that most humanities and social science majors will not have taken. Changes to the LSAT in the 1980s assisted this trend by eliminating the math section and decreasing the number of logic questions.[62]

Law has always been a respected and learned profession in America. Applicants also think that lawyer unemployment has always been quite low, although as noted in chapter 7 that may be because of JD-holders leaving the profession rather than because of an abundance of law jobs. Cooley Law School has a whole portion of its website dedicated to convincing students that lawyer unemployment is, and will remain, low.[63]

As a psychological matter, law school tends to draw risk-averse students and law has been seen as a safe haven for humanities college graduates.[64] Most applicants to law school have been told that "you can do a lot with a law degree,"[65] further encouraging students who are unconvinced that they want to be lawyers to attend law school.

There are two supply-side reasons for tuition inflation. First, ABA and AALS accreditation requirements make starting and maintaining a law school more expensive than they would otherwise be. Both the AALS and the ABA have a mass of complicated and very expensive requirements for accreditation.[66] ABA accreditation standards mandate a bevy of expensive items, like a minimum number of full-time teaching faculty who also produce scholarship, teaching loads, and volumes of books in a law library.[67] AALS membership is voluntary and generally a matter of prestige, although more than three-quarters of American law schools are members.[68] ABA accreditation standards matter tremendously. Forty-five states require graduation from an ABA-accredited law school for admission to the bar.[69]

Nevertheless, the ABA and AALS standards have not changed that much over the last thirty years, so the accreditation standards cannot explain the run-up in tuition. The standards may have suppressed lower-cost competition, but they did not require tuition increases on the current scale.

A more likely explanation was the arrival of the *U.S. News* law school rankings in 1987.[70] Chapter 10 discusses the irony that the *Am Law 100* and the *U.S. News* rankings arrived in the same year, simultaneously undermining law schools and Big Law with jealousy and competition. In 2009, the Government Accountability Office concluded that "competition among [law] schools for higher rankings" was among the main culprits driving higher tuition.[71] Law schools began a "positional arms race," competing on the basis of scholarships, faculty, facilities, student-faculty ratios, and even "brochures bragging about our accomplishments."[72] Law schools raised tuition to pay for the competition. Some (many?) law schools also cooked the books for the rankings. The worst examples were embellished employment data, exaggerating both salaries and the number of employed students, since these exaggerations may have led more students to enroll in law school under false pretenses.

D.   Grad PLUS, IBR, and Loan Forgiveness

A change in the federal loan program has likewise made it easier for students to borrow large amounts. Under the Federal Graduate PLUS (Grad PLUS) loan program law students can borrow the entire cost of their education.[73] One of the very best portions of Brian Tamanaha's *Failing Law Schools* details how crippling the repayment of large loan amounts can be.[74] Tamanaha breaks it out by total debt load and projected salaries and shows that unless a student is attending a top-5 law school and is very likely to earn $160,000 per year or is attending a state school with low in-state tuition, it will be hard to make borrowing the cost of a law school education work.[75] Former Northwestern Dean David Van Zandt has calculated that in order to service the average amount of law school debt a graduate must earn at least $65,315.12. Unfortunately, more than 40 percent of the American law graduates that are able to get a law job start at lower salaries.[76]

Critics of Tamanaha's work have argued that federal income-based loan repayment (IBR) and loan forgiveness programs make condemning law school debt passé, because these programs mean that most law students will never repay their loans. Philip Schrag analyzes the income-based program in great detail, assuming a hypothetical student named Sarah, who has borrowed $120,000 to finance law school at a combined interest rate of 7.25 percent.[77] If Sarah gets a job paying $63,000 and attempts to pay back her debt in ten years she will struggle mightily. Nevertheless, with IBR and loan forgiveness Sarah will pay back relatively little of her loan:

> By electing [IBR] Sarah could limit her annual payment to 15 percent of her discretionary income, defined as her adjusted gross income minus 150 percent of the poverty level for a family of her family's size. Even if Sarah has no other family members, this formula would reduce her monthly repayment to $578 in the first year of repayment, about 11 percent of her actual income. Furthermore, the law that created IBR forgives any remaining debt after 25 years of repayment. If Sarah received 3 percent annual raises (and continued to have no other family members), in her 25th year she would pay $1,175 monthly, still only 11 percent of her income, and the remainder of her debt would be forgiven. If she were married with two children, her initial payments would be $355 per month, and her final payments would be $722 per month, 6.8 percent of her income.
>
> The terms of repayment under the 2007 legislation are more generous for those who are fortunate and self-sacrificing enough to do long-term public service. If, after graduating, Sarah spends 120 months working for a government entity or any non-profit organization described in Section 501(c)(3) of the Internal Revenue Code, she would have to repay at the IBR rate only for those 120 months. Under the federal Public Service Loan Forgiveness program (PSLF), forgiveness of the remaining balance would take place at the end of that ten-year period, and (unlike forgiveness for those who do not do public service) cancellation of the remaining debt would be tax-exempt.[78]

Moreover, recent changes in the law have made the deal even sweeter for students. The "pay-as-you-earn" plan lowers the rate of repayment from 15 percent to 10 percent of salary and shortens the forgiveness period to twenty years from twenty-five.[79] The ten-year public service timeframe for loan forgiveness remains unchanged.

There are several reasons to be skeptical of this solution, however. First, it is always a good idea to be suspicious of what looks like a scam. Schrag's description makes it seem like no one, not the schools, not the student, and not even the lender, ever expects the loan to be repaid. Sarah does not need to worry about what she borrows, because she will just pay 10–12 percent of her salary (whatever that salary is) for twenty to twenty-five years and then take her discharge.

One can imagine a more venal Sarah planning on a three-year vacation at a fourth tier law school in a fun location like San Diego or Miami. She could have lots of time on the beach, $12,000 a year or more for living expenses, and her parents can proudly tell their friends she is in law school. All she has to do is not fail out. When school is done, she can take whatever job she gets and pay a percentage back to the government, comfortable in the knowledge that she never planned to pay her loans back and she had a good three years.

Second, the loan repayment programs are not guaranteed to exist in their current form, or in any form. As time passes and more and more loans are not repaid there will be pressure to change or eliminate the law altogether. Congressional Republicans have already suggested reformatting student loan collections and eliminating the loan forgiveness programs.[80] Students borrowing today should be cautious about relying on future congressional largesse.

This is especially so because while the loan repayment programs appear to be a subsidy to students, they are actually a subsidy to law schools and other professional schools. For example, *BusinessWeek* crowed that the pay-as-you-earn plan is "a windfall for MBAs."[81] Grad PLUS loans allow law students to borrow any amount to cover the "cost of attendance" as "determined by the school."[82] With IBR and loan forgiveness all of the risk of law school is transferred from the student and the law school to the federal government. The student must only pay 10–15 percent of her income regardless of what she owes, and then must only hang in there until the federal government picks up the rest after ten or twenty or twenty-five years. The law school gets paid upfront. Because there is no cap on the Grad PLUS loans, tuition is bounded only by sticker shock, explaining why it has risen so steeply since the advent of Grad PLUS in 2005, even during the Great Recession.

In the 1990s, when I attended law school, federal Stafford Loans were capped, and if a student needed additional funds she had to borrow from a private lender. This acted as a brake on tuition, as students (including me) were loath to borrow more than the Stafford amount. Private loans had higher interest rates, more paperwork, and less favorable repayment terms, and seemed a lot scarier.

Matt Leichter demonstrated the effect in the *American Lawyer*, showing that since Grad PLUS launched, the number of law schools where tuition is more than the maximum amount that can be borrowed under a Stafford Loan has almost doubled.[83] Leichter argues that these subsidies have kept "zombie law schools" afloat, by keeping law schools that should have cut enrollment or tuition, or both, in business.

Third, even if IBR and loan forgiveness remain, they force graduates to carry a significant amount of debt for twenty to twenty-five years before forgiveness kicks in. Student loan debt is now the most common type of debt, surpassing both auto loans and mortgages.[84] These loan balances and repayment amounts can be considered in applications for other loans like mortgages or car loans. The Federal Reserve Bank of New York estimates that student loan debt slowed the rebound in the housing market because young professionals cannot or will not borrow more to buy a home.[85]

In 2013, more than half of student loans were delinquent or in deferral, also negatively affecting credit.[86] Loans in default are referred to collection agencies. Steven Harper reports that in 2011, the U.S. Department of Education referred more than $1.4 billion for collection.[87]

There is also the psychological freight of carrying around large balances. *USA Today* has reported on high levels of stress among the millennial generation, partially due to student loan balances,[88] and *U.S. News* published a guide on "how to de-stress from student-loan debt."[89]

E. The Upshot

American law schools, like the firms of Big Law, find themselves in unfamiliar waters. They have ridden a wave of more schools, with larger enrollments, charging tuition that has outpaced inflation, for years. Students came in droves, some based on a misunderstanding that they could work in Big Law (and 80–90 percent of them cannot) or on the more basic assumption that they would have the opportunity to work as a lawyer, and one-third of them likely cannot. The bait and switch is over, however, and what remains is to guess where law schools are going.

9

The Bleak Present and Near Future
for Law Schools

IN 2004, RICHARD MATASAR, who has been the dean of three different law schools, noted presciently that we were "reaching the end of a golden era for law schools [and] beginning a period of decline . . . putting many schools' survival at risk."[1] Schools are struggling with a public relations nightmare, fewer applications, lower enrollment, and growing public and internal criticism. We begin with a brief case study: Tennessee law schools. Two brand-new private law schools have been founded since 2008, both within 1.5 miles of an existing law school and both costing upward of $150,000 for a JD, despite the ugly employment and earnings picture for new Tennessee lawyers.

I choose Tennessee as a particularly galling example of over-expansion, but it is hardly unusual. For example, Indiana Tech opened a new law school in Fort Wayne, Indiana, in Fall 2013 with a smaller-than-expected inaugural class of twenty-four students and a student–to faculty ratio of 2 to 1.[2] Indiana already had two public law schools at University of Indiana–Bloomington and University of Indiana–Indianapolis and two private law schools at Notre Dame and Valparaiso. All told, the ABA has accredited twenty new law schools in the last fifteen years,[3] and four more are provisionally approved.[4]

A.   Tennessee Welcomes Two New Law Schools

In 2008, the state of Tennessee had three ABA-accredited law schools— the University of Memphis Cecil C. Humphreys School of Law,

The University of Tennessee College of Law, and Vanderbilt Law School—as well as the Nashville School of Law, a non-ABA-accredited school whose graduates may sit for the Tennessee bar. Each of these schools has been in existence for more than fifty years and serves its own niche within the state.

Memphis and Tennessee are state-supported law schools that charge a comparatively low, although ever-rising, tuition for in-state residents.[5] Memphis was founded in 1962 and is the only law school in Tennessee's largest city. It naturally has a large footprint in the local bar and throughout west Tennessee. It is consistently less expensive than Tennessee and is usually ranked in the middle or lower middle of law schools.

Tennessee was founded in 1890 in Knoxville and has been the flagship state law school since. It usually ranks between 50 and 75 in *U.S. News* and has alumni all over the state and the Southeast. It has the nation's oldest clinical programs and is a comparative bargain in-state.

Vanderbilt is an expensive, private, top-20 law school in Nashville, the second-largest city in the state. It prides itself on being the Harvard of the South. For years, Vanderbilt graduates were more likely to take the New York bar (and presumably work at a large firm there) than the Tennessee bar.[6] In the post-downturn years Vanderbilt has focused more on placement within the Southeast, and the current top state for bar admission is Tennessee.

The Nashville School of Law is accredited only in the state of Tennessee. It was founded in 1911 and was one of the original YMCA night law schools. It remains a night school staffed primarily by adjunct professors. It is the most affordable school in Tennessee, both because it is taught at night (allowing full-time work) and because it has low tuition ($5,292 per year in 2013–14, with four years of expected schooling).[7]

In 2009, 735 new lawyers passed the Tennessee bar examination.[8] The Bureau of Labor Statistics estimates that the total number of open law jobs in Tennessee from 2010–15 will be 389, resulting in a surplus of 346 new lawyers just in the bar class of 2009, let alone from the individuals who will pass the Tennessee bar between now and 2015. This phenomenon is not limited to Tennessee—eighteen other states had an even bigger surplus than Tennessee. In sum, even a cursory examination of the facts in the mid- to late 2000s reveals a surfeit of Tennessee law schools and law graduates.

Despite these trends, in 2008 Lincoln Memorial University (LMU) announced a new law school in Knoxville,[9] and in 2009 Belmont University announced a new law school in Nashville.[10] Both sought full ABA accreditation. Both schools planned on admitting 100–150 students in their inaugural classes, with room to grow in future years. For 2013–14, tuition at LMU was $30,984[11] and Belmont's 2013–14 tuition was $33,280.[12] With fees, books, and living expenses LMU is estimated to run $50,000 a year,[13] Belmont $57,495, bringing the three-year total cost for a JD to over $150,000 at either institution.[14]

LMU has had a rockier go of it so far. Both LMU and Belmont were accredited by the state of Tennessee before opening, so their graduates, like the Nashville School of Law's, can take the Tennessee bar exam. Both schools are also seeking ABA accreditation and LMU initially struggled. The ABA denied provisional accreditation in December 2011, followed quickly by an LMU lawsuit alleging antitrust and due process violations.[15] The ABA won the first round of that lawsuit by defeating LMU's request for a temporary restraining order.[16] Nine months later, LMU fired its dean and dropped its lawsuit to concentrate fully on reapplying to the ABA for provisional accreditation.[17] In the meantime, LMU enrolled a class of twelve students for Fall 2012 amid the uncertainty, and the school faced a lawsuit from a student alleging negligence.[18]

Did this cause LMU to reconsider? Hardly. It hired a consultant, Leary Davis, who had guided two North Carolina law schools through accreditation and a new dean, Parham Williams, who had guided Chapman University Law School through accreditation.[19] LMU officials announced that they would operate their law school, even at a loss, "indefinitely."[20] Dean Williams defended running the law school at a loss thusly: "the university regularly finances other academic departments that are not viable on their own—we wouldn't have oboe players if that was [not] the case."[21] In December, 2014 their faith was rewarded by provisional accreditation.[22]

Belmont received provisional ABA accreditation in 2013 after applying in 2012.[23] Belmont's journey was easier partially because its applicant profile was better than LMU's and the school built a brandnew $25-million law building and partially because its first dean was a veteran of past successful ABA accreditation applications at Elon and Appalachian.[24] The takeaway from Belmont and LMU? Hire an insider who knows how the system works if you want accreditation.

LMU and Belmont are less than 1.5 miles from existing law schools (Tennessee and Vanderbilt respectively) and are entering a market and state saturated with law schools. Both schools are significantly more expensive than the in-state tuition at the University of Tennessee or Memphis. Both schools faced immediate scrutiny upon announcing their intention to open, with a particularly pointed reaction to Belmont's announcement from *Above the Law*.[25]

Nevertheless, Belmont and LMU have pledged to plow ahead with the accreditation process and with a long-term commitment to operate a private law school, even in the teeth of a terrible market for lawyers and shrinking earnings. Moreover, these graduates will be competing for jobs in Tennessee without the benefit of any alumni in hiring positions. More Vanderbilt graduates are looking for work in Tennessee rather than New York or Washington, D.C., negatively affecting the job market for all Tennessee law schools.[26] Both law schools are very likely to be ranked at the bottom of *U.S. News* and other law school rankings (because name recognition among peers and the bar is 40 percent of the ranking),[27] at least for the foreseeable future.

The spate of recent law school openings is emblematic of much that is unfortunate about the legal academy today. These schools are cheaper than many private law schools, but still very, very expensive. Especially for what the students will receive: based on the experiences of other bottom-tier law schools in saturated markets there will be few graduates who get jobs that require a JD. These schools are made possible by the student loan structure, the hope/expectation that the graduates will not have to pay back the cost of their education, the blind insistence that the market for lawyers is better and improving, and the optimism bias/ignorance of the applicants.[28]

B. Bad Publicity and a Tale of Two "Law Profs"

These schools will likely struggle, because legal education is experiencing a spate of disastrously bad publicity. It started before the Great Recession with the law school "scamblogs."[29] These interlocking blogs complained about law schools inflating their employment numbers and drawing students into massive debt with the illusory promises of long and lucrative careers as lawyers.[30] These blogs have ranged in quality and tone, with *Third Tier Reality* the flagship for the low road, featuring pictures of fecal matter in toilets and scathing reviews of various law schools.[31] *Third Tier Reality* is also the progenitor of the "TTT" (third-tier toilet) designation for law schools and "TTTT" (fourth-tier toilet), and so on. At the high end, *Law School Transparency* and *The Law School Tuition Bubble* offer thoughtful and original research by recent law graduates, some of which is cited in this book.[32] The blogs are quite high profile: *USA Today, the New York Times, Slate,* and others have covered them.[33]

Some law professors have also joined the fray. At one extreme, Paul Campos has been stirring the pot since he started his blog, *Inside the Law School Scam* in 2011.[34] Campos started the blog anonymously under the pseudonym "lawprof." His first post praised other "scamblogs" and declared: "When people say 'law school is a scam,' what that really means, at the level of actual moral responsibility, is that **law professors are scamming their students**" (emphasis in original).[35] He followed up with posts arguing that law professors are overpaid, lazy, and poor teachers who often have only a surface understanding of the subjects they teach. He also attacked the law school emphasis on scholarship over practice experience in hiring and tenure decisions.[36] These posts caused quite a stir in academia and elsewhere[37] and eventually Campos revealed himself.[38] Campos subsequently wrote a book entitled *Don't Go To Law School (Unless)* that expanded some of the research from the blog and elsewhere and argued that it will not be worth it for most applicants to attend law school at the current prices and debt loads.[39] Campos has since retired the blog but seems likely to remain a strident critic of legal education.[40]

At the other extreme is Brian Tamanaha's excellent book, *Failing Law Schools.*[41] Tamanaha's work is measured, fair, and scholarly in its approach. Tamanaha comes across as quite calm and apologetic about the bad news he brings and is careful not to accuse anyone in particular of malfeasance. Nevertheless, he and Campos come to remarkably similar conclusions. Both Campos and Tamanaha lay out in painful detail the run-up in tuition and the concomitant rise in faculty salaries and student-debt burdens. They also note the poor market for law graduates and the role that the (relatively silly and self-defeating) competition over *U.S. News* rankings has played. Campos and Tamanaha both agree that the current structure is unsustainable and fundamentally immoral.

Campos and Tamanaha explicitly identify law professors as the villains in this morality play. Because of the nature of ABA and AALS accreditation, law school faculties have enormous input into how American law schools are run. Campos and Tamanaha argue vociferously that this control has meant that law schools are now tailored largely to the benefit of the faculty themselves.[12] They argue that many law professors do not work very hard and are poorly situated to teach law students due to limited practical experience. They assert that law schools over-emphasize scholarship at the expense of teaching or public service. And all of this is made possible by massive student loans. If you doubt the veracity of these arguments, watch the parody video of a law professor losing his mind when he is told he has to teach on a Friday.[43]

Campos seems to relish the role of gadfly, taking broad, and at times purposefully outrageous, swipes at legal academia. By comparison, Tamanaha seems pained to have to admit what to him is an inescapable truth: law schools are broken and he and his colleagues are at fault. Of the two, Tamanaha is the more persuasive because he tends to understate rather than to overstate. Tamanaha is also more effective because he is clearly a law professor's law professor, and yet he reached a crossroads in his professional life where he could no longer ethically support his own endeavors and responded with a measured and scholarly *mea culpa*.

C. Student Lawsuits

The blogs were the tip of the iceberg. In November 2011, the Anziska law firm filed a class action suit against New York Law School on behalf of graduates who claimed they were misled by the law school's employment statistics.[44] The firm followed up with a similar lawsuit against Cooley Law School,[45] and then twelve more schools (Albany, Brooklyn, Hofstra, Florida Coastal, Chicago-Kent, DePaul, John Marshall, California Western, Southwestern, Golden Gate, USF, and Widener).[46]

The cases follow the same basic template. Recent graduates of a law school sue and argue that the school's employment data posted on its website and given to the ABA and *U.S. News* were misleading because they listed the percentage of students employed nine months after graduation without separating out the jobs that were part time or did not require a JD. For example, according to the complaint, New York Law School reported 90–92 percent employment nine months after graduation for the years 2007–11, while the actual numbers for JD-required or JD-preferred jobs were much lower, as were the actual salaries for these jobs.[47]

So far, the success rate has been mixed, with courts dismissing the suits against New York Law School,[48] Cooley,[49] John Marshall,[50] DePaul,[51] and Albany.[52] Suits have been allowed to go forward against California Western, Golden Gate, USF, Southwestern, and Thomas Jefferson in California, and against Widener in New Jersey.[53] Even the suits that have been dismissed have hardly bathed those schools in glory. Courts have generally not disputed that the law school information was misleading, but rather held that law school applicants are savvy customers who should have known better.[54]

The lawsuits have likewise generated quite a bit of publicity, with coverage in the *L.A. Times*,[55] the *Wall Street Journal*,[56] and elsewhere. *New York Magazine* ran a particularly lengthy and unflattering piece that featured a picture of a birdcage lined with a feces-stained New York Law School diploma.[57]

This is all on top of the steady stream of stories recounting the sorry state of the job market for law grads in painful detail. For years, law school appeared to be a safe bet for a cushy life, almost regardless of price. In the Internet era the narrative can reverse quite quickly, however, and now potential applicants face a gauntlet of news stories, blog posts, and *YouTube* videos encouraging them not to go to law school.

D.   Fewer Applicants, Fewer Law Students

Conventional wisdom has finally caught up to market realities, and law school applications are way down. Fewer people are taking the LSAT and still fewer are applying to law schools. The LSAC provides the number of LSAT takers from 1988–9 to 2013–14, as shown in Figure 9.1.[58]

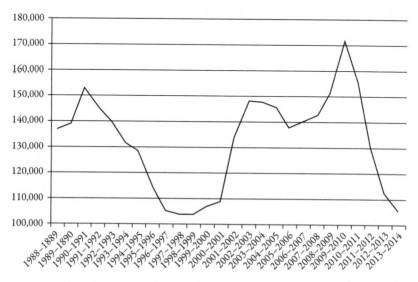

FIGURE 9.1 Total LSAT Takers

The high-water mark was 2009–10, as applicants fleeing the recession sought refuge in law schools. As the word got out that law school graduates were faring poorly, LSAT takers fell to the lowest level since 2000–1 and well below 1988–9 levels, when there were twenty-seven fewer ABA-accredited law schools and roughly 25,000 fewer American law students. The decline since 2009–10 has been precipitous, falling 34 percent between 2009 and 2013.[59] LSAT administrations declined another 6 percent in 2013–14, although there was a tiny 1.1 percent increase in the February 2014 exam, leading to hope of a thaw. The June and September 2014 LSAT administrations showed declines of 8–9 percent though, so we have yet to find the bottom, even after a decline of 45 percent from peak (2009) to trough (2014).[60]

Fewer LSAT takers means fewer applicants. The LSAC count for the number of applicants (Figure 9.2) shows a significant decline since 2004.[61]

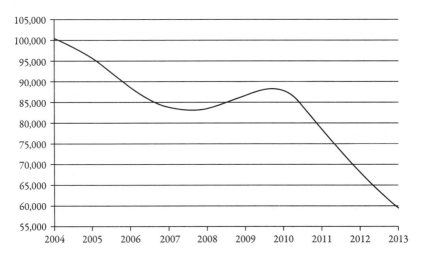

FIGURE 9.2 Law School Applicants

The number of law school applicants has declined 32 percent since 2004, with double-digit percentage declines in 2011, 2012, and 2013. In Fall 2013, 59,400 people applied to law school,[62] a little more than half the number of applicants just seven years ago. These applicants are filing fewer applications as well; applications are down 18.8 percent from 2012.[63] Over this same period fifteen new ABA-accredited schools opened, and ABA-accredited schools added roughly fifteen thousand more law students.

In 2010–11, 52,488 students enrolled at two hundred ABA-accredited law schools.[64] If the numbers follow the same trends, in 2014–15 fewer students will *apply* to law schools than *enrolled* just three years earlier.

E.   The Shape of Things to Come—Law Schools and the ABA

Fewer applicants means fewer students. In 2013 only 39,675 full-time students matriculated at an ABA-accredited law school, a decline of 11 percent from 2012 and the lowest number of first-year law students since 1977.[65] In 2013 ABA-accredited schools granted 46,478 JD degrees, so the difference between recent, current, and future enrollment is quite stark.

Observers have begun to predict a "death spiral" for lower-ranked schools.[66] Glenn Reynolds suggests that as many as twenty-five law schools could close in the near term.[67] Dean Philip Closius notes a crisis at American law schools, and lists only 68 law schools as immune (the top-25 and the 43 flagship state institutions), leaving 132 as vulnerable to closure.[68]

So what will happen? It seems likely that applications and enrollment will continue to decline, especially considering the continued bad news on the employment front. The students attending law school will also be more price-sensitive.[69] These changes will put tremendous pressure on law schools. Because the graduating classes of 2013 and 2014 will be the largest ever, the pain has yet to be really felt, because the three-year rolling total of paying students is still relatively high.

Top-25 and flagship state law schools will face less pressure. Unless the ABA somehow loses its vise-grip on accreditation the nature of law school will remain largely unchanged, albeit with a slightly greater focus on skills training and clinics. This is because the ABA will have no interest in loosening accreditation standards or allowing alternative models of legal education in the teeth of the current oversupply of law graduates. Extra law graduates are good news for consumers, but the ABA is not a consumer advocacy group. It is the nation's bar association.

The most vulnerable schools are expensive, fourth-tier, private, stand-alone law schools.[70] A stand-alone law school is not affiliated with a broader university. Stand-alone schools are more vulnerable because there is no central administration or larger body to ask for help or bridge loans during a down period. These schools rely heavily on tuition and have limited endowments. Many of these schools are relatively new, so they have fewer alumni to tap in a pinch. A December 2013 Standard & Poor's Report notes a deteriorating credit situation for stand-alone law schools, with Thomas Jefferson Law School being downgraded to junk bond status.[71] For a stretch it looked like Thomas Jefferson might close, but it surrendered ownership of its building, restructured its debt, and remains open for business.[72]

The list in chapter 8 of the top fifteen law schools in 2012 for student indebtedness included nine schools that fit some or all of the above criteria: Thomas Jefferson, California Western, Phoenix, New York Law School, Southwestern, Whittier, Florida Coastal, and the two John Marshall law schools. Average student indebtedness at graduation runs from

$142,000 to $168,800 and the tuition ranges from $35,000 to $49,000 a year at these schools. If fewer students come to borrow less money to pay the high tuition, the bottom line will be squeezed quite quickly.

These schools will likely reach the crossroads first, but the application/enrollment crunch will affect every law school in the country. Consider the Columbus School of Law (CUA Law) at the Catholic University of America, in Washington, D.C. CUA Law was founded in 1897 and was a relatively early adopter of the Harvard model, as it was accredited by the AALS in 1921 and the ABA in 1925.[73] It was rated 80th in the country by the 2013 *U.S. News* rankings and is widely considered a top-100 law school.

Nevertheless, in response to a drop in law school admissions and applications the *entire university* was required to take a 20 percent operational cut.[74] There are several remarkable aspects to this story. First, CUA Law's revenue/enrollment fell so much that the entire university is facing a 20 percent cut, suggesting a precipitous decline in law school revenue. Second, it highlights dramatically that law schools have been a cash cow for some schools. Being associated with a larger university thus may not offer much of a cushion to law schools, if the rest of the university depends on the law school's profit. Third, if it could happen at CUA, it could happen at any number of similarly well-regarded and long-existing law schools. The current downturn is going to affect every school from top to bottom.

Law schools have few options to address lower revenue. The biggest expense in American law schools by far is people, and the most expensive of these people generally have tenure, so easy options for trimming costs are relatively limited. Law schools now face one (or some combination) of the following unpalatable options:

(1) **Lower the Admission Standards.** Admit everyone who applies and facially meets the standards (i.e., any college graduate who took the LSAT). Worry about bar passage rates farther down the road. There is evidence that this is happening already at many schools. The number of law school applicants has been falling much more quickly than the number of law school enrollees, which means that some or all of the applicants who would have been denied admission in 2010 are now being accepted. This strategy alone cannot solve the problem if applications continue to

fall, as the number of applications (let alone enrollees) may soon fall below the necessary break-even enrollment at some schools.

(2) **Admit Smaller Classes.** Keep admissions standards where they are and admit a much smaller class. This is already happening at many schools.[75] This is only an option for schools that can afford the lost tuition.

(3) **Cut Tuition.** Cut tuition sufficiently to draw students away from other, more expensive law schools. The University of Arizona cut tuition by 11 percent for in-state students and 8 percent for out-of-state[76] and the University of Illinois has likewise discounted tuition across the board.[77] It will be interesting to see if this strategy proves effective. The "hallway chatter" suggests that law schools are already engaged in a costly price war over the most desirable students through scholarship offers.[78] Thus, the price of law school is now a little like the hourly rate in Big Law. It is a negotiation point rather than the true cost for most students. Unfortunately, this means that law school scholarship funds are more likely to be distributed based upon LSAT and GPA targets, rather than financial need.[79]

(4) **Merge.** Merge with another law school or join a larger university. Texas A&M has recently agreed to buy Texas Wesleyan Law School, a stand-alone, fourth-tier private law school in Fort Worth, Texas.[80] Cal Western has had recent merger negotiations with the University of California–San Diego.[81] Western Michigan University and Cooley Law School are considering a formal alliance.[82]

(5) **Cut Gradually.** Cut costs by encouraging retirements, freezing hiring, and raising teaching loads on the professors who remain. Hastings Law School, for example, has increased faculty teaching loads,[83] and multiple schools have frozen hiring.[84] New tenure-track track hiring is in free fall, shrinking more than 50 percent between 2011 and 2014.[85]

(6) **Cut Radically.** Cut costs by firing faculty or staff or eliminating a major cost center, like the law library. There is some evidence of this occurring, with the Appalachian School of Law instituting a substantial reduction in its library budget, cutting salaries, and laying off faculty and staff.[86] Vermont Law School

is cutting and buying out staff and looking to change faculty status from full-time and tenured to a "part time or class-to-class" status.[87] Hamline University School of Law has cut full-time faculty about 18 percent since 2010 through early retirement incentives, and twenty-one professors accepted buyout packages at Widener University School of Law. Most alarmingly, Seton Hall Law School recently notified its entire untenured faculty that it might not be retained in 2014–15.[88] Law libraries have already been cut radically[89] and James Milles speculates that they are headed for extinction altogether.[90]

(7) **Give Up.** Close the school and fire everyone. Many commentators have predicted a wave of law school closings, but that strikes me as the least likely of these strategies. It is hard to imagine that any American law dean is going to voluntarily close the doors on her law school. Consider the reaction of the largest law school in the country—Thomas M. Cooley—to the news of smaller entering classes at other law schools. Cooley did close its smaller campus in Ann Arbor, Michigan, but overall "isn't interested in reducing the size of its entering class on the basis of the perceived benefit to society. . . . Cooley's mission is inclusiveness."[91] *Above the Law* has a particularly hilarious reaction to this quote,[92] but it is emblematic of the survivalist ethic of law schools. They will try any combination of options 1–6 before closing up shop.

Cutting tuition or class sizes decreases revenue, so those solutions will not work for law schools on the edge of closing. Likewise, not every freestanding law school is going to be able to find a merger partner, especially if it is operating at a loss.

Many American law schools will combine lower admissions standards (admitting anyone even facially qualified) and cutting costs, even if it means closing the law library and firing most of its employees or replacing tenured faculty with adjuncts. A bare-bones law school that consists of a building and a small administration, and is staffed largely or exclusively by adjuncts, would be very inexpensive to operate, especially without any accompanying cuts to tuition. A law school could lose half or more of its enrollment and still turn a tidy profit under that strategy. Similarly, a law school could cut half or two-thirds of its full-time faculty and double or triple teaching loads and save a substantial amount.

This strategy would likely guarantee survival, but at a high cost. These law schools would likely cease to be in compliance with ABA accreditation standards. Letting in any and all applicants would likely result in lower bar passage scores. There is empirical evidence that lower LSAT scores correlate with lower bar passage scores, and that the effect accelerates as the scores get lower.[93] The first signs that the strategy of admitting anyone who applies has a downside is a steep decline in 2014 bar passage rates.[94]

Likewise, the ABA standards require a full-time law faculty dedicated to teaching, scholarship, and service.[95] If a law school were to cut its full-time faculty too much, or add so much teaching that scholarship and service were curtailed, the school would violate the standards. Nor would terminated law professors, or professors asked to teach twice their typical load, be likely to go gently into the night; the ABA would certainly receive notice and complaints.

Nevertheless, ABA accreditation runs on a seven-year cycle, and then allows any non-compliant school the opportunity to return to compliance or appeal any adverse decisions. In short, a law school could operate for years, if not a decade or two, in noncompliance before accreditation was fully removed.

These strategies would keep almost any law school in business, but would put the ABA between a rock and a hard place. On the one hand, the criticism of law schools and their accreditation standards is probably at the highest pitch ever, and *Above the Law* has been particularly persistent and persuasive on this point.[96] There is a sense that there are too many law schools that offer too little value for too high a cost, and that some law schools are taking advantage of their students. The ABA takes (and deserves) some or much of the blame.

There is also the fact of a collapsing market for legal services generally, and the concern of death from the side with each over-swollen law school class. The ABA of 1935 certainly knew how to react to a downturn in the market for lawyers (tighten entry), and the current ABA faces similar pressures.

On the other hand, disaccrediting a law school is a very drastic measure. The ABA has denied accreditation to new law schools several times[97] and has threatened disaccreditation with some frequency,[98] but it has never actually stripped an accredited law school of its accreditation.[99] Based on its recent somnolence in the face of false employment numbers, overwhelming student debt, falling bar passage numbers, and its choice of leadership for the accreditation team, it does seem that the ABA has little appetite for disaccreditation.[100]

When the ABA has denied accreditation it has faced lawsuits, but the ABA has consistently won those suits.[101] None of those cases dealt with disaccreditation, though, and a court might look less kindly on taking accreditation away rather than withholding it. Likewise, the ABA lives in continuous fear of further invasive antitrust oversight[102] and has seen increased congressional saber-rattling.[103] In 2011, Senator Grassley sent a sharply worded letter to the ABA with thirty-one detailed questions about its accreditation process.[104] The ABA may prefer to do nothing and hold on to its power to accredit law schools than to do something and lose that power altogether.

The ABA is likely to face this dilemma soon, as the unpleasant choices facing various law schools lead them to flout the ABA standards, forcing the ABA's hand. Based upon past practice, it seems likely that some law schools will face disaccreditation. The last time the legal establishment faced a long period of lawyer under-employment and shrinking wages, during the Depression, they responded by greatly strengthening entry barriers to dampen competition.[105]

Nevertheless, disaccreditation may be too blunt a tool. Between 2011 and 2012, bar passage rates (either first time, overall, or both) fell in thirty-nine states.[106] Falling bar passage rates and the denial of provisional accreditation to various schools by the ABA[107] may show the beginnings of a more subtle strategy.

Another possibility is that university administrators may close under-performing law schools on their campuses. Bill Henderson has advised that university presidents should either radically restructure their law schools or close them.[108] Former Emory Law Dean David Partlett reports that the Emory University president used to warn his deans that Emory had closed its School of Dentistry in 1992[109] and was not afraid to close other low-performing units.

This route seems unlikely, however, as many universities are opening or acquiring law schools as a prestige boost (as Belmont and LMU did in Tennessee), not closing them. Likewise, most law schools have been revenue centers for universities. Rather than closing these schools, university presidents will want to see a return to profitability, requiring some combination of the strategies listed above ahead of outright closure.

F.   The Remainder Will Try to Do More With Less

Every law school will face pressure to rein in tuition. Every law school will face more demanding and discerning students shopping for the best deals. Every law school will face the choice of shrinking class sizes or lowering the quality of its incoming class or both. The salad days are over, and law schools will have to make do with less.

Cutting costs will be hard because law schools are simultaneously being asked to do more and different things. Law schools face increasing pressure to produce more practice-ready graduates.[110] Calls for curricular reform have grown louder than ever. The myth that most law students learn how to practice law while they work as associates in big law firms has been largely discredited. At all but the very top law schools the majority of students do not work in Big Law; regardless, Big Law firms have largely ceded their training role.

Law schools will be asked to provide more skills training and clinical offerings. Most current tenured and tenure-track faculty are not qualified to do, or interested in, this work. Thus law schools will need to either hire more adjunct and non-tenure-track faculty (read: cheaper hires), which could affect accreditation if done on a mass scale, or hire tenured or tenure-track clinicians, skills teachers, and legal writing professors, which will put more pressure on the bottom line.

Law schools also face pressure to train lawyers for a brave new world of practice that involves computers and outsourcing and other trends that did not exist ten years ago. For example, Michigan State Law School has founded a Reinvent Law Center in an effort to marry law teaching and advanced technology.[111] Nevertheless, teaching legal technology will prove even more challenging than expanding skills training. Even the few law professors with a practice background do not have the experience or expertise to teach the computerization of legal practice.

Many law schools will remain engaged in the rankings competition. Students still strongly consider the *U.S. News* rankings. A recent Kaplan survey showed that despite the spate of publicity on the outlandish cost of law school and the importance of placement statistics, law students still see a law school's ranking as the most important selection criterion.[112]

With rising expenses and falling revenues, law schools will eventually put the squeeze on their tenured and tenure-track faculty members. Law professors seem likely to be asked to teach more and to be paid less, although at many schools this trend will likely start with new hires, rather than with the tenured faculty. Adjuncts will be asked to teach more classes, including core curricular offerings. The growth in law school staff and administration also seems likely to stall. Pay cuts, furloughs, and layoffs are possible. More teaching and less pay will result in some disgruntlement and may also signal erosion in the primacy of scholarship as the *sine qua non* of legal academia.

In presenting my research at law schools around the country, I have met many sincere and thoughtful faculty members who hope that the crisis will lead to some substantial restructuring of legal education (frequently in line with that professor's particular interest—be it skills training or clinic or intellectual property or immigration). These professors often ask me what I see in the redesigned law school of the future.

Sadly, I do not believe that the current crisis will result in a fundamental or thoughtful redesign of American law schools, regardless of how badly one is needed. Change is coming, but I think it will be painful (for the faculty at least), entailing forced cuts rather than carefully constructed new approaches. Given the nature of the faculties at these schools and how persistently American law schools have stuck to the Langdell model over the last 130 years, I foresee large changes will be made to cut costs, but only cosmetic changes will be made to improve the product. As long as graduation from an ABA-accredited school is required for bar admission and as long as law faculties drive accreditation, the only real changes will come from existential threats. Those challenges will force cost-cutting, not a radical redesign.

Part III

BIG PICTURE AND THE GLASS
HALF FULL

10

Big Picture and Parallels

BEFORE WE TURN TO the upshot of these myriad changes, it is worth discussing some themes and parallels that emerge. This chapter attempts to pull back from the trees to see a forest. It starts with a discussion of what lawyers and law professors are like, and then discusses how these essential natures help explain the mess we have created for ourselves and our profession. It then turns to situating lawyers and law schools within some broader economic and social trends.

A. Why Have Big Law and Law Schools Pursued the Same Self-Destructive Strategies? Because the Same People Run Them

If you have read this far, you have probably noticed some similarities in the self-destructive behavior of Big Law and legal academia. You have also probably wondered why judges, law professors, or bar associations have not stepped in to ameliorate the situation. There is a simple reason for both trends: all of these institutions are dominated by roughly the same people, trained and selected from the top of the class at the same elite law schools. The people who run lawyer regulation—high-level judges (federal judges and state supreme court justices), law professors, and Big Law partners—are all likely to have gone to a top law school and to have done very well in those schools.[1] Students at elite law schools tend to be from more affluent backgrounds[2] and are more likely to have gone to an elite undergraduate institution.[3] The upshot: a partner in Big Law is likely to have much more in common with a local federal judge or law professor than with a solo practitioner.

Judges, partners, and law professors also shared the searing experience of American law school. Justice Frankfurter once opined, "The law is what the lawyers are. And the law and lawyers are what the law schools make them."[4] The stated goal of American law school is to teach law students to "think like a lawyer," and this experience creates a number of shared heuristics and habits. Law professors, partners, and judges are likely to have done well in law school, so they are especially likely to have mastered and ingested "thinking like a lawyer." These shared heuristics carry on from law school and have very real consequences in practice. Obviously, academics, judges, and elite lawyers have different jobs and different interests, and many American law professors explicitly rejected a career in Big Law. Nevertheless, the similarities far outweigh the differences.

B. Big Law Partners, Law Professors, and High-Level Judges Are Naturally Path-Dependent, Hierarchical, and Competitive and That Explains Much of What Is Occurring in Big Law and Law Schools

These similarities result in remarkably consistent behavior by the elites that essentially run the legal profession. Here I am not making the broader claim that these elites have self-regulated the legal profession to their own benefit (although I have elsewhere),[5] but rather that when you consider the shared backgrounds, attributes, and education of these people it should not be surprising that the same flawed decisions pop up in different sectors. Path dependence, a keen sense of hierarchy, and a passion for high-stakes competition are three examples of shared heuristics that explain common behaviors.

1.   Path Dependence and the Unchanging Nature of Legal Institutions

The study and practice of American law is an inherently conservative and path-dependent endeavor. Students are taught to read cases from the past and to then reason out what legal rule might apply in the future to a slightly different fact scenario. The case method is backward looking and path dependent, meaning "that an outcome or decision is shaped in specific and systematic ways by the historical path leading to it."[6] In the common law system, every decision, and the law itself, is determined by what has come before. The past is the master of both the present and the future.

This has powerful effects on legal structures as well. Consider American courts, law schools, and Big Law. The last 130 years have seen an astounding number of technological and sociological changes, and most portions of the economy (and most portions of government and education) have changed substantially over those years. Nevertheless, law's institutions remain remarkably unchanged. American judges run their trial courts and appellate courts in a manner that a lawyer from 1880 would recognize. Law schools still follow the basic Langdell model of reading cases and teaching via the Socratic method. Law firms have changed the most, but still rely to a remarkable extent on the Cravath model.

Taken separately, the resistance to change seems somewhat puzzling. Taken together, the pattern emerges. In most areas of the economy it is not acceptable to answer the question "Why is it done this way?" with "We've always done it that way." In law that is not only an acceptable answer, it is the best and most basic answer. A lifetime of training in *stare decisis*, precedent, and the common law system actually dictates that answer. Jim Moliterno's excellent book, *The American Legal Profession in Crisis*, notes how lawyers have reacted conservatively to every crisis they have faced, from Watergate to the present day.[7] Lawyer resistance to change is more than a theme in lawyer regulation; it explains almost all of that regulation.

Path dependence has paid off nicely for American legal institutions for the last hundred years or so. Change has been very slow and frequently dictated by outside forces. For years lawyers, law professors, and courts have continued to behave as if legal services and legal problems cannot be routinized and can only be handled individually by a lawyer. This makes lawyers and law professors particularly ill suited to address a post-*LegalZoom* world: lawyers have been taught one way to do things and they have stubbornly stuck to it. For example, when tasked with how to increase the availability of legal services to the middle class and the poor, courts and bar associations tend to suggest more lawyers, not obvious solutions like computerization or non-lawyer assistance.

As customers vote with their feet, lawyers will face the uncomfortable task of changing how they do things or starving. In the areas where other lawyers are in charge, such as American courts, the changes will likely be more gradual. In the areas outside of direct judicial control, however, the ride will be much rockier and path dependence may be a liability rather than an asset.

2. *Hierarchy and Competition Define Legal Academia and Big Law*

But if path dependence is so strong, why have there been so many destructive changes to legal academia and Big Law over the last thirty years or so? The answer is hierarchy and competition.

From law school forward, lawyers see the world as an interlocking web of hierarchies. Each level of court has its own rules for what precedent controls and what precedent is persuasive and what sources are not to be considered at all. The same is true for the interaction between the common law, statutes, and regulations, or between local, state, and federal law. Lawyers are continuously required to slot certain governmental bodies or sources of law within a complicated hierarchy where one thing controls another. The ability to make careful distinctions between laws, regulations, governmental bodies, and even people is a critical legal skill.

A keen awareness of hierarchy naturally leads to competition. This is especially so for the "winners" of the law school rat race: the lawyers who eventually end up in Big Law or legal academia, or who become high-level judges. For these individuals, law school and practice is a series of ever-narrowing hoops to jump through, with stiff competition at every level. The first step is admission to law school, where hierarchy and competition dominate. Partially as a reaction to the *U.S. News* rankings, LSAT scores and undergraduate GPA now govern law school admissions. The first step of the journey is a numerical and hierarchical competition. Students know the range of schools they may be admitted to solely on their numbers, regardless of work or life experience or why they might want to pursue a law degree. The students return the favor to law schools: they tend to choose a school based on its ranking, above employment outcomes, price, or program.[8]

The hoops grow narrower once in law school, starting with class rank and law review membership. The law school class rank system debuted at Harvard in 1887 and has remained a mainstay of almost every American law school except Yale.[9] Class rank is exceedingly important. At most law schools it determines membership on law review and law school honors. Law firms, judges, and other employers will often use a class rank cutoff for their initial or callback interviews, so class rank is a prime gatekeeper for employment.

Because of the timing of law review applications and summer associate and clerkship hiring, class rank at the end of the first year of law school is frequently determinative. At most law schools first-year grades are based on a single, end-of-semester exam, so eight to ten exams may serve as a sorting mechanism for the remainder of a student's legal career. Consider the strangeness of this system. A student whose GPA improves every semester of law school may already be locked out of a clerkship or Big Law, even if her graduating GPA is better than a student who did worse every semester of law school. This effect is compounded by how hard it is to "transfer in" to Big Law or legal academia if one was not on law review or did not do a clerkship.

For the students who win these "prizes," the competition continues after graduation. Lawyers in Big Law immediately start on the tournament of lawyers. In some firms they may have to fight a two-tiered competition, first to non-equity partner and later to equity partner. The same competition that defined every step from applying to law school forward actually ramps up in practice. Even equity partners now face ruthless competition over firm size, profits, and their individual share.

Academia is almost worse because at least Big Law has a clear scorecard: money. Academics compete hard over the number of publications and the quality of their placements, all with an eye on the quality of the school where they teach and potential lateral moves up the chain. There are probably not two more similar people in the world than a torts professor at a top-10 law school and a torts professor at a top-100 law school, and yet snobbery and condescension are hallmarks of academia.

Ironically, Big Law and law schools are probably smart to compete hard in their respective rankings, even if they disagree with the methodology or think it is detrimental to their mission. The individuals currently running these institutions likely chose their original law school and their later jobs based upon prestige and hierarchy, so they naturally expect potential law students and associates to do the same. I've heard law professors bemoan the effects of the *U.S. News* rankings in the same conversation where they brag about publishing in a "top 25" law review, using the same, otherwise objectionable, rankings as the benchmark.

3. A Tale of Two Rankings

Law firms and law schools know that students will choose jobs or schools based on rankings, so they naturally compete on those measures, regardless of whether the rankings actually measure quality. As a result these competitions are very narrow and homogenous. Instead of competing through differentiation, law schools and law firms compete on the narrow band of qualities measured by the dominant outside ranking: the *Am Law 100* and *U.S. News.*

In 1986, the *Am Law 100* debuted, listing for the first time the total revenues and profits per partner for the 100 biggest firms. Chapter 4 described the immediate and powerful impact: salary numbers that were opaque before were suddenly publicly available. Given the nature of lawyers, a highly foreseeable arms race was launched. Firms attempted to move up rankings by hook or by crook.[10] Some of the decisions were business decisions to increase profits per partner or to grow bigger, but many of the decisions were explicitly based upon competing in the rankings. The rankings game became an end unto itself.

One sign of the seriousness of the competition is that many firms cheat. The *Am Law 100* numbers are all voluntarily supplied to *The American Lawyer.* Many of the same law firms also supply financial information to the Citi Private Bank Law Firm Group (Citibank). The Citibank financial information tends to be quite accurate because Citibank is a major lender to law firms, and many of the data are associated with that lending. Citibank gathers, aggregates, and publishes its law firm financial information as part of a public discussion of overall market trends.[11] Firm names are not used. Citibank compared its numbers to *The American Lawyer's* and came to the conclusion that more than 50 percent of the firms are overstating the numbers they send in for the *Am Law 100.*[12]

The *U.S. News* ranking is the law school equivalent to the *Am Law 100.* It debuted in 1987 and immediately revolutionized how law schools viewed themselves.[13] Before the ranking there were 15 schools that considered themselves top 10 and 35 schools that considered themselves top 25. Schools competed on the basis of prestige and publications, but without a joint measure the competition was more muted and based on non-standardized and unquantifiable measures of "quality."

Brian Tamanaha's *Failing Law Schools* dedicates two chapters to how hard law schools have competed for the rankings since 1987 and the multiple ways it has affected/warped law school priorities.[14] Law school deans have resigned or been fired over the rankings. The rankings have spawned an ever-deepening obsession with scholarship and scholarly productivity, including a boom in lateral hiring and what some call "law porn," glossy brochures or postcards trumpeting a law school's scholarly productivity or symposia.[15] The rankings have radically changed admissions and scholarship decisions, with schools offering scholarships based on improving their LSAT and undergraduate GPA numbers rather than financial need.

The *U.S. News* rankings have also inspired cheating. Some of the cheating was pretty straightforward, with Villanova and Illinois simply faking many of their numbers altogether.[16] Other cheating has been subtler, with schools hiring their unemployed graduates for part-time work so that employment statistics are improved or taking a mass of transfer students because their LSAT/GPA numbers do not count for *U.S. News*.

The reaction of Big Law and legal academia to their rankings reveals something important about the people running these longstanding legal institutions: given a rubric for competition, they were off and running hard, with any and all strategies allowable. Many of these strategies are corrosive to these institutions and their collective reputations. At the same time, these same institutions continue to claim significant moral and regulatory authority in the legal profession. Just as law firms have been short-selling their reputations for profits through lateral hiring and increased leverage, Big Law and law schools have placed their own competitive gain ahead of their standing within the profession and the standing of the profession as a whole.

4. *What Competition Cannot Override*

Given the competitive nature of lawyers and their burning desire to be slotted as highly as possible within any hierarchical structure, there must be great diversity among law schools and firms as they try to differentiate themselves in a crowded market, right? Weirdly, no. As noted above, both law schools and law firms have largely stuck to the same template since the late nineteenth century. Even when they have departed from those templates (like law firms focusing on lateral hiring or law schools adding externship or clinical programs) they have done so largely in a herd.

Visit the website for any American law school. While there may be differences in the production quality, the messages are likely to be remarkably similar. The website will trumpet a school's focus on teaching, new technologies, clinical offerings, and so forth. There is rarely, if ever, any head-to-head comparison with competing law schools or any explicit description of being a different type of law school. The exceptions prove the rule: CUNY and Northeastern have long been somewhat different law schools. Washington and Lee has redesigned its third year of law school to require clinics and simulation courses, a somewhat obvious innovation, and it has received a mass of good press and an uptick in applications as a result.[17]

The same goes for law firms. Bruce MacEwen calls his version of this game "Guess Which Firm's Website!"[18] Choose any three or four firms at random, visit their websites, ignore the firm logo, and guess which firm it is solely on the basis of the text or pictures. It cannot be done; the websites are indistinguishable. Big Law websites mention size, expertise, office locations, client-focused services, and so forth. The websites do not try to differentiate the product, however. Again, the exceptions prove the rule. *Axiom*'s website boldly promises "We Do Legal Work Efficiently,"[19] and the entire website is an aggressive comparison between *Axiom* and Big Law.

Nor have Big Law or law schools changed much in their hiring over the years. Each tries to hire the best-credentialed students (based on the competitions described earlier) from the highest-ranked law schools. Applicants who prove their worth post–law school are often stymied. Big Law is notoriously difficult to enter post-graduation regardless of later career success. Academia is even worse. Bill Henderson calls this "The Pedigree Problem": law schools and Big Law are obsessed with pedigree.[20] The irony is that the determinants of entry to, and success within, an elite law school are only partially correlated with success as a lawyer.[21] Like the rankings game, however, law firms and law schools compete within the narrow bands of the hierarchy that birthed them, reproducing themselves along historical criteria without any real data to support their approach or any critical assessment of the process.

Two hiring stories are apt examples. There is a funny scene in the first episode of *L.A. Law* in which Harry Hamlin's character decides to hire an associate to help in his criminal practice. To find this new associate, he goes to a prosecutor he knows and asks whom she would recommend from the public defender's office. He eventually hires the Jimmy Smits character. The funny part of this scene is how unrealistic it is: Big Law would never go out and find the best possible lawyer regardless of pedigree to fill an opening. They would choose from the usual suspects of new law graduates or lateral candidates with the same credentials who had worked at another law firm. The unreality of this common sense approach speaks volumes about the irrationality of Big Law hiring. Big Law behaves as if how a twenty-two-year-old did on ten exams in her first year of law school is a better hiring criterion than actual success in the practice of law.

Law faculty hiring is even worse. Every law professor who has been on a hiring committee knows a version of the following story. A graduate from a non-top-15 law school applies for a faculty position. She did well in law school, but did not graduate in the top 10 percent and did not do law review. The applicant has written several well-placed and well-written law review articles. She has taught successfully as an adjunct professor and has good teaching evaluations. She has also excelled in the practice of law at the same time. When presented to the hiring committee they object, "We never hire from *that* school and, good lord, this person was not even on law review!" When it is explained that membership on law review and attending a top law school are just proxies for success as a law professor, and this person has actually already demonstrated an ability to do the job well, the hiring committee harrumphs, "we just do not hire people with this thin a record of achievement."

Nor do law schools or law firms compete much over the nature of their workplaces. An associate at one Big Law office in a city probably has an extremely similar job to an associate at another firm in the same city. Law firms tell us that they are involved in a death battle for the best talent possible. And yet they ignore the most obvious way to differentiate themselves: the nature and conditions of the work. Big Law seemingly has no interest in creating part-time positions, or flexible work for less pay, or other obvious structures that might attract different sorts of talent or might keep the talent they already have.

The monolithic approach to starting salaries demonstrates this quite nicely. Several times since the 1960s, Cravath has unilaterally raised its starting salary and a significant number of firms have jumped to match. The matching firms, however, are very unlikely to have the same cash flow or profitability as Cravath. The cost to the least-profitable firm of matching the Cravath starting salary is steep for those partners because high associate pay comes directly off the bottom line. Nevertheless, these firms feel obliged to compete with Cravath and fear that differentiation in pay would make them look like second-class citizens. The puzzling thing is that only a few boutique firms, and now *Axiom* and *Valorem*, have positioned themselves as lifestyle alternatives: same or more interesting work, more flexible hours, lower pay.

Law professor jobs are similar. A tenure-track law professor at the 150th-ranked law school and another at the 15th-ranked law school have almost the same job. The professor at the lower-ranked school probably has a slightly higher teaching load (often four courses per year rather than three), lower expectations for scholarship (a smaller amount of scholarship at relatively lower-ranked journals), and a lower salary, but these are differences in degree, not kind. One might expect law schools engaged in a no-holds-barred competition over students to have different-looking faculties from varied backgrounds, teaching a different mix of classes. Instead, law school competition has largely been on the basis of imitation.

C. These Changes Are Bigger than Us

Much of the writing and thinking about the current law school and lawyer crisis has described the current situation as unprecedented or unforeseeable. The opposite is true. The legal profession and law schools are a small part of a much bigger story.

1. *Law School Seems Like a Bad Choice for Twenty-Somethings. But What's Better?*

Chapters 8 and 9 outlined what a bad deal many law schools are for their students, the recent spate of bad publicity, and the resulting collapse in applications. Nevertheless, if you ask twenty-something Americans about their job prospects or their professional aspirations, you will find that there are no easy alternatives these days. Between 2000 and 2011 the percentage of Americans aged 25–34 who are not working (what the *New York Times* calls the nonemployment rate) rose from 18.5 percent to 26.6 percent. Over the same period, the American nonemployment rate shot past Japan, France, and Germany's. Japan, France, and Germany actually saw a small decline in young adult nonemployment over the same period.[22] I have a colleague with an unemployed 24-year-old son with a college degree. Her take on the state of the economy for the millennial generation: "It sucks. When did we all move to Italy?" The situation is bad enough that the *Onion* recently mocked a millennial interviewing for a job at a small non-profit in the "Most Depressing Job Interview You'll Ever See Currently Taking Place at a Starbucks Table."[23]

What about other professions? It turns out there are no safe harbors. Virtually every profession feels pessimistic about its present and future. Doctors are increasingly unhappy: insurance, paperwork, and lower incomes have killed their profession.[24] Architects have never felt properly appreciated or paid; young architects are regularly quitting the profession.[25] Engineering is a flavor du jour, and yet engineers do not seem very happy or hopeful either.[26] A short review of *Dilbert* comics gives you a sense for how engineers experience their work. Business school has its own "tuition bubble": business school tuition and potential future earnings may be more out of whack than law school tuition.[27] If you search for the name of any profession with the words "tuition bubble" on *Google* you will find an argument that every graduate program is a bad deal.

In many science fiction visions of the future, robots or computers do all of the unpleasant work, while humans live the "life of Riley" or do only really interesting work. Unfortunately, economic reality has dictated the opposite. There are plenty of humans to do unpleasant jobs. So many in fact that unpleasant jobs are also very low paid. Instead, computers and robots are deployed where the cost of designing, buying, and operating them makes the most sense—that is, to replace expensive humans. As venture capitalist Marc Andreesen has argued, in the future there will be two kinds of workers: "People who tell computers what to do, and people who are told by computers what to do."[28] It is not hard to guess which of those categories of work will pay better.

In short, twenty-somethings face a menu of declining prospects. Law is facing the reality of computerization and globalization, but so is the rest of the economy. Any job (in law or elsewhere) that is relatively straightforward to perform is likely to be computerized, delegated, or outsourced. Young people must find a niche where they are especially valuable or uniquely qualified in order to make a decent living going forward. Comfortable and secure jobs that pay a healthy salary to smart college graduates are few and far between these days, and the transition is quite jarring for everyone involved. Millennials are on the front line of all of this.

2.   *The Winner-Take-All Economy*

There is another upshot of globalization and computerization: the winner-take-all economy. In 1981, the economist Sherwin Rosen wrote a groundbreaking article entitled "The Economics of Superstars."[29] Rosen argued that certain segments of the economy were superstar-driven and thus did not behave like normal markets. For example, if there are 200 professional comedians in the U.S., one might expect their earnings to look like a bell curve, with a few earning top dollar, most earning a middling wage, and some starving. In a superstar market the few performers at the top earn a tremendous living and almost everyone else earns very little, even when the difference in quality between the twentieth-best comedian and the third-best comedian is relatively slight. In these markets the best performers get the "prize" and everybody else starves.

Globalization and technology are creating more superstar-driven segments of the economy. Economists Robert Frank and Philip Cook described this trend in their 1995 book *The Winner Take All Society*,[30] and the trend has only accelerated since. As computers replace people, prices drop tremendously, making the remaining humans working in the area poorer, while making the owner/designer of the computer process much wealthier than any individual human working in the area could be. Frank uses the example of *TurboTax* and accountants.[31] The corporate owners of *TurboTax* make a great deal from selling inexpensive tax preparation software, while the accountants who used to do that work lose business and must charge less for the work they keep. Or, they can focus on the portion of the market that cannot be (or has not yet been) computerized: high-end, complicated, and context-dependent work. If an accountant can do that work, then she will, like the remaining Big Law partners, earn a very good living. But, as computers get better and better at knowledge-based tasks, the volume of complicated, humans-only work shrinks and the competition for that work grows.

Globalization and outsourcing create the same effect. Workers in India or China are quite capable of doing some knowledge jobs that have been done by Americans. Document review and due diligence are legal examples. If you are a middle-class American who held one of those jobs you need to either lower your price radically or find other work. Again, the tasks that remain will be especially valuable and unique, creating a thin layer of superstar work that is lucrative and a mass of work that is poorly paid.

The end result in law—and the global economy—is growing income inequality, as the middle and low end of any segment of the economy is subjected to fierce wage competition. The high end, however, becomes a superstar market, where even relatively small differences in quality result in radically different rewards. Consider the bimodal salary distribution for law graduates. In chapter 4 we asked about the comparative quality difference between the last lawyer to get a job at a law firm paying $160,000 and the second choice for that job, who probably earns $50–60,000 a year instead. These lawyers are likely to be very close in quality, or at least not different by a magnitude of three. Nevertheless, in a winner-take-all economy a slight difference in perceived quality can result in a massive difference in remuneration.

3.   *The Law School Bubble Is Just Part of the Higher Education Bubble*

One hard thing about the winner-take-all economy is that it makes education less valuable for most people. In the near past an undergraduate degree or a law degree seemingly guaranteed at least a middle-class life. This is no longer true. Ironically, at the same time that higher education guarantees much less for most students, it has become a lot more expensive.

Glenn Reynolds has been on the cutting edge of commenting on what he calls the *Higher Education Bubble*.[32] College has gotten more expensive over the last forty years, outpacing inflation, family income, or the value (in terms of future earnings) of a degree. The excess cost has been taken on in debt, the same non-dischargeable and toxic debt that has fueled the law school boom. The trend is accelerating at an alarming rate. Between 2004 and 2013 aggregate educational debt almost tripled, rising to nearly $1 trillion. Over that period both the number of student loan borrowers and the amount they owe rose 70 percent.[33] These borrowers are having a very hard time retiring this debt. A Federal Reserve Bank of New York analysis estimated that as many as 47 percent of student loan borrowers were in deferral or forbearance periods in 2011.[34]

The percentage of the population who has attended college or has a degree has gone up continuously since the 1950s, partially due to government support and partially because of the perception of a degree's value. More people are borrowing and paying more for an asset that is worth less. Even with the higher cost, the educational experience at many universities has deteriorated. Undergraduate classes are increasingly taught by graduate students or adjuncts to free faculty resources for research. Faculty members are pressed to focus on garnering grants and writing scholarship, often to the detriment of their teaching. There is a proliferation of middle- and upper-management positions.[35] Faculties are paid more and are likelier to move laterally to other schools.

The law school bubble is just the higher education bubble on steroids. Law schools are the "canary in the coal mine."[36] Brian Tamanaha notes that the law school focus upon scholarship is just a part of the broader academic "prestige market" that values scholarly productivity above all else.[37] Every law school problem described in chapters 8 and 9 of this book is paralleled in higher education generally. Like law schools, universities cannot expect tuition and indebtedness to rise forever, especially as what they sell becomes less valuable.

4.   Villains, Short-Term Thinking, and Shortcuts

There are strong similarities in the behavior of the villains in this story. The behavior of Big Law partners, law school deans/faculty, and plaintiff's lawyers has been remarkably consistent. Each has mortgaged the future and sullied its reputations in pursuit of short-term gains and quick cash. This behavior is of a piece with broader American trends.

As chapter 4 demonstrated, many partners in Big Law are running their firms for maximum, short-term profit with little attention paid to firm culture, training the next generation of lawyers, or tending to the firm's reputational capital. Individual partners see themselves as free agents, making a lateral move for the best deal they can negotiate or wringing concessions out of their own firm.

Chapter 6 demonstrated that plaintiff's lawyers have done the same, pressing their legal advantages at every turn, filing silly lawsuits that eventually appear on *Overlawyered.com*, and advertising in the crassest manner possible. Each of these moves carries short-term gains: advertising can draw clients, filing a crazy lawsuit can get one's name in the paper, and pressing to maximize returns on each case is good business for that individual case. Nevertheless, these strategies maximize income today while damaging the business of the future, as tort reform gains political popularity.

Chapters 8 and 9 demonstrate that law school deans and faculties have done the same. In an effort to climb in the *U.S. News* rankings, American law schools have let the tail wag the dog, fudging or outright cheating. They have also relentlessly raised tuition as well as faculty salaries and perks. Law schools have been granted exclusive control over entry into the profession by the ABA and state supreme courts. Law schools have also been asked to be the front line of the professionalism effort. Yet, these institutions have short-sold their moral authority for money and a self-defeating rankings competition.

This trend, sadly, is just part of a broader American trend toward short-term thinking and shortcuts. Jonathan Macey's *The Death of Corporate Reputation* makes the case that throughout corporate America the focus has shifted from reputation-building and long-term growth to short-term thinking, ethical short cuts, and raising quarterly profits at any cost.[38] As in law, there are a few truly jaw-dropping examples of fraud like Enron or the most recent housing bubble. But, like law, the worst examples prove the rule. Some of the country's most important and longstanding institutions have abandoned a broader sense of responsibility to the common good in favor of wringing out every last penny.

5. *Devolution*

If one takes a longer view of the history of the profession, the anomalous period is the last fifty years when lawyers agglomerated into bigger and bigger firms. Internationally and pre-1960, it was very unusual for private lawyers to gather together into such big organizations. In 1960, there were only thirty-eight American law firms with more than fifty lawyers and only three had more than one hundred.[39] Likewise, most non-U.S. or U.K. law firms tend to be much smaller.[40]

Glenn Reynolds's *Army of Davids* and *Small Is the New BigLaw: Some Thoughts on Technology, Economics, and the Practice of Law* make this point more broadly.[41] The strange thing about the period from the industrial revolution until now is that people were gathered together into bigger and bigger organizations. Anyone who has ever worked in a large organization knows that there are significant costs to organizing large groups of humans. Overhead is also much more costly. Yet, in the industrial age, large-scale operations were the only way to mass-produce goods or build a railroad. Economies of scale were critical to industrial age success.

The information age has made economies of scale much less important, and devolution is in full bloom. From journalism to music to computer programming, individuals and small groups are becoming powerful competition. Through 2008 Big Law remained immune to these trends, with firms growing bigger through lateral hiring, and mergers.

The advantage of size is that more lawyers can reap the reputational benefits of the firm and that there will be sufficient lawyers and staff to handle big, emergency projects. But these large firms are very expensive to operate. Overhead and coordination costs are high, and it is very difficult to create a consistent culture in an international firm of more than one thousand lawyers. For the most lucrative work—large transactions or litigation—it makes sense to stay large to handle the peak load demands of clients. But for the more prosaic and regularized work, smaller groups of lawyers in virtual law firms can do the same work for much less. These lawyers may still earn more, because of radically lower overhead.

Today's 1,500-person law firms are actually an agglomeration of various practice groups located in various offices. These units are almost self-contained in some law firms, which means that the benefits of staying with the firm must outweigh the overhead and management costs.

Over time, some large law firms will survive and those that survive may grow even bigger, but it seems likely that others will atomize. This is especially so as the biggest and most profitable split off from the rest. Firms stuck in the middle will not have enough of the most valuable work to justify their overhead, nor will the reputational pull of their name be worth the costs. Thus, we may see a tapering of this anomalous period where corporate law is practiced in behemoth organizations and a partial return to smaller groups of lawyers.

C.   And Now for Some Good News

The economy is terrible, the gap between the rich and everyone else is structural and will just get worse, and lawyers and law professors are going to see worse times before they see better. Chapters 11 through 13 offer a welcome respite of good news.

II

The Good News for American Consumers

LAW PROFESSORS AND BIG Law partners have authored the primary analyses of the changes to the American legal profession. They are the parties most likely to be negatively affected, so there has been considerable handwringing. The titles of the recent books say it all: *Failing Law Schools, Declining Prospects, The Lawyer Bubble, The American Legal Profession in Crisis.*

It is important not to lose the bigger picture. Customers and the country itself will be much better off as access to legal information and work becomes less expensive. When digital photography replaced film photography, Kodak was quite distressed, but everyone else was better off. Likewise, the music industry has not enjoyed the Internet era, but consumers have access to more recorded music at a lower price than ever before.

A. When Transaction Costs Fall We Are All Better Off

It is an economic truism that when products grow cheaper through technology or efficiencies we are all better off because people can use the money they save to buy other things they want or need. This is one of the main defenses of a market economy; competition forces everyone to be more efficient.

Cheaper access to legal work carries an additional bonus though: lower transaction costs. Transaction costs are the various costs associated with economic activities—the cost of gathering information, contracting, and enforcing a contract are all examples. In buying a house there is the cost of the house itself, and then there are the associated transaction costs, such as hiring an inspector, hiring a lawyer, and bank fees. In a divorce there is the division of the property, but there are also the transaction costs of hiring lawyers (and accountants or private investigators) to determine who gets what.

One of the key insights of the study of law and economics is that transaction costs matter. When they are reduced, beneficial transactions increase and everyone is better off. This insight was developed from the Coase Theorem. Economist Ronald Coase imagined a world with no transaction costs. Assuming perfect information and functioning markets, every good or service would wind up with its highest-value user. So, as long as individuals act rationally and transaction costs are zero, legal rules are irrelevant to the efficient allocation of resources.[1] Without transaction costs, law serves a relatively limited purpose, setting the initial rights around which parties can negotiate, but having little effect on the ultimate outcome.[2]

We obviously do not live in a world where transaction costs are zero. Thus, Coase's work, and a great deal of the law and economics literature, is about how law, transaction costs, and efficiency interact.[3] As a general rule, law and economics scholars prefer legal regimes that minimize transaction costs and maximize private ordering and bargaining.[4] As the cost of transacting goes down, more productive transactions occur. If the actual market more closely approximates the imaginary world with no transaction costs, overall utility is maximized as assets flow to their highest-valued users. Coase argues that the most useful aspect of his analysis is not the behavior of a utopian, transaction-cost-free society, but rather the importance of considering how to minimize transaction costs through law and other means.[5]

Lawyers sometimes add value to a transaction by creatively drafting merger agreements or finding tax savings,[6] but, generally speaking, lawyers are quintessential transaction costs. Drafting contracts or IPO documents or litigating disputes are all transaction costs—market actors must pay these fees in order to settle disputes or complete sales or to head off future disputes.[7]

It seems very likely that between computerization, the ongoing oversupply of new entrants into the market, outsourcing, and new models of service delivery, the price of most legal services will continue to fall, with bet-the-company/bet-the-family cases and other particularly complex matters the exceptions to the rule. When corporations spend less on legal fees, they can allocate that money to shareholders or to consumers via lower prices. When individuals draft clearer and cheaper leases or wills or incorporation papers, the upfront costs of negotiation are lowered, and if the legal work is good (more on this later), the likelihood of future litigation is also lessened.

The argument that we will be better off with cheaper access to legal work is thus a simple Coasian syllogism: (1) markets work better and we are all better off when transaction costs are lower; (2) legal fees are transaction costs; (3) we are all better off when legal fees are cheaper.

This is especially so for private ordering. "Private ordering" describes situations where individuals create their own legal and economic relationships. "Public ordering," by contrast, is when the government controls the relationship. Law serves as a backdrop to private ordering, so legal advice or documents are frequently necessary to memorialize agreements or determine the parameters of a deal. Contracts, wills, deeds of trust, and leases are all examples of private ordering. As access to the law and the documents that govern private ordering become more affordable, we will see a great expansion of private ordering and will reap the benefits. If more Americans have an up-to-date and legally enforceable will, probate actions and custody battles over the children of deceased parents will become rarer. If it becomes easier and cheaper to form an LLC, more small businesses can move from sole proprietorships to more favorable entities, and so on. Markets function best when individuals voluntarily bargain and agree over their relationships. Inexpensive legal work makes these bargains cheaper and more likely to be reduced to writing and thus enforceable.

B.   The Law-Thick Society and Access to Justice

The argument above applies equally to Wal-Mart and the owner of a small business: low-cost legal work will make it easier to transact. Affordable legal work will have a bigger impact on the lives of the poor and the middle class, however. Large corporations and wealthy individuals have paid a lot for legal services, but they have been able to afford it. The poor and the middle class have largely had to go without, even as American law has grown more complex and pervasive.

America is what Gillian Hadfield calls a "law-thick society."[8] The combination of state and federal statutes, regulations, and the common law create overlapping and very complicated law. This law governs property rights, criminal prosecutions, familial relationships, and virtually every other aspect of American life. America relies upon courts and adversarial processes to handle a bevy of social and governmental interactions, from school discipline to disputes between neighbors. Federal Judge Alex Kozinski has argued that criminal law has grown so broad that "You're (Probably) a Federal Criminal."[9]

There is more than anecdotal evidence that America is unusually law dependent. A comparative international study of legal systems by political scientist Robert A. Kagan shows that American law is unusually expensive, expansive, complex, and uncertain. Kagan terms this "American legal exceptionalism":

> For one social problem after another, the studies show, the American system for making and implementing public policy and resolving disputes is distinctive. It generally entails (1) more complex bodies of rules; (2) more formal, adversarial procedures for resolving political and scientific disputes; (3) more costly forms of legal contestation; (4) stronger, more punitive legal sanctions; (5) more frequent judicial review of and intervention into administrative decisions and processes; (6) more political controversy about legal rules and institutions; (7) more politically fragmented, less closely coordinated decision-making systems; and (8) more legal uncertainty and instability.[10]

Kagan calls the American style of law "adversarial legalism" and traces its genesis to the social upheaval of the 1960s and the desire for a society marked by "total justice."[11] American courts, legislatures, and regulators greatly expanded their reach in an effort to bring justice to more people in more circumstances. The result was a massive expansion of the role of law in American lives.[12] America relies on legal structures more than its peers in an effort to govern a huge, complex, and diverse country.

Americans regularly run across situations where legal work is necessary. As noted in chapters 5 and 7, even in a market glutted with

lawyers, it is still quite expensive to pay an individual lawyer to research a legal problem, let alone to pursue litigation or draft a legal in-
strument. Derek Bok famously noted that "[t]here is far too much law
for those who can afford it and far too little for those who cannot."[13]
Gillian Hadfield has demonstrated the scope of the problem through
empirical calculation and a list of the many legal questions that confront the poor and the middle class.[14] Other empirical studies support
the claim that the poor and the middle class are forced to go without
necessary legal services because of price.[15] Deborah Rhode's *Access to
Justice* is a seminal work laying out how few Americans can afford legal
services, from writing a will to seeking a divorce.[16] Rhode estimates
that 80 percent of civil legal needs are not met for the poor, and 40–60
percent of civil legal needs are not met for the middle class.[17] Further
evidence is the flood of *pro se* litigation in American courts, frequently
over complicated issues like child custody or probate.[18]

The situation in divorce courts is particularly scandalous. The cost
of simple, agreed divorces is low and falling. But if a divorce is even
somewhat complicated—if there is a custody or property dispute, for
example—it is likely to be expensive. Truly poor persons may be eli-
gible for assistance from legal aid, but legal aid will often only handle
divorces where physical abuse is alleged because the demand for legal
services so far outstrips the supply of available lawyers.[19] Some poor
people with simple, agreed divorces can get court-supplied forms or pay
$500 for forms and a lawyer. If the divorce is in dispute, or if one of the
spouses is out of state (or has been deported), the process is likely too
expensive and complicated to handle *pro se* or for a small fee and the
unhappy individuals are stuck.

In short, most Americans cannot afford to hire a lawyer to do necessary, let alone helpful, legal work. Bar associations and advocates for
the poor have long argued that the solutions are increased legal aid
funding, required or expanded *pro bono* service, or a civil *Gideon* right.
For example, in 2006, the ABA House of Delegates unanimously approved a report calling for a national civil *Gideon* to "provide legal
counsel as a matter of right at public expense to low income persons in
those categories of adversarial proceedings where basic human needs
are at stake, such as those involving shelter, sustenance, safety, health
or child custody."[20] The ABA has also come out strongly in favor of

increased *pro bono* work[21] and more funding for legal aid.[22] These are the traditional responses to legal need: more bespoke legal services by government-supported or *pro bono* lawyers.

This is a backward-looking, 1960s-era response to a very real problem. These intended solutions have also been failures. Civil *Gideon* has proven quite illusory. In 1981, the Supreme Court declined to find a right to appointed counsel in a termination of parental rights case in *Lassiter v. Department of Social Services*.[23] In 2012, by a 9–0 margin, the Court refused to require an appointed attorney in a child support case, despite the petitioner serving actual jail time.[24] State courts have likewise declined to create a broad right to appointed counsel in civil matters.[25]

Free or reduced-price legal services for the poor or the middle class are also a tough political sell. Legal aid funding has been cut continuously since the 1980s. Even returning legal aid funding to 1970s-era levels would fail to meet the need.

Pro bono service alone is insufficient. There are not enough lawyers with the needed expertise, and those lawyers who are willing cannot do enough free legal work to even begin to address the problem. Much *pro bono* work is for the arts or museums and not for the indigent. The current state of the access-to-justice "crisis" is thus like the movie *Groundhog Day*: the same impracticable solutions are pitched for the same insoluble problem.

And, of course, legal aid, civil *Gideon*, and *pro bono* work are only for the indigent. When it comes to legal work for the middle class, bar associations, law schools, and others have no suggestions. Law students are trained to offer individual services by the hour, and cheaper, non-lawyer options are repressed or prosecuted as the unauthorized practice of law (UPL).

C. Technology and Access to Justice

Technology is the best bet for solving these problems. We are at the very beginning of the application of computer power to legal services and we have already seen much that will help increase access to justice: free or low-cost access to the law itself (statutes, regulations, and cases), free or low-cost legal forms, low-cost access to legal advice, and so forth. Moreover, we are only in the early stages of the technological revolution in law, harvesting the lowest-hanging fruit of computerization.

As programmers gain confidence and get creative we may see technology fundamentally reshape the market for legal services.

Two caveats. First, for potential clients who are illiterate or lack access to a computer with Internet access, computerization is unlikely to be much help. Access to the Internet is continuing to grow, however. Approximately 70 percent of Americans have a broadband connection at home, including more than half of households with incomes below $30,000.[26] Almost all public libraries provide free access to the Internet and computers as well.[27] Chicago-Kent Law School's A2J project is beginning to make smartphone versions of their Internet access-to-justice programs,[28] and 61 percent of Americans own a smartphone.[29]

Despite the possibility of access, there are significant numbers of Americans incapable of self-help, regardless of technological advances. But if technology can handle some or many of the legal needs of the middle class and the working poor, legal aid and *pro bono* efforts could focus more narrowly on the neediest Americans.

Second, technology will not reach all of American legal need equally. The legal needs of the poor and the middle class can be roughly sorted into four different categories. Computers will not help equally in each category.

The easiest case is access to the raw materials of American law. Thanks to the work of state, local, and federal governments, as well as non-profits like Cornell Law School's Legal Information Institute,[30] Americans with a computer and an Internet connection now have more access to the laws that govern them than ever before. *Google* and other search engines also make these raw materials easier to find than ever.

Legal drafting will also be cheaper. Simple wills, powers of attorney, incorporation documents, and divorce papers can all be done much, much more cheaply online than an individual human ever could. Commercial providers like *LegalZoom*, and free providers like *legalhelp.org* and various state court websites all provide access to a variety of legal forms. As of now many of these forms are basic and must be filled out by individuals. Interactive forms are an obvious improvement and are increasingly available.

Legal advice is harder, but growing more available as well. This work tends to be more contextual, and also more protected by rules against UPL; so legal advice will be harder to commoditize and sell cheaply. Nevertheless, we have already seen free or reduced-cost legal advice on the Internet, and there is reason to believe that trend will accelerate.

The hardest case is in-court litigation work. American judges have always enforced this lawyer prerogative most jealously and it is here that protections against UPL are at their most powerful. Nevertheless, judges struggling with large *pro se* dockets are increasingly willing to make it easier to operate in their courts without a lawyer, and online dispute resolution offers a wholly different manner to settle disputes, bypassing courts and lawyers altogether.

The danger to many of these solutions comes from restrictions on UPL, hostile judges, lawyer recalcitrance, and letting the perfect be the enemy of the good. The greatest danger to the power of technology is the beneficiaries of the status quo. That said, there are early signs that technology is poised to triumph, to the benefit of us all.

1.   *Access to Legal Materials*

Because America is a federalist, common law system, American law comes from a dizzying variety of sources, including statutes, regulations, and case law from federal, state, and local governments. This has always made it hard for Americans to find what laws apply to any particular situation.

In the nineteenth century, before the advent of public law libraries and legal publishing companies, ordinary Americans had very limited access to the laws that governed them.[31] From that time forward it has become easier and easier, first for lawyers and then for everyone. The founding of West Publishing in the late nineteenth century and the publication of its case and statutory digests made finding applicable statutes and case law vastly simpler, although the books were expensive and made for lawyers, not ordinary people. Law libraries at public law schools opened in the twentieth century, offering easier access to the books themselves.

Starting in the 1990s, electronic search engines like Westlaw and Lexis offered even better and cleaner access to these various materials. Because they were online, these databases also eliminated the need for a physical library for research. Nevertheless, Westlaw and Lexis were expensive and again designed for use by lawyers. The search terms and codes were clumsy and particularly non-intuitive for ordinary people.

Over the last twenty years or so, however, free access to law on the Internet has become a reality. Federal, state, and local governments have made statutes, regulations, and cases available for free online. Non-profits like the Legal Information Institute (LII), have gathered them in one place.

The LII was founded in 1992. Its mission is to provide free online access to law. The website is advanced enough now that it has statutes, court opinions, and regulations from the federal government and all fifty states. It also offers an online legal encyclopedia and other general legal help publications.[32] Wikipedia also includes a great number of sections devoted to legal cases and concepts.[33]

The availability of these materials is helpful, but the addition of advanced search engines like *Google* or *Yahoo* is the true added value. These search engines allow easy access to particular statutes, regulations, or rules if you have the citation (just *Google* a Federal Rule of Evidence, for example). More importantly, it also allows for relatively accurate natural language search. *Google* has gotten good enough at natural language legal search that Westlaw and Lexis are responding to the competition by creating their own natural language search engines.

None of these resources are perfect, and someone with a legal issue should certainly hesitate before relying on *Wikipedia* or a *Google* search. Nevertheless, like Internet medical information, knowledge is power, and simply having access to the raw materials of American law is a significant improvement on the past. Think of it this way: a contemporary American with a smartphone now has easier access to the laws that govern her than any judge or lawyer in 1980, let alone 1880.

2. *Document Drafting*—Probono.net, *A2J, and State Supreme Courts*

Access to the law itself is one thing; access to court filings and other legal documents is another. There has been considerable progress on this front as well. Between free documents provided by state supreme courts, *probono.net*, legal aid societies, and low-cost document providers like *LegalZoom* and *Rocket Lawyer*, ordinary Americans have more access to legal forms than ever before.

The most obvious use of technology is to simply post forms and instructions on the Internet for download and use. In many cases these forms are posted for free and are available to anyone with Internet access and a printer. State supreme courts all over the country have started to offer free online forms in a multitude of areas. For example,

Tennessee has a court-supported self-help website that offers PDFs that can be filled in online and used for uncontested divorces,[34] orders of protection,[35] and various defenses in collection matters.[36] Tennessee is not unusual in this regard; the National Center for State Courts has a page with links to free, online court forms from forty-nine states and the federal government.[37] Much of the work on these forms has been done by state access-to-justice commissions. The ABA lists thirty-four different states with such commissions.[38]

How does it work? The Tennessee site for uncontested divorces is pretty typical. It has five pages of instructions in English or Spanish.[39] The very first set of instructions describes who may use the form: uncontested divorces with no children or property. The instructions walk the applicant through the various forms, explain what to expect in court, and provide answers some common questions. The applicant then fills out the necessary forms, including the Request for Divorce, the Divorce Agreement, the various filing documents and a draft Final Decree of Divorce. I have served as the faculty supervisor to the student-run University of Tennessee Homeless Legal Advocacy Project since 2001, and while these forms do not work for every divorce, we have used them regularly since they came online a few years ago, and they have been a life saver. We would previously send the homeless to Legal Aid of East Tennessee, knowing that unless the divorce involved domestic abuse the client was likely to wait for years or forever before gaining a divorce.

Interactive forms are the next level of technical sophistication. *Pro-bono.net* and Chicago Kent Law School's A2J project have worked together to create LawHelp Interactive (LHI), an online repository of guided legal form drafting.[40] Since 2009, LHI has created over 145,000 different forms in twenty-eight different states. The forms cover issues like child support and custody, domestic violence, debt collection, foreclosures, evictions, and divorce. The A2J software is especially designed to deal with self-represented litigants who may be uncomfortable filling out a legal form or otherwise confused by legal processes.[41] It takes the user through a guided online "interview," where questions are asked and answered. The program reacts to the questions by guiding the user to the proper form. Once the correct form is selected, the program asks the questions necessary to fill out the form. At the end, the user has a completed legal form.

Consider the program for an Illinois name change application, designed by A2J and *probono.net*.[42] The first page asks the user to agree to the terms of use. With that out of the way, an attractive, picture-based road to a courthouse appears, with a series of signposts laying out the steps to completing the form. Figure 11.1 shows a generic version from the A2J website.

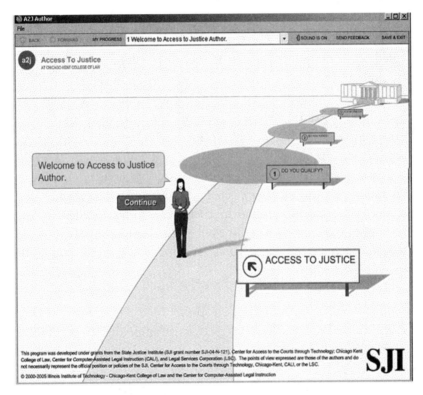

FIGURE 11.1 A2J Welcome Screen

The first page announces what the program is: the Illinois Legal Aid's Online Petition for Change of Name. The next pages collect personal information (name, date of birth, address, phone number), the proposed new name, as well as eligibility information. Have you lived in Illinois for longer than six months? Are you a convicted sex offender? Each of these questions is asked in a simple, straightforward manner. Many include pop-up explanations about why the particular question is necessary.

The program asks if you would like to access the forms to waive the filing and publication fees. It also gives instructions about the requirement to publish notice of a name change in a newspaper and how to do it. It then asks about finding a witness for the affidavit section of the form. Once these questions are answered, the form is ready to be printed out and filed. I proceeded through the steps (using made-up Illinois state information) in under fifteen minutes and then printed out the forms.

Legal aid societies are also turning to the Internet to try to reach more potential clients. *LawHelp.org* has an interactive map of the United States that sends the user to the relevant legal aid website in all fifty states.[43] Twenty-five states use *probono.net*'s LawHelp platform for their websites.[44] *Probono.net* created the platform to provide a uniform structure for legal aid websites. Each of these sites contains a mix of forms, general information, and specific legal advice. For example, *texaslawhelp.org* offers advice and forms on a bevy of subjects, including divorce, domestic violence, bankruptcy, eviction, housing discrimination, estate planning, veteran's benefits, and many other topics.[45] Legal aid has long provided printed materials and forms to clients whom they cannot individually help. Just putting all of these publications and forms online is a tremendous leap forward.

3.   *Private Companies Offering Legal Forms*—LegalZoom

LegalZoom offers similar services to those listed above, for a fee. Like the A2J software, *LegalZoom* takes users through a series of questions and then generates legal documents. For many documents *LegalZoom* provides a review by a non-lawyer scrivener at the end to ensure consistency and to avoid typos.[46] *LegalZoom* also sells a lawyer's review of some documents for as little as $39.[47]

The list of *LegalZoom* documents covers almost every type of non-court document you can imagine, including entity formation, trademark searches, contracts, leases, wills, living trusts, powers of attorney, divorce papers, patents, and promissory notes, just to name some.[48] All told, *LegalZoom*'s page of available products lists more than seventy documents.[49]

Take, for example, drafting a living will. The basic living will is $39.[50] *LegalZoom* offers a helpful page that differentiates between a Last Will and Testament, a Living Trust, and a Living Will, explaining what each is for.[51] When you select "living will" you begin to answer a series of relevant questions: name, address, county of residence, and so forth.

Then, the site asks a series of questions about life support. Would you want it if you are unconscious and have a terminal condition with no hope of recovery? What care would you like if life support were withdrawn? Do you have any additional comments or instructions? Next, you decide whether to appoint a health care agent and what powers you wish to grant the agent. It closes by asking for your burial wishes. After spending $39 *LegalZoom* creates a document from your answers and then prints it out and mails it to you.[52] The process is simple, inexpensive, quick, and straightforward.

More contested matters are harder. *LegalZoom* offers documents and support for uncontested divorces only and includes a description of the difference between an uncontested and contested divorce.[53] Uncontested divorces start at $299.[54] Bankruptcy by *LegalZoom* actually requires a lawyer and a higher fee ($1,599 in Tennessee, for example).[55]

LegalZoom also offers over 160 documents "crafted by top attorneys" for download that the user can fill in herself.[56] The documents come with instructions and are listed from A to Z (or from "Academic Letter of Recommendation" to "Workplace Injury and Illness Report"). The individual forms are mostly priced at $14.95. *LegalZoom* also offers unlimited access to the forms for $7.99 a month or unlimited access plus "attorney support" from the Legal Advantage Plus attorney plan for $14.95 a month.[57] The plan offers lawyer document review and legal consultations.

LegalZoom is just one of the many websites offering these types of services for a fee. Between free and inexpensive legal forms, drafting of basic legal documents will be simpler and easier than ever before.

4.   *Hybrid Lawyer/Forms Arrangements*

Lawyers have responded to the threat of forms providers by getting into the game themselves. There are now a bevy of online forms providers that explicitly include lawyer review in the price. The most basic are lawyer/form hybrids, where the customer fills in the legal forms and a licensed lawyer "reviews" them. Richard Granat was a pioneer in the field with his fixed-fee divorces in Maryland at *mdfamilylawyer.com*.[58] A simple divorce for a couple with children can be handled by a lawyer for as little as $229, without children $199.[59]

Other sites offer legal advice upfront, followed by forms, so the on-line client can know what forms might work best for her. For example, *SmartLegalForms* offers legal forms and legal advice by a lawyer in a package deal.[60]

Last, even when a client goes to meet with a flesh-and-blood lawyer, it is very likely that lawyer will use some sort of form on the client's behalf. State bar associations and the National Law Foundation both offer a blizzard of forms that can be filled in for virtually any kind of legal drafting.[61] Savvy lawyers are already starting to use technology to streamline their practices, lower their overhead, and to allow them to focus on the parts of their job that cannot be replaced easily online: human interactions and work where the human complications are at least as important as the legal ones.

5. *Legal Advice*

First, there is a great deal of free legal advice on the Internet. For ex-ample, a *Google* search for "How do I write a will on my own?"[62] leads to ads from *LegalZoom* and *Rocket Lawyer*, but the first result is from *wikihow.com* and is entitled "How to Write Your Own Last Will and Testament (with Will Template)."[63] *Avvo* and *Freeadvice.com* offer free answers to user questions with an eye toward generating paying work for the lawyers. It is true that like anything else on the Internet you get what you pay for. Some advice is wrong or too broad. It is also true that you could pay a lawyer much more and get even worse, off-the-cuff advice.

Second, similar to many other services, online providers are lowering the price of legal advice. For example, *LegalZoom* and *Rocket Lawyer* and other online providers are starting to sell legal services and advice by flesh-and-blood lawyers through a subscription model or a fixed-price model.[64] The *LegalZoom* subscription model is aggressively priced to try to draw middle-class users. For $11.99 a month *LegalZoom* prom-ises a lawyer will "review your last will, power of attorney or other legal documents. Get help when you need it from an attorney who knows the laws of your state. Get unlimited number of consultations on new legal matters for one low monthly rate."[65] *Rocket Lawyer* charges "pre-negotiated fees" in its "Rocket Lawyer On Call" program.[66]

Internet sites like *LegalMatch* also seek to connect clients and lawyers, for the lowest price.[67] I briefly signed up for *LegalMatch* as a lawyer just to see how it worked and was flooded with potential client matters to review and bid on. If I was an under-employed solo practitioner, I certainly would have been sorely tempted to pitch some of these potential matters. But *LegalMatch* provides customer reviews and my proposed fees to each potential client, so I would face significant pressure on both price and customer satisfaction. Lawyers desperate for work and clients looking for the best deal naturally drive down costs.

In short, even with the protections of UPL, Internet suppliers are likely to drive the price of legal advice down. Like the provision of forms by *LegalZoom*, much current online provision of legal advice is hardly a threat to lawyers. Much of the advice now given for free online was given for free to acquaintances in years past, with a similar "this is not legal advice" disclaimer. But, like *LegalZoom*'s forms business, the advice business is a serious matter. Websites are explicitly targeting middle-class consumers who might otherwise hire small-firm and solo practitioners. As the technology improves, anyone with access to the Internet may be able to get fairly nuanced legal advice for free or very cheaply.

6.   In-Court Litigation

LegalZoom, *LawHelp*, and other online forms providers do not offer any in-court legal services. Their forms are to be used *pro se* or the users are to hire a lawyer to appear with them in court. In-court litigation looks likely to stay a lawyers-only activity for the foreseeable future. In-court representation of clients is the easiest type of UPL for judges to police and it is the area least likely to be attacked by political opponents or lawyer competitors. Since the turn of the twentieth century, American judges have insisted that only lawyers may represent clients in their courts and that will not change anytime soon.

Appearing *pro se* is always an option.[68] But, many American courts have been relatively hostile to *pro se* representation, expecting *pro se* litigants to handle their case the way a lawyer would.[69]

Nevertheless, there are cracks in the armor, especially in America's *pro se* courts. Judges and advocates for the poor are realizing that it makes little sense to operate courts that are overrun by *pro se* litigants as if every case involved a lawyer on both sides. It is frustrating to the judges, unfair to the litigants, and inefficient for everyone involved.

Reforms have come in several flavors. From inside the judiciary, there has been a conscious effort to push *pro se* courts to operate in a manner friendlier to their clients—the litigants who appear before them. For example, the American Judicature Society published a guide entitled *Reaching Out or Overreaching: Judicial Ethics and Self-Represented Litigants*.[70] It includes a long list of common-sense steps that judges can take to help *pro se* litigants, including making procedural accommodations, being courteous, eschewing legal jargon, heading off procedural snafus before they arise, explaining the process, avoiding over-familiarity with lawyers in the courtroom, and training court staff so they provide patient, helpful service to self-represented litigants.[71] The American Judicature Society has also published a set of core materials that gathers the best and most innovative approaches to *pro se* reform.[72] The National Center for State Courts published *The Self-Help Friendly Court: Designed from the Ground Up to Work for People without Lawyers*.[73] While these guides are not perfect or particularly visionary, if *pro se* courts around the country adopted their suggested reforms it would make a huge difference in the lives of the poor and the middle class, as well as making those courts fairer and more efficient.

There are a number of individual courts trying quite innovative approaches. For example, Lois Bloom and Helen Herschkoff describe the creation of a special federal magistrate position in the Eastern District of New York assigned to hear significant categories of *pro se* matters, the first federal district to assign a single magistrate in this manner.[74] Ronald Staudt and Paula Hannaford have gathered a number of innovative court processes into one National Center for State Courts–supported research project.[75] San Antonio and other cities have established specialized *pro se* courts adopting many of the suggestions for court structure listed above.[76]

Court systems, legal aid offices, and other advocates for the poor have also been working hard on offering legal advice and form preparation assistance for *pro se* litigants. California has a 900-page Online Self-Help Center sponsored by their supreme court.[77] Utah, Maryland, and other states have followed suit.[78]

Some court systems are beginning to experiment with using online dispute resolution (ODR) to fully replace court procedures. Recall the discussion of *Modria* in chapter 5. The company uses the *eBay* ODR system for all sorts of disagreements. For example, *Modria* built an ODR system for property assessment appeals in the Canadian province of British Columbia.[79]

This process was successful enough that British Columbia asked *Modria* to design an ODR process for consumer complaints to their consumer protection bureau.[80] Consumers with a complaint about a business are invited to try ODR. If they agree, Consumer Protection British Columbia contacts the business and invites them to participate.[81] From there, the *Modria* ODR platform does the rest. Small claims court is saved a matter. If the ODR platform matches the performance of *eBay*'s complaint resolution software, both the business and the consumer should be happier with the outcome.

UNCITRAL, the U.N. working group on international law, has also sought to make this model industry standard for cross-border e-commerce and business-to-business disputes.[82] Like all of these technological advances, ODR is radically cheaper than using humans to resolve disputes and theoretically it could replace lawyer-driven courts for dispute resolution when a lawyer is too expensive.

Modria's process could be used as a precursor to, or a full replacement of, traditional *pro se* courts. Other online providers of legal services also have an incentive to work with courts to improve the *pro se* experience. For example, *LegalZoom* already does a good business in selling do-it-yourself divorces. Over time they may find it lucrative to work with courts to help streamline the divorce process to include contested divorces or other, more complicated issues. Currently, in-court work is a natural bottleneck to expansion. If *LegalZoom* or *Rocket Lawyer* could convince courts to standardize procedures and make it easy to proceed *pro se*, the companies would gain a new market for its forms, the courts would profit by streamlining their processes and addressing the *pro se* crisis, and the many litigants who cannot afford a lawyer would benefit as well.

6.   A Brief Detour into Science Fiction

If courts could ever be convinced to adopt computer-assisted dispute resolution, the results would be exceptional: a simple, transparent court system aimed at assisting litigants in a considerate and efficient manner. Ask any poverty lawyer if any of those adjectives describe the courts where she practices, and the answer will be an emphatic no.

This is where the possibility of *pro se* court reform veers off into science fiction. Imagine a world where the courts meant for the poor and middle class are *better* than the courts where the wealthy and corporations litigate.[83] If *pro se* courts embrace technology while more traditional, lawyer-driven courts do not, this scenario could come true. The pitch to legislatures and courts writes itself: this approach could alleviate the *pro se* crisis, make better use of precious judicial resources, save money, and (as a bonus) produce better, fairer outcomes.

Nevertheless, in-court change will be slow because lawyers will fight it tooth and nail, arguing procedural justice and consumer safety, not protectionism. Naturally conservative judges will also resist any large-scale technological change. For example, British legal futurist Richard Susskind has predicted a computer-led revolution in legal services and court processes for years. His biggest disappointment? The slow pace of change in Britain's courts.[84]

Consider the incredibly slow adoption of electronic filing for court documents in America. While e-mail and electronic documents have been in widespread use since the 1990s, courts have resisted allowing electronic filing of papers. This was not an insignificant decision: physically filing paper copies of all legal papers means extra costs in filing and storing, as well as the costs of lawyers producing and delivering the documents. Nevertheless, it took until approximately 2003 for some Federal courts to start allowing electronic filing, and state courts are behind even that slow progress.[85] Many of these jurisdictions still allow paper filing as well, which retards the change and reduces the cost savings. Even in jurisdictions where electronic filing is allowed, a majority of lawyers report that they still paper-file.[86]

Nevertheless, even if courts remain mostly unchanged, access to justice should improve. Using an individual lawyer for in-court work will become much cheaper, thanks to a flood of new law grads, unemployed lawyers going solo, and lawyers gradually adopting *LegalZoom*-like forms practices as their own. Because litigation is so much harder to systematize or computerize, it seems unlikely that these costs will fall enough to reach all of the pent-up demand, but middle-class consumers should eventually find it somewhat more affordable to litigate.

So, just as with corporations, private ordering through law should become cheaper, more accessible, and eventually better for the poor and the middle class. Litigation will remain relatively expensive, subject to the natural downward pressure of increased supply.

Access to justice for the poorest Americans, those without access to the Internet or those who cannot read or write, will take longer and may never be solved. These people are also most likely to need in-court help. Legal aid offices are trying to help by utilizing self-help and computerization to reach the greatest number of their most self-sufficient clients, allowing them to focus on the neediest.

We should also not let the perfect be the enemy of the good. Will poor people or the middle class get the same level of representation as the wealthy? Obviously no. Will the poor and the middle class have more access than they have now? Absolutely yes, and that should be celebrated as progress.

D.   Objections—Quality/Consumer Protection

One obvious objection is that *LegalZoom* and other Internet sources of law are currently unregulated and may prove dangerous to clients. A 2011 letter to the *New York Times* by ABA President William Robinson objecting to non-lawyer assistance for the poor and the middle class is emblematic:

> The American Bar Association strongly agrees that our nation must expand access to justice for low-income Americans. However, a rush to open the practice of law to unschooled, unregulated nonlawyers is not the solution. This would cause grave harm to clients. Even matters that appear simple, such as uncontested divorces, involve myriad legal rights and responsibilities. If the case is not handled by a professional with appropriate legal training, a person can suffer serious long-term consequences affecting loved ones or financial security. It also could lead to a violation of the law. . . . We must expand legal services for those in need, provided by first-rate trained lawyers.[87]

The ABA agrees that there is an access-to-justice problem, but strongly warns that "first-rate trained lawyers" are the only solution. Anything less is too dangerous.

A modified version of this argument suggests that anything less than an individual lawyer for the indigent is second-class justice. Self-help, modified *pro se* courts, and online legal advice are deficient. Only when the poor have the same advantages as their opponents (an individual lawyer) will there be true access to justice. This argument is extremely divisive because the proponents of free, high-quality, individualized legal services by lawyers for the poor and the middle class cannot answer how or who will possibly pay for these services.

The Internet offers a panoply of information on every imaginable topic, some of which is incomplete, misleading, or even harmful if misused. Medical diagnosis sites are a classic example. It is likely that anyone reading this book has looked up a set of symptoms on the Internet. These medical sites are potentially much more harmful than legal sites because it is much harder to undo physical injury or death than a legal error. This is not to ignore the possibility that Internet legal information could harm consumers. Rather, the medical websites show that the value of access to good information on the Internet usually outweighs the potential damages from the bad information. If this is the case in medicine, it is even more likely to be the case in law.

Consider the speculative nature of the claimed harm. Historically, lawyers and courts have stated that they prosecute UPL for consumer protection. Yet the vast majority of UPL complaints have come from injured lawyers, not injured clients, which suggests protectionism.[88] Likewise, the more recent UPL complaints against *LegalZoom* appear to arise out of bar association and lawyer concerns, not consumer complaints.[89] The discovery in these suits is not publicly available, but the complaints are, and those complaints do not allege any specific harm to any customers, just that *LegalZoom* is involved in UPL.

Given *LegalZoom's* high profile and the threat it presents to existing lawyers, if its legal work had caused a flood of serious injuries, one would expect lawsuits or significant publicity by bar associations or both. The absence of this publicity or lawsuits is telling. For what it is worth, *LegalZoom* claims high customer satisfaction: "LegalZoom surveys every customer who completes a purchase and over 96% of those who respond say they would refer LegalZoom to friends and colleagues. LegalZoom is a Better Business Bureau ('BBB') accredited business and participates in the BBB's OnLine Reliability Program. LegalZoom has an 'A' rating with the BBB."[90] The relative dearth of reported harm from *LegalZoom*, which has existed since 2001, speaks volumes. If we are going to ban or curtail vastly less expensive online legal services for consumer protection, we need actual evidence of harm, and as of yet it has not arrived.

The danger of harm on the Internet is, ironically, greatly reduced by the availability of the Internet. The Internet is the single greatest engine of consumer information ever created, and online merchants and sites are now assiduous about maintaining a good reputation. For a hotel, one online story of bedbugs can be devastating. For a restaurant, an online picture of mice droppings can close the doors. Lawyers are finding this out as they confront online ratings at *Avvo* and other sites. If there are very harmful legal forms or legal advice on the Internet, it will not be long before customers will be warning others about it, blunting the potential for harm. A *Google* search for "LegalZoom complaints" or "Rocket Lawyer complaints" offers multiple, pertinent responses.

Lawyers made the same quality-control arguments when title insurance companies largely replaced lawyers on residential real estate closings. Real estate law was too complicated, and the danger to the clients too great, to allow non-lawyer involvement.[91] These concerns have proven to be largely unfounded, and by 1986 even the ABA gave up the ghost, admitting "it can no longer be claimed that lawyers have the exclusive possession of the esoteric knowledge required and are therefore the only ones able to advise clients about real estate closings."[92]

There is also a great irony in lawyers and bar associations complaining about the danger online providers pose to potential clients: the lawyer disciplinary system itself does not offer much protection. The American legal profession is very hard to get into, but it is also very hard to get tossed out of. The ABA itself has concluded that attorney discipline is, and always has been, a neglected area.[93] Attorney discipline procedures are under-funded,[94] backlogged,[95] and generally held in secret.[96] Historically speaking, up to 90 percent of complaints against lawyers have been summarily dismissed, partially because many complaints are over fee disputes or "mere negligence" that is not generally covered by the Rules.[97]

Even with recent improvements, discipline is rare. In 2009 (the latest year the ABA completed its Survey on Lawyer Disciplinary Systems), there were 125,596 complaints made to American lawyer discipline agencies.[98] There were roughly 1.2 million licensed lawyers that year,[99] so there was more than one complaint for every ten American lawyers. The complaints were not likely to be evenly distributed. Few complaints were likely filed against the licensed lawyers who were not practicing, the 8 percent of lawyers who work in private industry, the 8 percent for the government, and the 2 percent in the judiciary or at a law school.[100] The lawyers in Big Law also rarely draw official complaints from their corporate clients.[101] The great majority of these complaints dealt with the small-firm and solo practitioners who routinely represent the poor and the middle class. These "first-rate trained lawyers" that the ABA trumpets received one hundred thousand or more disciplinary complaints in 2009 alone. The number of complaints probably greatly understates the actual scale of the problem because filing a formal complaint is notoriously difficult.

Nor are complaints against lawyers taken very seriously. Of the total 2009 complaints, 66,160 (53 percent) were dismissed without any investigation.[102] After investigation, only 6,900 (5 percent) of the complaints resulted in formal charges.[103] Public sanctions were given to 5,009 lawyers, and only 798 lawyers were disbarred nationwide.[104] Thus, in 2009, only 0.6 percent of complaints against lawyers resulted in disbarment, and only 0.06 percent of licensed lawyers were disbarred. Further, in most jurisdictions the only publicly available information is a public sanction, so as many as 120,000 of the 125,000 complaints were hidden from public view.

There is thus good reason to doubt the sincerity of bar association warnings about the potential harms to clients by non-lawyers. Clients have been complaining about licensed lawyers for years, with very limited results.

Last, even if *LegalZoom*'s forms and advice are not currently as good as a live lawyer (and everyone probably knows a lawyer who is already worse than *LegalZoom*), over time they will continue to improve as experience guides changes to the programs and the forms. Regardless of comparative quality, *LegalZoom* and *Rocket Lawyer* are definitely better than nothing, which is what most poor and middle-income Americans can currently afford. It is easy for a bar association to stand up for consumer protection by requiring everyone to pay full freight for a licensed lawyer. These lawyers are not forced to choose between needed legal work and other critical expenditures. They are unlikely to be too poor to be able to afford to get divorced, for example. For the poor and the middle class, however, the consumer protection argument is not a shield, but a devastating sword.

Whether purposeful or not, the disgraceful treatment of *pro se* litigants is one of the very best advertisements for legal services. When middle-class or poor people come to a typical American court without a lawyer they often see chaos. Judges, clerks, and represented parties roll over confused, unrepresented parties. These individuals learn that if they can afford a lawyer they *need* to get one. If these courts were run for the benefit of *pro se* litigants (transparently, simply, and fairly), the opposite would be true. Even people who could afford a lawyer might go forward without one. The harder it is to operate *pro se*, the better it is for lawyers.

E. Objections—Maybe Less Expensive Legal Work Will Prove Harmful

Daniel Currell and Todd Henderson suggest a cloudy picture for the effect of cheaper law. Possibly we already have an efficient price for lawyers or maybe making lawyers cheaper will make society worse off because litigation imposes costs that exceed its benefits, and maybe cheaper legal work means more harmful litigation.[105] Cheaper litigation costs could, in fact, make it more likely that litigation will be launched or maintained, a possible societal detriment. Currell and Henderson do agree that non-litigation legal advice and work is more likely to be socially beneficial at a reduced price.

As noted above, the current waves of changes will have a relatively limited effect on the cost of litigation because the lawyer's monopoly is strongest in court and weakest in private ordering. The changes buffeting the legal profession might actually be optimal for Currell and Henderson's concerns. Private ordering will become cheaper and much more widely accessible, while litigation will remain the primary province of more expensive lawyers. Thus, the costs of avoiding litigation are likely to shrink much faster than the costs of pursuing litigation.

The burden is on those objecting to come up with evidence that cheaper law will be harmful in and of itself. Stating that less expensive access to legal services will help all Americans is a truism of the market economy: competition incentivizes efficiency and drives down the costs of services, benefiting consumers. There may be a persuasive story about why legal services are radically different, but as of yet there is little empirical evidence to support it.

F.   Upshot

The easiest glass-half-full case is to just reread chapters 4–8 and ask if the public at large is better off as lawyers suffer their downturn. The honest answer in most cases is yes. America has increasingly turned to law and its legal system to govern a diverse and far-flung country. This has benefited lawyers tremendously, as the growth in the size of the profession and its earnings from 1960 to 1990 demonstrate. But increasing legalization has harmed the poor and the middle class, who need legal services and cannot afford them. Current trends are making legal services significantly more affordable, a considerable benefit to the majority of Americans who cannot afford a lawyer.

Moreover, note the relatively basic nature of the current interactions of law, the Internet, and artificial intelligence. We are in the very early stages of the computerization of legal services and what appears to be state of the art today is likely to seem crude and rudimentary in the near future. Right now, computerization is reaching low-hanging fruit: using predictive coding and search engines to mechanize electronic discovery or using the Internet and interactive forms to draft simple legal documents. These relatively basic uses of computing power are already displacing the work of lawyers, but they are really only the tip of the iceberg. The best is yet to come. Richard Susskind differentiates between computer processes that automate—reproduce what humans do more cheaply—from those that innovate—that is, allow us to do completely different things.[106] We are just beginning with the automation of law. Innovation will take longer but will offer significantly more benefits.

12

The Profession and Law Schools That Emerge Will Be Stronger and Better

THIS CHAPTER COVERS THE more difficult glass-half-full argument: that the profession and law schools that emerge from the current, wrenching changes will be better and stronger than the ones that entered. Lost jobs and shrinking salaries are not to be taken lightly. Some law schools will close or downsize in the near term, which will be challenging for the faculty, staffs, administrations, and alumni. The so-called "lost generation" of law graduates from 2008–13 will remain underemployed. Many lawyers who have made a decent living for many years will make less and some may be forced out of the profession altogether. Nevertheless, when the new normal has settled in, those of us who remain will be better off. This chapter starts by discussing the profession and then turns to law schools.

A. Lawyers Will Have Better, Happier Jobs—Big Law

One irony of the boom years is that Big Law lawyers earned more, but many of them enjoyed it less. It was not always thus. The lawyers of the so-called golden age of law firms had exactly the types of jobs that creative humans love and that generate happiness. Big Law's transformation since then increased both remuneration and misery.

Most current surveys show relatively high levels of lawyer unhappiness as well as high incidences of depression, alcoholism, and even suicide.[1] Consider the titles of some recent books on the topic: *The Unhappy Lawyer,*[2] *Way Worse Than Being a Dentist,*[3] and *The Destruction of*

Young Lawyers.[4] Nancy Levit and Douglas O. Linder have written the best of these books, *The Happy Lawyer.*[5] It lays out the problem crisply and then suggests solutions. One key to Levit and Linder's analysis is that lawyers are not equally unhappy. The lawyers in Big Law are the least happy and government lawyers are the happiest. Only 44 percent of Big Law lawyers report satisfaction with their career, while 68 percent of public sector lawyers do.[6] First, a note of caution: almost half of survey respondents in Big Law *are* satisfied with their careers. Moreover, there are no comparable surveys from the golden age of Big Law, so cross-generational comparisons should be taken with a grain of salt. This is especially so because many of the data we have on the law firms of the 1960s come from retrospective interviews. That said, there are good reasons to think that the current structure of Big Law may lead to more unhappiness than the structure of the golden age firms.

Unhappiness in modern Big Law comes as no surprise to anyone who has read the happiness[7] literature. The first lesson is that people are very bad at determining what will make them happy.[8] Notably, people tend to think that earning more money, buying certain goods, or winning competitions will make them happy.[9] Generally speaking, happiness does not increase at income levels above $70,000.[10] "Those with incomes over $90,000 were nearly twice as likely to report being 'very happy' as those with incomes below $20,000, although there is hardly any difference between the highest income group and those in the $50,000 to $89,999 bracket."[11] It turns out that relatively well-off humans adjust very quickly to new material items or to a raise in income. After a short-lived boost in well-being, people return to seeking more income or goods.[12]

These studies speak volumes about the nature of Big Law since at least the 1980s. The competitive hiring process, the tournament of lawyers once hired, and the all-important inter-firm and intra-firm battle over higher profits per partner are all examples of competitions over things that people think will make them happier, but do not. Worse yet, "promoting materialism can promote status competition, selfishness, and envy, and marginalize quality-of-life factors correlated with greater well-being."[13] It is not just that the monetary focus of Big Law fails to bring happiness; it actually promotes unhappiness and is "negatively correlated with social interest (care and concern for others, friendliness, empathy), agreeableness, self-esteem, self-actualization, intelligence, religious values, family-oriented values, environmentalism, and aesthetic values."[14]

Leaving aside the competition over status and money, the job itself promotes unhappiness. Given the basic elements of a modern Big Law job—constant pressure to bill more, limited control over one's schedule, reliance upon third parties (partners or clients) for career advancement, forced personal responsibility for the well-being of (frequently irascible and implacable) clients—it is no wonder happiness rates are down.

Daniel Pink's *Drive*[15] offers an overview of the state of current research on motivation and career satisfaction, and offers two insights that explain the current emotional state of many lawyers in Big Law. First, Pink defines satisfying careers along three axes: mastery, autonomy, and purpose.[16]

"Mastery" refers to a career that offers a lifetime of intellectual challenge. Most law jobs fit this criterion, especially in Big Law. First-year associates doing due diligence might argue, but senior lawyers would agree that their work is intellectually challenging.

"Purpose" refers to working with a group of people toward a common and important goal. Purpose is not necessarily charity work (*Drive* is a book for business people), but it does require a sense of working together toward a shared goal. Descriptions of the golden age of law firms suggest workplaces filled with purpose, as partners and associates worked together hand in hand with their clients to create a lasting legacy. Larry Ribstein's trenchant description of reputational capital in Big Law describes the same experience.[17] High-functioning law firms operated as partnerships in corporate form, but also in spirit.

Practicing law, even at a big firm, *should* lend itself to a shared sense of purpose. Lawyers work in a helping profession. This should mean a joint sense of identity as professionals, and the natural sense of purpose that comes from helping clients solve problems. Firm culture can also create purpose, an ethos that unites a group of creative humans working together on the same team. This sense of common purpose, or really any purpose beyond maximizing profits, is what has been diluted since the golden age. Size itself dilutes purpose. Consider Malcolm Gladwell's "rule of 150." The maximum size of a group of humans that can have real social relationships with each other is 150.[18] The recent spate of lateral hiring also destroys firm culture and purpose. Lateral hiring encourages each lawyer to consider her value individually, rather than collectively. Many lawyers neglect mentoring or firm building and focus on their own bottom line.

But the biggest impediment to Big Law happiness is autonomy. Unlike mastery and purpose, "autonomy" is pretty straightforward: you need to be able to control what you do at work, with whom, when, and how.[19] The happiest and most productive workers have a great deal of control over the nature of their work. Happy workers are measured by their outputs (the work itself) not by how long it took them, or whether they did the work at home or the office. Big Law runs on the exact opposite understanding. Pink uses hourly lawyering as his main example of a job that lacks autonomy:

> Alas, at the heart of private legal practice is perhaps the most autonomy-crushing mechanism imaginable: the billable hour. Most lawyers—and nearly all lawyers in large, prestigious firms—must keep scrupulous track, often in six-minute increments, of their time. If they fail to bill enough hours, their jobs are in jeopardy. As a result, their focus inevitably veers from the *output* of their work (solving a client's problem) to its *input* (piling up as many hours as possible).[20]

This phenomenon accelerates as lawyers age, because lawyers in their forties or fifties experience time differently than twenty-six-year-olds. I have a friend from law school who is a Big Law partner, and he explains that the reality of selling his time to clients is particularly painful—the metaphor and the reality blend to make clear that what he actually sells in Big Law is a precious part of the balance of his life.

Levit and Linder have a section in their book that describes ways law firms can promote happiness. Their first suggestion is increasing autonomy and decreasing the reliance on billable hours.[21] Big Law has resisted alternative billing and any flexibility in working conditions tooth and nail. They want to bill every case by the hour and they want their associates to be physically at work, billing as many hours as can be charged to clients and realized. Until 2008, this was a very successful strategy for increasing profits, but it came at a significant cost in happiness.

B.   The Golden Age

I worked as a summer associate at a white-shoe Wall Street law firm in 1995. A long-time partner who shared my undergraduate *alma mater* and had started at the firm in 1950 took me out to lunch. He described the firm to me as a family: "This firm, our clients, and the people in the firm have been my life's work," he said. He could not have been more proud of what they built and he sincerely wanted to pass that sentiment on. From the summer associate's point of view it was an amazing outpouring of emotion for what appeared to be primarily a very successful and very cutthroat money-making operation, and hardly a fount of familial emotions. Michael Trotter's book about Atlanta law firms likewise dedicates a section to "the firm family" in the 1960s.[22]

And yet, many of the lawyers who worked during what Galanter and Palay call the "golden age" of the American law firm, the late 1950s and early 1960s, would report the same.[23] This period was marked by rampant discrimination against women, African Americans, LGBT persons, and non-Protestant religious groups, so no one should take it as an actual "golden age." The term refers to business structure, not despicable personnel policies.

While it is a good idea to be skeptical of a previous generation making note that everything was better in the past, a close examination of the business practices of law firms in the 1960s suggests that they likely would have been happier places to work. Most lawyers of the golden age billed by the transaction or periodically "for services rendered."[24] Even the hourly billing system was more civilized. Partners were paid on the basis of seniority, rather than the hours they billed or the clients they brought in. Associates were measured for the quality of their work as much (or more) than for their annual billings. Because of the long-term relationship between firms and clients, lawyers filled an independent counselor role, and had the autonomy to disagree with clients, or even call them a "damned fool" when necessary. Competition was at a low ebb: lawyers rarely left one firm for another and many clients were happy to stay with a single law firm in a single city. Lateral hiring was rare. If associates left the firm or failed to make partner they found suitable work in-house or at another law firm. They worked together in a partnership and built the reputational capital that many firms are still riding today. Everyone earned significantly less money. Some of these lawyers were classic lawyer-statesmen, traveling between government service and practice regularly, with less of a noticeable salary loss, because partners made somewhat comparable salaries to government lawyers.

Law firm lawyers in the 1960s had exactly the kinds of jobs that creative humans love. The work was challenging. They worked together on building a firm and helping their clients. They had significant autonomy. It is not an exaggeration to say that every aspect of the job except for the pay has gotten worse since then, a quintessential mistake of trading happiness for remuneration.

C.   And the Work Itself Has Likely Suffered

Big Law managers and corporate clients might take more interest in the happiness of their lawyers if they consider Daniel Pink's other primary insight. Pink gathers a series of studies on creativity and motivation to show that the motivational tools of the industrial age—essentially the carrots and sticks of higher pay for desired outcomes and punishments or termination for bad outcomes—have the *opposite* effect in jobs requiring creativity.[25] Carrots and sticks tend to extinguish intrinsic motivation and crush creativity. They foster short-term thinking and encourage short cuts and cheating.

Pink describes psychologist Sam Glucksberg's famous experiment with the "Candle Problem."[26] The experiment requires participants to use creative problem-solving to mount a lit candle on the wall using only a box of tacks, a book of matches, and a candle. Glucksberg offered one group a financial incentive to solve the problem and had the other group do it for free. The paid group actually took nearly three-and-a-half minutes longer than the unpaid group. The financial incentive was not just neutral; it was counterproductive. Later experiments confirm that incentivizing by punishment also slowed creative thinking.

Pink's argument is tailor-made for Big Law. Piling on extrinsic rewards like money and partnership, and extrinsic punishments like "up or out" partnership determinations or targeted layoffs do not motivate creative thinking. And, creative thinking, not mere time, is exactly what corporate clients seek from their lawyers. Extrinsic punishments and rewards lead to unhappiness and corner-cutting, with bill-padding and other shortcuts likely. In one particularly embarrassing example, consider the lawsuit over fees between Adam Victor and DLA Piper. Internal e-mails from DLA Piper lawyers exclaim that they had "random people working full time on random research projects in standard 'churn that bill, baby!' mode" and that the "bill shall know no limits."[27]

In sum, over the last forty years corporate law firms changed from being the types of workplaces that creative humans enjoy working in— places filled with highly motivated professionals working together on intellectually stimulating joint projects with a sense of purpose—to nearly the opposite. Associates and partners work seven days a week, often motivated primarily by the money, with an eye toward the door and little loyalty toward the clients or each other.[28] This is damaging to the individual lawyers, but also to the quality of the work.

D.   It Will Get Better—For Big Law and Others

The current slowdown will change much of this. Law firm partners and corporate clients have increasingly adopted alternative, non-hourly billing arrangements,[29] exactly the kind of billing that encourages autonomy, efficiency, and creativity. Lawyers will find working as efficiently as possible to achieve the best possible results on projects much more likable than grinding out as many billable hours as they can on the cases they have. Task-based billing will encourage ingenuity, lessen friction with clients, and better align the lawyer's and client's interests.

The work itself will be more interesting. Insofar as some lawyers have felt unchallenged by their work, or have been stuck doing document review or other repetitive work, the future will look quite a lot brighter. The legal work that American lawyers do will be much, much more individualized, because routine work will be done by a computer or a lawyer in Bangalore for $10 an hour. Small-firm and solo practitioners will also have to adjust the work they do, working "at the top of their license," as Richard Granat puts it. This means doing the sort of work that cannot be handled online or by a paralegal: in-court work, complicated drafting, and so forth. This is cold comfort to the unemployed, but it is a benefit to the lawyers that remain.

Many lawyers will enjoy the challenge of responding to shifting market forces. For the first time in years, the practice of law and the market for legal services are undergoing seismic changes. The lawyers that relish the chance to innovate and are entrepreneurial will face more opportunities in the 2010s than they would have in previous decades. Radical change creates winners along with losers, and in many cases the winners will come from unexpected places. The Internet generally lowers the price of routine or interchangeable services. But the so-called "long tail effect" means that unique or distinctive services can reach more consumers, driving up the price or earnings or both. Innovative lawyers will certainly benefit. By contrast, recent law graduates, even those from top schools who go to work in Big Law or a corporation, who want to have a steady, large salary and not have to innovate or sell themselves are in for a rough ride.

Axiom- and *Valorem*-style alternative law firm arrangements will also blossom. This will be bad news for non-lawyers working as staff in the legal sector and for commercial real estate in large cities, but great news for lawyers. Clients will grow accustomed to measuring lawyers on criteria other than the mahogany in their office or the size of their staff. The "back room" expenses of Big Law will be slashed. The lawyers working in these new "firms" will bill out less and work less, but by reducing overhead may actually make more money. This is not to suggest that these new style firms will replace Big Law altogether, just that these sort of arrangements will become more common.

The trend will spread beyond Big Law as well. Small-firm and solo practitioners who do not need an office or a secretary will not have one. Virtual law firms will also be much less wedded to the Big Law hiring model and the crossover between different portions of the profession may become more fluid.

Alternative law firms may also be able to square the circle of increasing the representation of women at the highest rungs of the profession. Since 1990, women have made up half of American law graduates, yet as of 2010 only 20 percent of Big Law partners were women.[30] This is at least partially because Big Law and the tournament of lawyers is not particularly family-friendly and women still bear a disproportionate burden of bearing and raising children. Alternative law firms offer the flexibility and autonomy to work more or less, as circumstances allow, and enable women lawyers to stay in the game even during times of heavy family duties. *Forbes* recently published a five-step guide to opening a virtual law office, with special attention to its advantages for the women pushed out of Big Law.[31]

This change will benefit lawyers of all stripes as well. Big Law's inflexibil-
ity on the terms and conditions of work has long been puzzling. Turnover
and unhappiness have been high for years. Surveys of Big Law associates
show large majorities desiring more flexibility and less work, coupled with
a willingness to make less money.[32] More flexible aggregations of lawyers
offer these benefits. They may also bring pressure on Big Law to adjust.

Some law firms will go back to the golden age. For example, Bartlit
Beck is a litigation boutique in Chicago founded by former Big Law
partner Fred Bartlit.[33] The firm's work is traditional: it does almost
nothing except try cases. Its structure is radically new school, however.
It only hires lawyers it expects to make partner. There are more partners
than associates. They use alternative-billing arrangements almost exclusively. Firm culture recalls a golden-age law firm, filled with lawyers who
train and support each other, and who work in a partnership with each
other and the clients. Atlanta's Taylor English Duma LLP and Cleve-
land's Tucker Ellis LLP are also examples of "new model" law firms,
emphasizing high-quality services, low leverage, and low overhead.[34]

While many lawyers will make less, the lawyers at the top will make
much more. If there is one lesson of the information age and the new winner-take-all markets, it is that the lawyers who find ways to deliver legal services more efficiently and cheaply, while also improving quality, will be very,
very wealthy indeed. Even the wealthiest partner in the most successful
law firm does not have the earnings potential of the lawyers who founded
LegalZoom. For all of the effort that Big Law expends on leverage and billing rates and realization, it is still at heart an hourly business. In the future
the most financially successful purveyors of legal services will not be hourly
workers, but entrepreneurs. Whether this is a good or bad development will
depend on your perspective. It will likely force law back into a more recog-
nizable bell curve of earnings. It will also likely increase an already-marked
income gap between the very top earners and the rest of the profession.

Entrepreneurialism will be required at every level of private practice.
I now make a point of telling every class I teach that they are embark-
ing on a career where entrepreneurship is critical. It is not enough to
hang up a shingle and wait for the clients to roll in. Lawyers of all
stripes will need to convince clients that they add value beyond what is
available online. We are all in sales now, and the lawyers who embrace
that reality will be those that survive and thrive.

Last, the profession itself will find this a galvanizing period. Times of crisis bring people together, and this will unify the legal profession. Lawyers and bar associations will look back on arguments about civility and professionalism with fondness as they face meetings about saving practices from online threats and increased competition from all sides.

In fact, it seems likely that in ten years the managing partners of law firms and the deans of American law schools will gather over drinks to discuss with bemusement the rankings and other silliness that obsessed the profession during the 1990s and 2000s. Existential threats will bring needed perspective to each of our endeavors. When the dust settles we will have a happier, healthier profession, energized by the opportunity to do the challenging legal work that remains.

E. Today's Law Students Are Better Prepared and Better Suited for the New Normal

There is another reason to be optimistic about the future of the profession. Today's law students are much better suited and prepared to be lawyers than students from even five years ago. This is not because law schools are getting better, although the continued growth in practical training may prove helpful. This is because the students coming into the profession truly want to be lawyers and are better apprised of what it means to be a lawyer.

There will be fewer law students. Because there are still many more law graduates than jobs there will be a painful transition, but as matriculation decreases the mismatch should improve. Right now, only 50–65 percent of America's law graduates can get work as a lawyer. Law graduates unable to work as lawyers carry a significant debt of wasted time and money. If applications continue to decline (which is likely given the current public relations nightmare for law schools), the number of law graduates may more closely match, or even fall below, the openings for lawyers. Even if enrollment stalls at 2013–14 levels, it will help close the gap.

Current and future law students face a tremendous headwind on their way to law school. Friends and family warn them not to go. The *Wall Street Journal* and the law school "scamblogs" echo the sentiment.

A *Google* search for the words "law school" brings a relatively negative article entitled "Should I Go To Law School?" on the first page of results.[35] The article tartly notes that: "You probably know this already, but I'll say it again. America has too many law schools charging too much tuition and turning out too many lawyers."[36]

The responses to a *Google* search for "don't go to law school" are even less encouraging, including the *Huffington Post*'s "Tucker Max: Why You Should Not Go to Law School"[37] and a Steven Harper *Salon* essay entitled "Law School Is a Sham."[38] *Forbes* published an article entitled "Why Attending Law School Is the Worst Career Decision You'll Ever Make."[39] This is the advice from reputable sources. The law school scamblogs and *YouTube* offer more pointed and scatological advice to potential students.[40]

Incoming law students should also have a better sense of the reality of the legal profession. In the past a student might watch *The Practice* or *The Good Wife* and decide that the life of a lawyer looks fun and lucrative. Five years ago these impressions would have been confirmed by the employment data published on law school websites and in *U.S. News*. Thanks to lawsuits and public shaming, law schools have been forced to publish more realistic placement statistics to potential students. The myth that Big Law is what most lawyers do has been thoroughly debunked. The reality is sinking in that few law graduates will work in Big Law, and of those who do, few stay for a lifetime. Incoming students will know that the legal profession is not a safe route to riches.

Given a more realistic understanding of the cost of law school, job prospects, the pain of repaying debt, and what most lawyers actually do and earn, only students who really want to be lawyers will come to law school. These will be the students who always wanted to be a lawyer, not history or English majors with nothing else in particular to do. These students will be more likely to enjoy law school and practice.

Smaller law school classes are also a boon to the country. Having more law graduates than there are law jobs is a tremendous loss to society as a whole. Very able college graduates have been wasting a small fortune and three years of their life to pursue a degree that they are not well suited for, in a field with limited employment options. These students can now apply their talents in other fields.

The mismatch between who has been coming to law school and who should be coming to law school has been a significant drag on the profession. The gap between expectations and reality contributed to the disillusionment of many lawyers. Some of lawyer unhappiness is a result of the expectations of individuals who went to law school based on misunderstandings of the lawyer's life. Some came because they thought that lawyers have an easy time getting steady, lucrative employment. Others came to make a fortune working in Big Law. Some came hoping to work in areas like sports law or public interest environmental law that in fact have few openings. Still others enjoyed reading John Stuart Mill and thought being a lawyer would be similar. Some just came because they did not know what else to do. Lowered, more realistic expectations are one key to life satisfaction,[41] and today's law students and lawyers will benefit from lowered sights.

The law school experience itself will be cheaper and better. As fewer students apply to law school, there will be increased competition for students in terms of tuition and scholarships. The *Wall Street Journal* reports increased scholarship competition for applicants and increased cost haggling by incoming students.[42]

As some law schools move away from competing over *U.S. News* rankings to the serious business of keeping the doors open and the lights on, the student experience may also improve. There will be pressure to spend less on faculty scholarship (which is quite expensive) and to increase the teaching of practical legal skills. Competition has already created some small innovations, like Northwestern's two-year program or Washington and Lee's experiential-learning third year of law school. Increased competition may result in further experimentation and pedagogical improvements. Any changes that break up the current, monolithic approach to law school will be positive overall, even if some of the innovations are less successful or are simply cost-saving measures.

The general scarcity of law jobs may engender a sense of perspective and gratitude for students who are able to secure employment. I have already noticed that students who get relatively low-paying jobs in small firms or as district attorneys, public defenders, or legal aid lawyers are much less likely to grumble than in years past. Recall the discussion in chapter 4 of the relative unhappiness of silver and bronze medalists. Bronze medalists are happy to have made it into the medal round. They compare themselves to all of the competitors below them. Silver medalists fixate on the gold medalist above them and dwell on their failure. The current market has made all employed law students bronze medalists, just happy to have made it. These changes could also lessen the divisiveness that comes from the double-hump salary chart for new graduates. Eventually the legal market may return to something approaching a more normal, bell-shaped curve.

The downward pressure on costs and borrowing may also allow law students to choose jobs that they like, rather than jobs to repay loans. Critics of the rising cost of law school and student debt have argued that idealistic students who came to law school to serve justice are driven into the arms of Big Law against their will, and then remain as a result of golden handcuffs.[43] Most students will not work in Big Law, but due to the expense of law school they may still choose a job based largely on salary, rather than aptitude or interest. More transparency about debt and employment, along with wiser student behavior, will ameliorate this problem.

If the loan repayment programs do not change, law students may face a different problem: the ten-year loan repayment program for government or non-profit work is too good a deal to pass up. Given the sheer size of the average indebtedness at a private law school, it is likely a better deal for a student to work as a district attorney or public defender for ten years than as an associate in Big Law. The work is likely to be more meaningful, over fewer hours, and it might be easier to repay law school debt sooner.

Between the loan repayment program and the shrinkage in Big Law, open lawyer jobs in government and non-profits are suddenly very attractive, and competition for these jobs has grown increasingly stiff. For example, the public defender's office in Knoxville, Tennessee, reports that it now receives applications from Harvard and Yale for summer positions. Deborah Rhode similarly describes that top students at Stanford Law School are struggling to find government or non-profit work in the Bay Area. Insofar as one believes that students who attend top law schools are more able as lawyers, this trend will also help the public at large, as public service and loan forgiveness draw the best and brightest to public service.

F. Law Faculty

Happier students should make for happier faculty. But, even if it does not, a correction in the salaries and perks for law school professors has been a long time coming. Brian Tamanaha's *Failing Law Schools* is at its most powerful in its chapter on a law professor's job ("Teaching Load Down, Salary Up"), precisely because legal academics have been so slow to recognize their own role in the trends of the last thirty years. Law professors work less and are paid more than they used to, and yet seem mystified over why tuition and debt loads have risen so precipitously. Some law professors have a "let them eat cake" response to the suffering of recent law graduates, noting that law has always been a competitive market and these graduates are just poorly suited to it. Others have resisted efforts to train more practice-ready students, arguing that skills training is below them and a waste of time for law schools. Still others think that the cost of law school is fair enough in a free market, conveniently forgetting that much or all of the "demand" for law school comes from the government requirement of graduation from an ABA-accredited law school in order to hold a law license.

These attitudes will fade somewhat as the pain in the legal market is shared by legal academia. If it is true that the worst part about living a lie is wondering when everyone will find out, the hardest part is over for legal academia. The law faculty who survive the retrenchment will, like the students who are happy to be employed, experience gratitude for what they have, rather than jealousy for what they do not. The mania of rankings competition and lateral professor hiring will also slow, increasing satisfaction. Of course, Deborah Rhode's *In Pursuit of Knowledge* warns us that jealousy and status competition is not a byproduct of current academia, it is its essence,[44] so progress may be limited.

The shakeup will likely have helpful effects for legal scholarship as well. Commentators from Chief Justice Roberts to Federal Judge Harry Edwards have noted that current legal scholarship is too theoretical to be useful to most lawyers and judges.[45] Previous generations of law professors taught more, and they wrote treatises and shorter, more practical law review articles (or nothing at all). Currently, the rankings race and other institutional incentives have pushed law professors into a one-size-fits-all approach to scholarship: sixty- to seventy-five-page articles of highly theoretical work of little practical value to bench and bar. At some schools it is unthinkable for a faculty member to write a treatise, and even casebooks and hornbooks are discouraged or demeaned as not "real scholarship."

If teaching loads go up and money dries up for scholarship, several things might occur: (1) law school might get cheaper as the cross-subsidy to scholarship from tuition shrinks; (2) some folks might not write at all, which would be good if they write only because it is required for money/tenure reasons; (3) faculty may be free to write what they want, be it a treatise, bar journal article, or the like, without suffering any sanctions for not doing approved "scholarship;" (4) teaching might become a more important part of decisions on hiring and tenure; and (5) some hiring might shift toward judges or lawyers with significant practice experience, rather than a narrow focus on future scholarly productivity.

G.   The Upshot

It is true that the glass will not be half full for the lawyers who cannot find work or for the law professors who lose their jobs. Nevertheless, it is worth remembering the wisdom of Arthur Leff: "the radically unknown is always frightening (at least to those making out all right as is), especially considering how many lives can be lashed to pieces as a new distributional curve flails about, desperately seeking a new equilibrium."[46] Nevertheless, what economists call "creative destruction" is perhaps the most important benefit to a functioning market economy. Old business models and processes are replaced with cheaper, better alternatives. Jobs are lost, skills become outdated, but progress is made.

13

Conclusion

WITH THE GLASS HALF full in mind, this conclusion will discuss some potential benefits that are unlikely to occur, despite the highest hopes of advocates. It is doubtful that either law schools or lawyer regulation will be radically reshaped in the midst of a brutal downturn. This is because state supreme courts have claimed a constitutional power to regulate the legal profession, and they have historically worked very closely with the ABA and state bar associations. State supreme courts are not going to cede that power or work to disempower bar associations any time soon. The changes at hand are so profound, the possible effects of any new regulations so unclear, the antipathy of the public toward lawyer self-interest is so deep, and the profession is sufficiently divided and demoralized that the regulatory status quo will likely appear the safest route.

Which leads us to the one under-discussed note of caution. Hard times can bring bad regulation. The Depression was the last time that the American legal profession faced an existential threat. State supreme courts and the ABA responded by ratcheting up entry regulations and prosecuting UPL. If the protectionist approach repeated itself today, much of the glass-half-full case would be lost. For example, the California State Bar Association has been lobbying for the power to independently prosecute UPL, a clear threat to online and do-it-yourself legal services.[1] Because lawyer regulators are unlikely to explicitly approve of computerization and outsourcing, however, our best-case scenario is continued desuetude and silent acquiescence. If that happens we will see continued innovation and improved access to legal services for all Americans.

Whither American lawyers? The book concludes with a short rumination on the most basic reason to be optimistic about the American legal profession going forward: lawyers have faced much worse and triumphed.

A.   The Current Roil Will Encourage Incremental Changes, But Will Probably Not Revolutionize Legal Education or Lawyer Regulation

Rahm Emanuel reminded us in 2009 that we should never let a crisis go to waste, and the critics of legal education have taken that advice to heart. Lawyer regulation has long been subject to withering critique and in response to market changes there have been increased calls for the slackening of UPL,[2] allowing non-lawyers to provide simple legal services[3] and allowing the corporate ownership of law firms.[4]

Law schools have also faced a bevy of suggestions. Some of the criticisms of American law schools are longstanding and obvious, such as that law school does too little to prepare students for practice. In 1921, Alfred Zantzinger Reed wrote a report for the Carnegie Foundation entitled *Training for the Public Profession of the Law.*[5] Reed noted that "[t]he failure of the modern American law school to make any adequate provision in its curriculum for practical training constitutes a remarkable educational anomaly."[6] Eighty-six years later, Roy Stuckey's *Best Practices for Legal Education*[7] and a second Carnegie Foundation report entitled *Educating Lawyers* made essentially the same point.[8]

Neither the Socratic nor the case methods have any empirically demonstrated pedagogical advantages, and they have some clear disadvantages. Jerome Frank and other legal realists savaged the use of the case and Socratic methods in the 1930s,[9] and those criticisms have hardly subsided since then.[10]

Deborah Rhode and others have criticized the utility of the third year of law school.[11] These standard criticisms have been joined by the more recent concerns over cost, debt loads, and employment opportunities.

The current crisis offers the perfect opportunity for critics to trot out their preferred solutions. For example, Brian Tamanaha suggests, among other things, a less expensive, two-year law school program,[12] and President Obama may agree.[13] The Chief Judge of New York's highest court has also expressed some interest in the possibility.[14] John McGinnis recommends making law an undergraduate degree, as it is in the U.K. and Australia.[15] Brent Newton suggests that law schools be required to hire professors with practice experience to teach a more practice-oriented curriculum.[16] Ray Campbell (echoing Deborah Rhode) wants to allow licensing of non-lawyers for some legal tasks to ameliorate the access-to-justice problems.[17] David Barnhizer hopes that the ABA will approve large-scale online courses, allowing law schools to pool teaching resources, shrink their faculties, and possibly use the additional resources to require clinics or other experiential learning.[18] David Lat has suggested replacing the third year of law school with apprenticeships.[19] John Farmer suggests a mandatory "residency" year after law school.[20] And so on. The solutions are as legion as the problems.

There are four reasons to doubt that much will come of the proposed changes to lawyer or law school regulation.

1. Many of the Critiques and Solutions are Stale

Many of the proposed responses address general, longstanding problems and are not a response to the current crisis. For example, teaching law graduates the basics of actually practicing law has been an obvious need since Socratic/case-method law schools replaced apprenticeships. Graduating practice-ready lawyers might help that school's students compete in a tough market, but it does nothing to address the baseline problem: there are too few jobs. It also begs the question of what "practice ready" means in a radically shifting market.

2. The ABA and Supreme Courts are Still in Charge

Barring a change in who regulates law schools (the ABA and state supreme courts) none of these changes is likely to happen in the near term. Why? Because any of these large-scale changes would cost a lot of money, reduce tuition, or increase competition in a crowded market. If history is our guide, licensing will tighten during a crisis, not loosen. State supreme courts and the ABA control admission to the profession and the accreditation of American law schools. These bodies have proven predictably responsive to their main constituencies (lawyers and law schools),[21] so for each proposed solution, ask: "Would ABA members or law school faculties and administrators object to this change?" If the answer is yes, the change is unlikely to occur.

Take the idea of a two-year law school program. Northwestern allows one, but those students pay full freight and attend school full-time through two or three summer sessions.[22] That two-year program is just a three-year program squeezed into two full years. Likewise, the ABA has allowed William Mitchell Law School to offer an "online" law degree, where students earn half of the credits online and earn the other half in a few intensive weeks of in-person classes per semester. It is an innovative program in every respect except for the price, which is currently the same as attending full time. A true two-year or online program would require fewer credit hours and would be cheaper and faster. That would result in more law graduates or fewer total students per year, or both. In short, an ABA-accredited two-year program would be a disaster for already struggling law schools and a saturated job market. Even if state supreme courts and the ABA thought these ideas were good, the opposition from law school deans and the rank and file would be excruciating.

The same analysis applies to law as an undergraduate study or the replacing of the third year of law school with apprenticeship. The former would result in more potential lawyers, and the latter would cost law schools a year of tuition and might provide more low-cost competition in the form of law "apprentices."

Ironically, the most likely solution is the one requiring a residency *after* three years of law school: (1) it would be harder and more expensive to become a lawyer, decreasing competition; (2) it would not cut into law school tuition; and (3) the "residency" might be aimed at serving the indigent. Like other historical changes to licensing, it is a win-win all around, except for the new entrants, who are generally not at the table to negotiate.

There is also the problem of faculty governance of law schools. Brian Tamanaha's *Failing Law Schools* is absolutely correct when it says that American law schools have largely been run by and for law professors.[23] Not surprisingly, law deans are finding their faculties disinterested in any sweeping changes that will make their jobs harder. An aptly titled *Chronicle of Higher Education* article says it all: "As They Ponder Reforms, Law Deans Find Schools 'Remarkably Resistant to Change.'"[24] Schools facing closure will obviously have a mandate for a change. Schools that face struggles, but not extinction, will likely stay the course as long as they can.

The ABA has created a Task Force on the Future of Legal Education that appears to be considering some or all of the more radical suggestions above.[25] The hearings and announcements sound promising, but the recommendations have proven controversial[26] and time will tell if they have much effect when they reach the broader membership of the ABA. Law professors are already having conniptions,[27] so if you believe Brian Tamanaha that they have a powerful effect on the ABA regulations, these suggestions may be dead on arrival.

Similarly, based on the Washington State "Limited License Legal Technicians"[28] (LLLT) program there is much hope that non-lawyers may finally be able to compete with lawyers in providing legal services. The Washington program is less than it appears, however.

In Washington State non-lawyers will be licensed and allowed to draft legal instruments in limited areas (at first just domestic relations) and offer related advice. The LLLTs will not be allowed to appear in court. At first blush, this appears to be a significant and unexpected concession by the Supreme Court of Washington. There have been unsuccessful efforts to loosen strictures against UPL to address access-to-justice concerns for years. Deborah Rhode led a very persuasive and successful one-woman charge against the prosecution of UPL in the 1970s and 1980s.[29] In 1995, the ABA Commission on Nonlawyer Practice was finally persuaded. It released a report describing the legal work that legal paraprofessionals already safely performed and suggested that the ABA reconsider its ethics rules and its definition of UPL.[30] The ABA ignored the reports and many local bar associations have since ramped up UPL prosecution.[31]

So maybe Washington's action is a significant deregulation? Not so much. The State Bar of Washington (and not the Washington Supreme Court) will license and regulate LLLTs in the first instance, making any radical new competition from non-lawyers unlikely. The rules for becoming an LLLT are quite stringent, including years of school and apprenticeship, making a flood of new entrants unlikely. In some ways the regulations are already stricter for LLLTs than lawyers. LLLTs must carry malpractice insurance, for example, and lawyers do not. The new program is not a loosening of restrictions on UPL. To the contrary, it is an attempt to regulate *more* of the market for legal services, by essentially regulating paralegals. Thus, the entire program may be a stalking horse for greater tightening of lawyer control. Even with these caveats, any "lawyer-light" licensing is a hopeful sign. If significant numbers sign up and charge less that would certainly help access to justice for the middle class.

3. When You Hit a Storm, You Batten Down the Hatches

Remember Clayton Christensen's study of disruptive technologies. When legacy companies face radical market changes, they tend to hold fast rather than attempt to adopt the disruptive technology. Established providers tend to double down on what they have always done, because uncertainty breeds inertia, and it is hard to teach old dogs new tricks. The legacy industry is expert at one way of doing business; the disruptive innovation presents a radically different model.

The reaction of lawyers to their changed circumstances has been straight out of this playbook: they ignored computerization at first. Then they pooh-poohed it. Now, they deride it as substandard, but have largely failed to meet the competition head-on. This provides a market opportunity for the lawyers that have adopted virtual and online law practices. But, it presents a significant challenge to everyone else. Frequently, these sorts of challenges have been met by paralysis rather than action.

4. The Public is Watching

If bar associations or state supreme courts took any radical actions, like prosecuting UPL more aggressively, they would face a significant public backlash. *LegalZoom* and other computerized providers of legal services have grown prevalent and profitable enough to present a strong challenge to any UPL enforcement effort. Generally speaking, UPL enforcement has been at its most robust when aimed against individuals. For example, one of the few UPL prosecutions for using a computerized form actually punished an individual who filled out an electronic will form for an elderly neighbor, rather than the form provider itself.[32] Similarly, publishers of legal forms have had more success fighting UPL than individual non-lawyer scriveners.[33] This is because individuals often lack the funds or political power to defend themselves. So, UPL prosecutions of small legal websites are likelier to proceed and succeed than any prosecution large enough to slow the current tide.

The alternative—a full-scale attempt to bring non-lawyers, outsourcing, and computerization to heel via UPL or more aggressive regulation—would require a great deal of political will and capital from state supreme courts. Truly aggressive moves would be likely to draw federal antitrust and congressional attention. If push came to shove, state supreme courts and lawyer regulators would face a potentially existential crisis: attempts to maintain their inherent authority to regulate lawyers would come up against an angry populace and an engaged federal government. It is beyond the scope of this book to determine whether federal supremacy would overrule bedrock state constitutional law in such a showdown. Simply describing the parameters of the potential showdown helps explain why lawyer regulators have stepped lightly and why they will continue to do so.

B.   Desuetude or Tightening?

Nor are we likely to see a broad deregulation of the legal profession, as has occurred in the U.K. and to a lesser extent in Australia.[34] Legislatures have much more control over the legal profession in those countries, so the interests of the public are likelier to prevail. Here, courts and bar associations will not consider this the right time to embark upon wholesale changes. Consequently, hopes that the ABA or state bar associations will suddenly deregulate the profession are unfounded.

The relevant question is whether bar associations and courts will remain relatively passive as the market for legal services changes (or collapses) around them. More aggressive prosecution of UPL or enforcement of the Rules of Professional Conduct could challenge a number of recent trends, including computerization, outsourcing, and settlement mills; or immigration, bankruptcy, and disability firms where one or two lawyers front for a mass of non-lawyers who do almost all the actual work.

During the Depression, the concerns over the survival of the profession grew to the point that the prosecution of UPL boomed and bar associations and state courts erected a number of new barriers to entry. If the market for lawyers continues to shrink, we may see a return to these policies. An alternative may be lower-profile moves like quietly adjusting the bar passage rate downward or disaccrediting some law schools. In Tennessee, the bar examiners subtly changed the way they scored the bar exam two years ago, coincidentally resulting in a tumble in the bar passage rates during a horrible market for lawyers. This strategy appears to have caught on-bar passage rates tumbled all over the country in 2014. Some combination of low-profile tightening seems much more likely than any large-scale loosening or any radical changes.

The likeliest result is that law schools and lawyer regulation stay basically the same but grow less relevant, as everything except for in-court and other bespoke legal work is swamped by competition from computers, outsourcing, and non-lawyers. Rather than try to regain lost ground, lawyers and law schools will try to hold on to what they still have, even as it shrinks around them. I think of it as a sand castle facing a rising tide: the outer walls will be lost, but perhaps the citadel can be maintained.

There is the possibility for some targeted deregulation to allow lawyers to compete more effectively with the explosion of non-lawyer services on the Internet. Right now, regulatory sluggishness is keeping many lawyers on the sideline, while unregulated non-lawyers are rushing in. For example, the ABA and most state bar associations continue to drag their feet on changes to ABA Rule of Professional Responsibility 5.4, which bars non-lawyer ownership of law firms and sharing legal fees with non-lawyers.[35] As Bill Henderson has noted, this ban is allowing non-lawyers to provide-legal type services in multiple guises and with creative financing, while leaving law firms hamstrung.[36] Gillian Hadfield has argued that loosening Rule 5.4 would also greatly increase access to justice because non-lawyer owners could leverage economies of scale and logistics to streamline the types of representation needed by the poor and the middle class.[37]

Regulatory bans on multijurisdictional law practice likewise make it hard for licensed lawyers to compete on the Internet. *LegalZoom* and *Rocket Lawyer* are available in all fifty states. A lawyer-run virtual law practice, however, must satisfy licensing requirements of each jurisdiction, making a national virtual law firm competitor a very difficult proposition.[38] Nevertheless, bar associations have asked the band to play on as the ship sinks, arguing over ethics rules that only bind a very limited group of lawyers, leaving the ever expanding online market for legal services largely unregulated.[39]

C.   You Can't Stop Us, You Can Only Hope to Contain Us

This book tries to present a fair view of the challenges but is ultimately optimistic about where American lawyers are going. This is partially for the reasons outlined in chapters 11 and 12, but also because the

American legal profession has survived and thrived through more trying times. There is and always has been a strong strain of disdain for
lawyers in this country, and there has been quite a bit of *schadenfreude*
recently.[40] Nevertheless, every time the American legal profession has
appeared down for the count, it has come roaring back.

America is an unusual country. Our legal profession is especially
prominent in social, civic, and governmental affairs. Lawyers founded
these United States. Thirty-two of the fifty-five framers of the Constitution and twenty-five of the fifty-six signers of the Declaration of Indepen-
dence were trained or practicing lawyers.[41] Twenty-five out of forty-four
American presidents have been lawyers. The trend was even stronger in
the eighteenth and nineteenth centuries: three of the first four, six of
the first eight, ten of the first thirteen, and twelve of the first sixteen
presidents were lawyers.[42] Lawyers have always been a dominant force in
Congress and state legislatures.[43] Even in an era of relative lawyer unpop-
ularity, the 113th Congress included fifty-five senators and one hundred
and fifty-six representatives who were current or former lawyers.[44] Every
Supreme Court Justice and federal judge has likewise been a lawyer.

In 1830, De Tocqueville noted that "American aristocracy is found at
the bar and on the bench":[45]

> Lawyers in the United States constitute a power which is little feared
> and hardly noticed; it carries no banner of its own and adapts flex-
> ibly to the demands of the time, flowing along unresistingly with all
> the movements of society. Nevertheless it wraps itself around society
> as a whole, is felt in all social classes, constantly continues to work
> in secret upon them without their knowing until it has shaped them
> to its own desires.[46]

De Tocqueville praised the inherent conservatism of lawyers and judges
as a bulwark against the tyranny of the majority. Why? Because "innovation can only damage them, which adds an interest in conservation
to the natural liking for order."[47] De Tocqueville's commentary is 180
years old and startlingly accurate today. Lawyers and law are central to
this country's DNA. It has always been thus.

The exceptions prove the rule. Jacksonian democracy came immediately on the heels of De Tocqueville. Every effort was made to reprogram

America and to break the hold of courts and lawyers. In the middle of the nineteenth century it looked more likely that the law would be fully open to practice by lay people than that lawyers would rise from the grave and reorganize to create the profession we have today. The practice was virtually unregulated in a majority of states, and legislatures passed new codes of civil procedure to further erode lawyer hegemony. Judicial elections were introduced. After the Civil War, lawyers who were already facing deregulation confronted the loss of the lucrative business of conducting title searches.[48] Times looked grim.

Lawyers responded by becoming irreplaceable partners with all levels of businesses, working hand in hand with the makers of the industrial revolution. As Lawrence Friedman describes the post–Civil War era:

> Nevertheless, the lawyers prospered. The truth was that the profession was exceedingly nimble at finding new kinds of work and new ways to do it. Its nimbleness was no doubt due to the character of the bar: open-ended, unrestricted, uninhibited, attractive to sharp, ambitious men.[49]

When confronted with extinction the profession has continuously re-invented itself.

Lawyers again faced an existential threat during the Depression when the economy crumbled and earnings collapsed. The situation was dire enough in 1935 that 1,500 lawyers, in a country that only had 160,000 lawyers,[50] took a pauper's oath in order to join a legal relief project under the Works Progress Administration.[51]

Bryant Garth has written an article comparing the profession's Depression-era crisis with today's. He notes that in the Depression there was talk of a "crisis" of "too many lawyers."[52] Lawyers faced competition from non-lawyers on a number of fronts:

> Title companies took over the searching of titles. Workmen's compensation began to eliminate litigation over industrial accidents. Summary trial, probation, and penal boards are removing much of the importance of the defense of criminals. Practice in taxation matters and before the Interstate Commerce Commission has fallen into

the hands of specialists. The bank and trust company has threatened to poach on the sacred fields of the drafting and probating of wills.[53]

Nevertheless, this period laid the foundation for the growth from the 1950s through the 1970s, as tightened entry standards and World War II resulted in drastically reduced competition.

There is the question of lawyer agency amongst these challenges and changes. My colleague, Dana Remus, notes that this book presents lawyers as relatively passive victims to larger market forces. She also notes that "passive" is not the adjective she would use to describe the majority of the lawyers she knows. It does seem likely that some lawyers and lawyer regulators will cling to the past as hard and as long as they can. But, other lawyers will do what American lawyers have always done: they will find a way to make a good living advising clients, or finding loopholes, or suing wealthy defendants, or guiding complicated transactions. Throughout this book, I have noted that entrepreneurial lawyers and law graduates will have the opportunity to flourish in this brave new world. The good news for lawyers is that many of them are, in fact, clever, hard-working, and entrepreneurial. These are exactly the attributes that will lead to surviving and thriving in the future.

Take Big Law's international standing, for example. Growth has slowed and a restructuring is in progress, but America's law firms are still the envy of the world. The United States is the largest exporter of legal services in the world and has consistently run a trade surplus in law.[54] In 2001, the United States legal services industry ran a $2.4 billion trade surplus.[55] The surplus grew to $4.9 billion in 2007[56] and $5.3 billion in 2011.[57] The competition for the highest-end, bet-the-company legal work, is international, and America has been winning. American lawyers are concerned with the effects of computerization and globalization. Foreign lawyers are worried about those things *and* American lawyers.

Consider also the endless ingenuity of the American lawyer. Following the terrorist attacks of 9/11, America reeled and sought to use any and all tools to battle international terrorism. Plaintiff's lawyers, among others, convinced Congress that lawsuits would be an effective remedy, and the Antiterrorism Act of 2001 was born.[58] The act allowed Americans to sue for treble damages if they were "injured in his or her person, property, or business by reason of an act of international terrorism."[59] Lawsuits have proliferated, and plaintiff's lawyers have had some notable successes in trying to track down the money trail behind international terrorism.[60] It is telling that when faced with a crisis America turned to one of its most potent weapons: lawyers and courts.

Lastly, consider what Richard Posner has called "the appalling complexity of American law."[61] Elsewhere, I have railed against this trend,[62] but it does not appear to be slowing down. Computers, lawyers, and legal complexity are thus involved in a convoluted race. Computers, non-lawyers, and outsourcing will continue to try to peel off simpler legal tasks and more basic legal questions and commoditize them. Lawyers will try to make all legal work so complex that clients need an expensive human guide. As overlapping laws, court decisions, and regulations proliferate, lawyers will continue to be needed to navigate complicated issues, for those who can afford it. This is especially so because judges, not computers, will interpret the law, making a nuanced understanding of human judgment critical.

America and its legal profession have been intertwined from the beginning, and lawyers—sharp-elbowed and ambitious—will find a new purchase in these changed times. They have before. They will again.

NOTES

⇒•⇐

Chapter 1

1. CHARLES DICKENS, BLEAK HOUSE (Signet Classic Edition 1980).
2. *Id.* at 22.
3. Bespoke was originally a tailoring term, denoting custom-made clothes for individuals. It has since come to be used more broadly to refer to any individualized, custom service. Richard Susskind uses the term to describe the individualized legal work of British solicitors and barristers in RICHARD SUSSKIND, TOMORROW'S LAWYERS (2013) and RICHARD SUSSKIND, THE END OF LAWYERS? (2010).
4. SUSSKIND, TOMORROW'S LAWYERS, has a great visualization of this process at 25.
5. ROBERT H. FRANK & PHILIP J. COOK, THE WINNER-TAKE-ALL SOCIETY (1995).
6. Robert H. Frank, *Why Has Inequality Been Growing?*, SLATE, December 6, 2011, http://www.slate.com/articles/business/moneybox/2011/12/how_technology_and_winner_take_all_markets_have_made_income_inequality_so_much_worse_.html.
7. Larry E. Ribstein, *The Death of Big Law*, 2010 WISC. L. REV. 749 (2010).
8. *Id.* at 753–60.
9. *Cf.* Jacob Gershman, *More Than 50% of Graduates Aren't Making a Living—Study*, WALL ST. J., April 4, 2013, http://blogs.wsj.com/law/2013/04/04/more-than-50-of-graduates-arent-making-a-living-study/.
10. STEVEN J. HARPER, THE LAWYER BUBBLE (2013); BRIAN Z. TAMANAHA, FAILING LAW SCHOOLS (2012); MICHAEL H. TROTTER, DECLINING

Prospects (2012); Paul Campos, Don't Go to Law School (Unless) (2013), James E. Moliterno, The American Legal Profession in Crisis (2013).

11. *See, e.g.,* Benjamin H. Barton & Stephanos Bibas, *Triaging Appointed-Counsel Funding and* Pro Se *Access to Justice,* 160 U. Penn. L. Rev. 967 (2012) and Benjamin H. Barton, *Against Civil* Gideon *(and for* Pro Se *Court Reform),* 62 Fla. L. Rev. 1227 (2010).

12. Glenn Reynolds, *Higher Education Bubble, Law School Edition,* Instapundit, April 17, 2013, http://pjmedia.com/instapundit/167222/.

Chapter 2

1. Morton J. Horwitz, The Transformation of American Law, 1780–1860 140–59 (1977); Maxwell Bloomfield, *Law vs. Politics: The Self-Image of the American Bar (1830–1860),* 12 Am. J. Leg. Hist. 306, 307–8 (1968). Please note that the "golden age" meme for this period has been criticized by modern legal historians. *See* Charles W. Wolfram, *Toward a History of the Legalization of American Legal Ethics—I. Origins,* 8 U. Chi. L. Sch. Roundtable 469, 471 & n. 14 (2001).

2. A great example is W. Raymond Blackard, *The Demoralization of the Legal Profession in Nineteenth Century America,* 16 Tenn. L. Rev. 314 (1940). The works of Warren, Pound, and Chroust cited herein are in the same vein.

3. Francis R. Aumann, The Changing American Legal System 23–30 (1969).

4. Robert G. McClosky, *James Wilson, in* The Justices of the United States Supreme Court 55–72 (Leon Friedman and Fred L. Israel eds. 1995) (hereinafter Justices).

5. Fred Israel, *John Blair, Jr., in* Justices 74–80; Leon Friedman, *John Rutledge, in* Justices 22–38.

6. Jay F. Alexander, *Legal Careers in Eighteenth Century America,* in The Legal Profession 2–9 (Kermit L. Hall ed., 1987).

7. Anton-Hermann Chroust, The Rise of the Legal Profession in America, Volume 2 146 (1965).

8. Chroust, The Rise of the Legal Profession, at 201.

9. Bruce Frohnen, *The Bases of Professional Responsibility: Pluralism and Community in Early America,* 63 Geo. Wash. L. Rev. 931, 931–8 (1995).

10. Edward P. Weeks, A Treatise on Attorneys and Counsellors at Law 144–223 (1892). In keeping with modern trends, however, this power was infrequently invoked. See Fannie M. Farmer, *Legal Practice and Ethics in North Carolina 1820–1860,* in The Legal Profession, Major Historical Interpretations 274, 350 & n. 101 (Kermit Hall ed., 1987) (noting that "prior to 1868, no court, so far as the records show, was called upon to disbar an attorney" in North Carolina).

11. Alex B. Long, *Attorney Deceit Statutes: Promoting Professionalism Through Criminal Prosecutions and Treble Damages,* 44 U.C. Davis L. Rev. 413, 444–9 (2010).

12. ALEXIS DE TOCQUEVILLE, DEMOCRACY IN AMERICA (Gerald Bevan, trans. 2004).

13. *See* ALFRED Z. REED, TRAINING FOR THE PUBLIC PROFESSION OF THE LAW 87–8 (1921).

14. *See* EZRA POUND, THE LAWYER FROM ANTIQUITY TO MODERN TIMES 227–8 (1953).

15. JAMES WILLARD HURST, THE GROWTH OF AMERICAN LAW: THE LAW MAKERS 282 (1950).

16. *Id.*

17. Larry C. Berkson, *Judicial Selection, in* THE UNITED STATES: A SPECIAL REPORT, IN JUDICIAL POLITICS: READINGS FROM JUDICATURE 50 (Elliot E. Slotnick ed., 2005).

18. Joanna M. Shepherd, *Money, Politics, and Impartial Justice*, 58 DUKE L.J. 623, 631–2 (2009).

19. CHARLES WARREN, A HISTORY OF THE AMERICAN BAR 508–39 (1966).

20. *See, e.g.*, POUND, THE LAWYER FROM ANTIQUITY TO MODERN TIMES at 223–49.

21. LAWRENCE M. FRIEDMAN, A HISTORY OF AMERICAN LAW 303–10 (2nd ed. 1985).

22. *Id.*

23. EDWIN ARTHUR MILES, JACKSONIAN DEMOCRACY IN MISSISSIPPI 42 (1960).

24. Bloomfield, *Law vs. Politics*, 307.

25. *See* CHRIS FARRELL, DEFLATION 35 (2005); GARY M. WALTON & HUGH ROCKOFF, HISTORY OF THE AMERICAN ECONOMY 369 (2009).

26. FRIEDMAN, HISTORY OF AMERICAN LAW, at 633. The U.S. population roughly tripled over the same period (from 23 million to 76 million). *See U.S. Population through History,* http://geography.about.com/od/obtainpopulationdata/a/uspop.htm (last visited March 25, 2014).

27. RICHARD ABEL, AMERICAN LAWYERS 280 (1989).

28. *Id.*

29. B. Peter Pashigian, *The Number and Earnings of Lawyers: Some Recent Findings*, 1978 AM. B. FOUND. RES. J. 51, 64–5 (1978).

30. FRIEDMAN, HISTORY OF AMERICAN LAW, at 642–3.

31. Roscoe Pound, *The Etiquette of Justice, in* 3 PROCEEDINGS OF THE NEBRASKA BAR ASSOCIATION 231–5 (1909).

32. ABEL, AMERICAN LAWYERS, at 180.

33. *Id.* at 635–9.

34. WAYNE K. HOBSON, THE AMERICAN LEGAL PROFESSION AND ORGANIZATIONAL SOCIETY, 1890–1930 168 (1977).

35. For an example of a leading firm in this vein, *see* Robert T. Swaine, THE CRAVATH FIRM AND ITS PREDECESSORS, VOLUME I, 1819–1947 (1947).

36. HOBSON, THE AMERICAN LEGAL PROFESSION, at 195–203.

37. ROBERT SWAINE, THE CRAVATH FIRM AND ITS PREDECESSORS, VOLUME 2, 1819–1947 1–12 (1946)

38. *Id.* at 4.
39. *Id.* at 7.
40. *Id.* at 8.
41. Marc Galanter & Thomas Palay, Tournament of Lawyers 9–11 (1991).
42. Swaine, The Cravath Firm, Volume 2, at 1–3.
43. Alpheus Mason, Brandeis: A Free Man's Life 83–5 (1946).
44. Cravath, Swaine & Moore, LLP, *Philosophy: The Cravath System,* http://www.cravath.com/cravathsystem/ (last visited January 16, 2014).
45. Thomas Paul Pinansky, *The Emergence of Law Firms in the American Legal Profession*, 9 U. Ark. Little Rock L.J. 593, 609–13 (1986–87).
46. *Id.*
47. *See* Friedman, History of American Law, at 640.
48. *See id.*
49. *See* Lawrence M. Friedman, A History of American Law (3rd ed. 2005).
50. Richard Posner, Federal Courts 32 (1985).
51. *See* Abel, American Lawyers, at 173.
52. *See* Kate Sayan Kirkland, Captain James A. Baker of Houston, 1857–1941 76–7 (2012)
53. Friedman, History of American Law, at 640 ("[F]irms of this size made up a tiny percentage of the total practice.").
54. This outsized footprint is seen in the extraordinary influence of the American Bar Association, which was founded in 1878 from the elite of the profession. From the founding to the current day the ABA has been the engine behind the regulatory and educational changes to come. *See* Benjamin H. Barton, The Lawyer-Judge Bias in the American System 113–5 (2011).
55. Abel, American Lawyers, at 180.
56. Robert Stevens, Law School 24 (1983).
57. Jerold S. Auerbach, Unequal Justice 94 (1976).
58. These trends will be discussed at greater length in chapter 8.
59. Stevens, Law School, at 73–91.
60. These charts and data come from Benjamin H. Barton, *An Empirical Study of Supreme Court Justice Pre-Appointment Experience*, 64 Fla. L. Rev. 1137 (2012).
61. Friedman, History of American Law, at 648–52.
62. Reed, Training for the Public Profession of the Law, at 220.
63. W. Hamilton Bryson & E. Lee Shepard, *The Virginia Bar, 1870–1900*, in The New High Priests: Lawyers in Post-Civil War America 171–2 (Gerald W. Gawalt ed., 1985).
64. 2 A.B.A. Rep. 212 (1878).
65. Edson R. Sunderland, History of the American Bar Association and Its Work 72–3 (1953).

66. Auerbach, Unequal Justice, at 40–73.
67. 14 A.B.A. Rep. 301–60 (1891).
68. 14 A.B.A. Rep. 349 (1891).
69. Benjamin H. Barton, *An Institutional Analysis of Lawyer Regulation: Who Should Control Lawyer Regulation—the Courts, Legislatures, or the Market?*, 37 Ga. L. Rev. 1167, 1171 (2003). Some state supreme courts have allowed minor legislative encroachment, and some federal agencies, like the SEC, have gotten more involved, but these have been small encroachments. The general rule is state supreme court control.
70. Nancy J. Moore, *The Usefulness of Ethical Codes*, 1989 Ann. Surv. Am. L. 7, 14–6.
71. Barton, Lawyer-Judge Bias, at 105–59.
72. The nineteenth-century collapse in entry standards demonstrates this, as the dilution of entry requirements was statutory or constitutional, not by courts. Barton, Lawyer-Judge Bias, at 116.
73. *In re* Day, 54 N.E. 646 (1899).
74. Thomas M. Alpert, *The Inherent Power of the Courts to Regulate the Practice of Law: An Historical Analysis*, 32 Buff. L. Rev. 523, 537 (1983).
75. *Id.* at 648.
76. *In re* Day, 54 N.E. at 648.
77. *Id.*
78. *In re* Day, 54 N.E. at 652–3. My favorite part of this section of the opinion is that the Illinois legislature apparently licensed "horseshoers" in 1899.
79. Blewett Lee, *The Constitutional Power of the Courts over Admission to the Bar*, 13 Harv. L. Rev. 31 (1899). There are a long series of inherent authority admission cases that follow similar reasoning. *See, e.g., In re* Disbarment Proceedings of William L. Newby, 107 N.W. 850, 852 (Neb. 1906); *In re* Bailey, 248 P. 29, 30 (Ariz. 1926); Ex Parte Steckler, 154 So. 41, 45 (La. 1934); *In re* Sparks, 101 S.W.2d 194, 197 (Ky. Ct. App. 1936); Ayres v. Hadaway, 6 N.W.2d 905, 908 (Mich. 1942); *In re* Thatcher, 22 Ohio Dec. 116 (Lucas Co. Common Pleas Ct. 1912).
80. Henry M. Dowling, *The Inherent Power of the Judiciary*, 21 ABA J. 635, 635–7 (1937).
81. Terry Radtke, *The Last Stage in Reprofessionalizing the Bar: The Wisconsin Bar Integration Movement, 1934–1956*, 81 Marq. L. Rev. 1001, 1007 (1998); Richard Abel, Lawyers in Society: The Common Law World 199 (1988).
82. *See* Abel, American Lawyers, at 159.
83. B. Peter Pashigian, *The Market for Lawyers: The Determinants of the Demand for and Supply of Lawyers*, 20 J. L. & Econ. 53, 63 (1977).
84. *See* Abel, American Lawyers, at 159–62.
85. These figures come from Bureau of the Census, U.S. Department of Commerce, Historical Statistics of the United States: Colonial Times to 1970, 176 (Bicentennial ed. 1975).

86. ABEL, AMERICAN LAWYERS, at 280.
87. *Id.* at 277–8.
88. *Id.* at 55.
89. *Id.* at 40–73.
90. See Terry Radtke, *The Last Stage of Professionalizing the Bar: The Wisconsin Bar Integration Movement, 1934–1956*, 81 MARQ. L. REV. 1001, 1001 (1998).
91. *See, e.g.*, Application of the Montana Bar Ass'n, 368 P.2d 158, 162 (Mont. 1962) (integrating the bar by court order because "[t]here is need for improvement in our court, the district and justice courts, and the bar of which we are members"); *In re* Integration of the Nebraska State Bar Ass'n, 275 N.W. 265, 267–8 (Neb. 1937) (approving integration because "the court has an immediate interest in the character of the bar, for the court's own sake"); Petition of the Florida State Bar Ass'n, 40 So. 2d 902, 908–9 (Fla. 1949) (same).
92. Barton, *An Institutional Analysis of Lawyer Regulation*, at 1208–9.

Chapter 3

1. You can find a list of the numbers at ABA, *Total Licensed Lawyers*, http://www.americanbar.org/resources_for_lawyers/profession_statistics.html (last visited February 27, 2014). These data are the source for the next two graphs, Figures 3.1 and 3.2.
2. Comparing the ABA lawyer count and the Census Bureau population data for the given years generated these data and chart.
3. Milton Z. Kafoglis, *Commentary, in* THE CHANGING ROLE OF THE CORPORATE ATTORNEY 54–5 (William J. Carnet ed., 1982).
4. Personal Consumption Expenditures is a Bureau of Economic Affairs measure of expenditures by market sector. For a fuller description, see Bureau of Economic Analysis, *Personal Consumption Expenditures*, http://www.bea.gov/national/pdf/methodology/ch5%202012.pdf (last visited February 27, 2014).
5. RICHARD L. ABEL, AMERICAN LAWYERS 160 (1989).
6. *Id.* at 160.
7. Marc Galanter, *Law Abounding: Legalization Around the North Atlantic*, 55 MODERN L. REV. 1, 5 (1992).
8. *See* CLIFFORD WINSTON, ET AL., FIRST THING WE DO LET'S DEREGULATE ALL THE LAWYERS 21 (2011). The data for the next two charts, Figures 3.5 and 3.6, come from the Bureau of Economic Analysis.
9. JOHN P. HEINZ ET AL., URBAN LAWYERS: THE NEW SOCIAL STRUCTURE OF THE BAR 25 (2005).
10. ABA, *Lawyer Demographics*, http://www.americanbar.org/content/dam/aba/migrated/marketresearch/PublicDocuments/lawyer_demographics_2011.authcheckdam.pdf (last visited March 26, 2014).
11. HEINZ ET AL., URBAN LAWYERS, at 3.

12. MARC GALANTER & THOMAS PALAY, THE TOURNAMENT OF LAWYERS 20–36 (1991).

13. *See* W. Bradley Wendel, *Morality, Motivation, and the Professionalism Movement*, 52 S.C. L. REV. 557, 566–7 (2001).

14. GALANTER & PALAY, THE TOURNAMENT OF LAWYERS, at 20–36. Support for the rest of this paragraph can be found in this source.

15. ERWIN SMIGEL, THE WALL STREET LAWYER: PROFESSIONAL ORGANIZATION MAN? 58 (1964).

16. *Id.* at 183 & n. 13.

17. *See* Richard Sander, *Hidden Transformation of the Legal Industry*, ABA YOUNG LAWYERS DIVISION, http://www.americanbar.org/publications/young_lawyer_home/young_lawyer_archive/yld_tyl_june08_sander.html (last visited March 25, 2014).

18. GALANTER & PALAY, THE TOURNAMENT OF LAWYERS, at 30–1.

19. SMIGEL, WALL STREET LAWYER, at 18, 92.

20. MICHAEL H. TROTTER, PROFIT AND THE PRACTICE OF LAW 9 (2012).

21. Eli Wald, *The Rise and Fall of the WASP and Jewish Law Firms*, 60 STAN. L. REV. 1803, 1818–19 & n. 72 (2008).

22. TROTTER, PROFIT AND THE PRACTICE OF LAW, at 11–12.

23. GALANTER & PALAY, THE TOURNAMENT OF LAWYERS, at 34.

24. Matt Leichter, *A Profession in Decline: BEA Legal Sector Data (1977–)*, http://lawschooltuitionbubble.wordpress.com/original-research-updated/a-profession-in-decline/ (last visited March 25, 2014). Note that this graph is based on the pre-2014 calculation of GDP. The BEA updated half of this data in 2014, but since the old data cover a longer period of time we use those data here for comparative purposes.

25. Sander, *Hidden Transformation of the Legal Industry*.

26. *See The Am Law 100, 2012: 25 Years*, THE AMERICAN LAWYER, May 2012.

27. The statistics in the rest of this paragraph all come from Michael D. Goldhaber, *The Long Run*, THE AMERICAN LAWYER, May 2012, at 99–101.

28. These numbers were generated using THE AMERICAN LAWYER counts and the ABA's total licensed lawyer count.

29. Judith H. Collins, *Class of 2011 Has the Lowest Employment Rate Since Class of 1994*, NALP BULLETIN, July 2012, http://www.nalp.org/0712research (last visited March 25, 2014).

30. The NLJ 350 by the Numbers, http://www.law.com/jsp/nlj/PubArticleNLJ.jsp?germane=1202489565842&id=1202548783905 (last visited March 25, 2014). The rest of the facts in this paragraph can be found in this source.

31. Robin Sparkman, *The Haves and the Haves Less*, THE AMERICAN LAWYER, May 2012, at 92.

32. *Id.* at 99.

33. Dan Slater, *At Law Firms, Reconsidering the Model for Associates' Pay*, N.Y. TIMES, March 31, 2010, http://www.nytimes.com/2010/04/01/business/01LEGAL.html?pagewanted=all&_r=0

34. NALP, *Class of 2012 Summary Report,* http://www.nalp.org/uploads/ NationalSummaryChart2012.pdf (last visited May 15, 2014).

35. JOHN HEINZ & EDWARD LAUMANN, CHICAGO LAWYERS: THE SOCIAL STRUCTURE OF THE BAR 3–5 (1982); *see also* Mark Green, *The Gross Legal Product: "How Much Justice Can You Afford?,"* in VERDICTS ON LAWYERS 63, 64–5 (R. Nader & M. Green eds., 1976)("[T]here are two distinct legal professions in the United States today. Large corporate law firms [that] generate vast fees and lush incomes [and solo] practitioners or small-firm lawyers in small towns . . . who handle personal [matters and] have moderate incomes.").

36. *See* ABEL, AMERICAN LAWYERS, at 158–63, 202–7.

37. JOHN P. HEINZ ET AL., URBAN LAWYERS xv–xx (2005).

38. *Id.* at 3–28.

39 *Id.*

40. NALP Bulletin, *Salaries for New Lawyers: How Did We Get Here?* (2008), http://www.nalp.org/2008jansalaries (last visited March 25, 2014).

41. ABA, *Enrollment and Degrees Awarded,* http://www.americanbar.org/ content/dam/aba/administrative/legal_education_and_admissions_to_ the_bar/statistics/enrollment_degrees_awarded.authcheckdam.pdf (last visited March 25, 2014).

42. *See* NALP, *The NALP Salary Curve Morphs with the Class of 2010,* http:// www.nalp.org/salarycurve_classof2010 (last visited March 25, 2014) ("[M]ore complete salary coverage for jobs at large law firms heightens this peak and diminishes the left-hand peaks.").

43. ABA, *Total Licensed Lawyers.*

44. NALP, *A Picture Worth 1,000 Words,* http://www.nalp.org/apictureworth 1000words (last visited March 25, 2014).

45. NALP, *The NALP Salary Curve for the Class of 2011,* http://www.nalp. org/salarycurve_classof2011 (last visited March 25, 2014).

46. NALP, *Class of 2011 National Summary Report,* http://www.nalp.org/ uploads/NatlSummChart_Classof2011.pdf (last visited March 25, 2014).

47. ABA, *J.D. and LL.B. Degrees Awarded, 1981–2011,* http://www. americanbar.org/content/dam/aba/administrative/legal_education_ and_admissions_to_the_bar/statistics/jd_llb_degrees_awarded. authcheckdam.pdf (last visited March 25, 2014).

48. *See* NALP, *Class of 2013 Salary Distribution Curve,* http://www.nalp. org/class_of_2013_bimodal_salary_curve; NALP, *Class of 2012 Salary Distribution Curve,* http://www.nalp.org/class_of_2012_salary_ distribution_curve (last visited December 13, 2014).

49. *See* NALP, *Salaries for New Lawyers: How Did We Get Here?,* http:// www.nalp.org/2008jansalaries (last visited March 25, 2014).

50. Bill Henderson, *Distribution of 2006 Starting Salaries: Best Graphic Chart of the Year,* September 4, 2007, http://www.elsblog.org/the_empirical_ legal_studi/2007/09/distribution-of.html.

51. Richard Sander, *Hidden Transformation of the Legal Industry,* http://
www.americanbar.org/publications/young_lawyer_home/young_
lawyer_archive/yld_tyl_june08_sander.html (last visited
March 25, 2014).

52. Henderson, *Distribution of 2006 Starting Salaries.*

53. Anne VanderMey, *MBA Pay,* BLOOMBERG BUSINESS WEEK, September 9,
2009, http://images.businessweek.com/ss/09/09/0928_mba_pay/1.htm.

54. Clifford Winston and Vikram Maheshri, *An Exploratory Study of the
Pricing of Legal Services,* draft on file with author.

55. Inflation calculation performed here using 2013 dollars: http://www.bls.
gov/data/inflation_calculator.htm (last visited January 16, 2014).

56. PAUL CAMPOS, DON'T GO TO LAW SCHOOL (UNLESS) 5–6 (2013). The
2009 survey can be found here: http://www.alabar.org/media/news/
images/04042012_Economic-SurveyofLawyersinAlabama2010Report.
pdf (last visited March 25, 2014).

57. William D. Henderson & Rachel M. Zahorsky, *Law Job Stagnation
May Have Started Before the Recession—And It May Be a Sign of Lasting
Change,* ABA J., July 1, 2011, http://www.abajournal.com/magazine/
article/paradigm_shift/.

58. Bill Henderson, *From Big Law to Lean Law,* draft on file with author, at
9. In 2007, the top twenty law schools sent 55 percent of graduates to big
firms; in 2011, that percentage was down to 36. Karen Sloan, *It's Tough
Out There,* NAT'L L. J., February 27, 2012, http://www.law.com/jsp/nlj/
PubArticleNLJ.jsp?id=1202543428380&et=editorial&bu=National%20
Law%20Journal&cn=20120227nlj&src=EMC-Email&pt=NLJ.com-%20
Daily%20Headlines&kw=It%27s%20tough%20out%20there.

59. James G. Leipold & Judith N. Collins, *Class of 2012 Employment and
Salary Findings Show First Positive Signs Since 2008,* http://www.nalp.
org/0813_selectedfindings_bulletin_article (last visited January 13, 2014).

60. Joe Palazzo, *Law Grads Face Brutal Job Market,* WALL ST. J., June 25,
2012, http://professional.wsj.com/article/SB10001424052702304458604577
486623469958142.html?mod=ITP_pageone_0&mg=reno-wsj#project%3
DLSCHOOL20120625%26articleTabs%3Darticle.

61. Paul Campos, *Two Out of Three 2011 Law School Graduates
Did Not Get Real Legal Jobs,* LAWYERS, GUNS & MONEY BLOG,
June 8, 2012, http://www.lawyersgunsmoneyblog.com/2012/06/
two-out-of-three-2011-law-school-graduates-did-not-get-real-legal-jobs.

62. *Law Firms: A Less Gilded Future,* THE ECONOMIST, May 5, 2011, http://
www.economist.com/node/18651114.

63. Bill Henderson, *Rise and Fall,* THE AMERICAN LAWYER, June 2012, at 60.

64. Sparkman, *The Haves and the Haves Less,* THE AMERICAN LAWYER, May
2012, at 87.

65. Robin Sparkman, *Spring Awakenings,* THE AMERICAN LAWYER, May
2012, at 94.

66. Aric Press, *Am Law 100 Analysis: the Super Rich Get Richer*, THE AMERICAN LAWYER, April 28, 2014, http://www.americanlawyer.com/id=1202651706887.

67. The data in this paragraph all come from Citi Private Bank and Hilldebrandt Consulting LLC, *2013 Client Advisory*, http://online.wsj.com/public/resources/documents/CitiHildebrandt2013ClientAdvisory.pdf (last visited July 25, 2013).

68. Jennifer Smith, *Law Firms Press to Get Bills Paid by Year-End*, WALL ST. J., December 22, 2013, http://online.wsj.com/news/articles/SB10001424052702304773104579270470475326780?mod=ITP_marketplace_3

69. Daniel G. Currell & M. Todd Henderson, *Can Lawyers Stay in the Drivers' Seat?*, http://papers.ssrn.com/sol3/papers.cfm?abstract_id=2201800## (last visited March 25, 2014).

70. Citi Private Bank, *2013 Client Advisory*.

71. *Id.* at 12.

72. *Id.*

73. Sparkman, *The Haves and the Haves Less*, at 87.

74. Sparkman, *Spring Awakening*, at 96.

75. Aric Press, *Am Law 100 Analysis: the Super Rich Get Richer*, THE AMERICAN LAWYER, April 28, 2014, http://www.americanlawyer.com/id=1202651706887.

76. Citi Private Bank, *2013 Client Advisory*, surveyed law firm managing partners and 72% reported pursuing this strategy.

77. Michael Simkovic & Frank McIntyre, *The Economic Value of a Law Degree*, http://papers.ssrn.com/sol3/papers.cfm?abstract_id=2250585 (last visited March 25, 2014).

78. *See, e.g.*, Brian Tamanaha, *How "The Million Dollar Law Degree" Study Systematically Overstates Value: Three Choices that Skewed the Results*, BALKINIZATION, July 23, 2013, http://balkin.blogspot.com/2013/07/how-million-dollar-law-degree-study.html.

79. *See* Jennifer Smith, *Survey Says Post-Recession Shifts are Here to Stay*, WALL ST. J., May 16, 2012, http://blogs.wsj.com/law/2012/05/16/brave-new-world-legal-edition-survey-says-post-recession-shifts-here-to-stay/.

Chapter 4

1. Larry E. Ribstein, *The Death of Big Law*, 2010 WISC. L. REV. 749 (2010).

2. Glenn Harlan Reynolds, *Small Is the New Biglaw: Some Thoughts on Technology, Economics, and the Practice of Law*, 38 HOFSTRA L. REV. 1 (2009).

3. Bill Henderson, *From Big Law to Lean Law*, draft on file with author.

4. Ribstein, *The Death of Big Law*, at 753–60.

5. Credence goods are hard for a consumer to gauge before or after consumption, like car repair or legal work. *See* Ribstein, *Death of Big Law*, at 309.

6. Reynolds, *Small Is the New Big Law*, at 6–9.

7. *See* Jennifer Smith, *Clearspire's Technology Outlives 'Virtual' Law Firm*, WALL ST. J., June 6, 2014, http://blogs.wsj.com/law/2014/06/06/clearspires-technology-outlives-virtual-law-firm/.

8. Robin Sparkman, *Spring Awakening*, AMERICAN LAWYER, May 2013, at 94.

9. LINCOLN CAPLAN, SKADDEN: POWER, MONEY, AND THE RISE OF A LEGAL EMPIRE 15–9 (1994).

10. Alexia Garamfalvi, *What Will Be the Fallout From the Failed Dewey-Orrick Merger?*, THE LEGAL TIMES, January 25, 2007, http://www.law.com/jsp/llf/PubArticleLLF.jsp?id=1169632955893.

11. Friederike Heine & Alex Novarese, *Our Lehman: How Dewey Went from Proud US Giant to the Largest Ever Legal Failure*, LEGALWEEK, http://www.legalweek.com/legal-week/feature/2186023/lehman-dewey-proud-giant-largest-legal-failure.

12. Peter Lattman, *Dewey & LeBoeuf Files for Bankruptcy*, N.Y. TIMES, May 28, 2012, http://dealbook.nytimes.com/2012/05/28/dewey-leboeuf-files-for-bankruptcy/.

13. Peter Lattman, *Dewey & LeBoeuf Said to Encourage Partners to Leave*, N.Y. TIMES, April 30, 2012, http://dealbook.nytimes.com/2012/04/30/dewey-leboeuf-said-to-encourage-partners-to-leave/.

14. Sara Randazzo, *At Deadline, New Batch of Dewey Dissenters Steps in to Challenge Partner Settlement*, February 13, 2013, http://www.americanlawyer.com/PubArticleALD.jsp?id=1202588110313&At_Deadline_New_Batch_of_Dewey_Dissenters_Steps_in_to_Challenge_Partner_Settlement&slreturn=20130115152640.

15. Lattman, *Dewey & LeBoeuf Said to Encourage Partners to Leave*.

16. Jacqueline Palank, *New Lawsuits Demand $9.8 Million from Ex-Dewey Partners*, WALL ST. J., December 3, 2013, http://blogs.wsj.com/law/2013/12/03/new-lawsuits-demand-9-8-million-from-ex-dewey-partners/.

17. James B. Stewart, *The Collapse,* THE NEW YORKER, October 14, 2013, at 80.

18. Matthew Goldstein, 4 Accused in Law Firm Fraud Ignored a Maxim: Don't Email, N.Y. TIMES, March 6, 2014, http://dealbook.nytimes.com/2014/03/06/former-top-leaders-of-dewey-leboeuf-are-indicted/.

19. Jennifer Smith, *Former Dewey Chairman Heads to Legal Post in United Arab Emirates*, WALL ST. J., December 31, 2013, http://blogs.wsj.com/law/2013/12/31/former-dewey-chairman-heads-to-legal-post-in-united-arab-emirates/.

20. Paul M. Barrett, *Howrey's Bankruptcy and Big Law Firms' Small Future*, BLOOMBERG BUSINESSWEEK, May 2, 2013, http://www.businessweek.com/printer/articles/113914-howreys-bankruptcy-and-big-law-firms-small-future.

21. Peter Lattman, *Mass Layoffs at a Top-Flight Law Firm,* N.Y. Times, June 24, 2013, http://dealbook.nytimes.com/2013/06/24/big-law-firm-to-cut-lawyers-and-some-partner-pay/.
22. Noam Schreiber, *The Last Days of Big Law,* The New Republic, July 21, 2013, http://www.newrepublic.com/article/113941/big-law-firms-trouble-when-money-dries#.
23. George B. Shepherd & Morgan Cloud, *Time and Money: Discovery Leads to Hourly Billing,* 1999 U. Ill. L. Rev. 91 (1999).
24. John Frank Weaver, *I am an Artisinal Lawyer,* McSweeney's, December 12, 2014, http://www.mcsweeneys.net/articles/i-am-an-artisanal-attorney.
25. Bruce E. Aronson, *Elite Law Firm Mergers and Reputational Competition: Is Bigger Really Better? An International Comparison,* 40 Vand. J. Transnat'l L. 763, 784 n. 44 (2007).
26. David Lat, *Breaking: Simpson Thacher Raises Associate Base Salaries,* Above the Law, January 22, 2007, http://abovethelaw.com/2007/01/breaking-simpson-thacher-raises-associate-base-salaries/.
27. Peter Lattman, *Debevoise & Plimpton's Trusts and Estates Group Finds a New Home,* N.Y. Times, March 19, 2013, http://dealbook.nytimes.com/2013/03/19/debevoise-plimptons-trusts-and-estates-group-finds-a-new-home/?src=recg.
28. NALP, *Partnership Tiers and Tracks,* http://www.nalp.org/feb10partnershiptiers (last visited March 25, 2014).
29. Marc Galanter & Thomas Palay, Tournament of Lawyers 59–62 (1991).
30. Galanter & Palay, Tournament of Lawyers, at 60–1.
31. *Am Law 100,* The American Lawyer, May 2012, at 125–37 (2012).
32. Henderson, *From Big Law to Lean Law,* http://papers.ssrn.com/sol3/papers.cfm?abstract_id=2356330 (last visited March 4, 2014).
33. NALP, *Number of Associate Hours Worked Increases at Largest Firms,* http://www.nalp.org/billable_hours_feb2012 (last visited March 25, 2014).
34. Jennifer Smith, *Law Firm Partners Face Cuts,* Wall St. J., January 6, 2013, http://online.wsj.com/article/SB10001424127887323689604578221891691032424.html.
35. There are ABA Opinions that suggest that firms may not profit on copying or other client disbursements. Firms cannot surcharge client disbursements and thereby earn a profit. So if a firm hires an independent copying center to produce documents for a client, the client should be charged only the amount the firm paid for such services. ABA Op. 93–379 (1993). Big Law tends to handle most of that work in house. For "in-house" services, such as the production of documents for the client internally, the client may properly be charged the actual cost of the services plus a reasonable amount of overhead expense. ABA Op. 93–379. If you think these ABA rules keep law firms from profiting on copying or other charges, please ask any general counsel for her opinion after reviewing a Big Law bill.

36. Jennifer Smith, *Law Firms Face Fresh Backlash Over Fees*, WALL ST. J., October 22, 2012, http://online.wsj.com/article/SB10001424052970203400604578070611725856952.html.

37. Jennifer Smith, *Law Firms Wring Costs from Back-Office Tasks*, WALL ST. J., October 7, 2012, http://online.wsj.com/article/SB100008723963904432949045780425928330116774.html.

38. Henderson, *From Big Law to Lean Law*.

39. *Id.*

40. Henderson, *From Big Law to Lean Law*.

41. Jennifer Smith, *Big Law Mergers Fuel Skepticism*, WALL ST. J., November 10, 2013, http://online.wsj.com/news/articles/SB10001424052702304672404579185983008199814.

42. Citi Private Bank and Hildebrandt Consulting LLC, *2013 Client Advisory*, http://online.wsj.com/public/resources/documents/CitiHildebrandt2013ClientAdvisory.pdf (last visited March 25, 2014).

43. William Henderson and Christopher Zorn, *Playing Not to Lose*, THE AMERICAN LAWYER, March 1, 2013, http://www.americanlawyer.com/PubArticleTAL.jsp?id=1202585323924.

44. *Id.*

45. Ribstein, *The Death of Big Law*, at 753–4.

46. Jennifer Smith, *Big Law Mergers Fuel Skepticism*, WALL ST. J., November 10, 2013, http://online.wsj.com/news/articles/SB10001424052702304672404579185983008199814.

47. Daniel Currell & M. Todd Henderson, *Can Lawyers Stay in the Driver's Seat?*, http://ssrn.com/abstract=2201800 (last visited March 25, 2014).

48. *See* Ashby Jones & Joseph Palazzo, *What's a First-Year Lawyer Worth*, WALL ST. J., October 17, 2011, http://online.wsj.com/article/SB10001424052970204774604576631360989675324.html.

49. Daniel T. Gilbert & Jane E. J. Ebert, *Decisions and Revisions: The Affective Forecasting of Changeable Outcomes*, 82 J. PERSONALITY AND PSYCH. 503 (2002).

50. BARRY SCHWARTZ, THE PARADOX OF CHOICE (2003).

51. *See* GALANTER & PALAY, TOURNAMENT OF LAWYERS.

52. Staci Zaretsky, *The Women of Biglaw Are Still Trapped in Staff Attorney Binders*, ABOVE THE LAW, October 23, 2012, http://abovethelaw.com/2012/10/the-women-of-biglaw-are-still-trapped-in-staff-attorney-binders/

53. Elie Mystal, *Departure Memo of the Day: Parenting Gets The Best of One Biglaw Associate*, ABOVE THE LAW, November 8, 2012, http://abovethelaw.com/2012/11/departure-memo-of-the-day-parenting-gets-the-best-of-one-biglaw-associate/.

54. David Lat, *Biglaw: It's Not All About the Benjamins*, ABOVE THE LAW, September 26, 2012, http://abovethelaw.com/2012/09/biglaw-its-not-all-about-the-benjamins/.

55. Peter Lattman, *Culture Keeps Firms Together in Trying Times*, N.Y. TIMES, September 24, 2012, http://dealbook.nytimes.com/2012/09/24/culture-keeps-firms-together-in-trying-times/.

56. *The Am Law 100: Firms Ranked by Profits Per Partner*, http://www.americanlawyer.com/PubArticleTAL.jsp?id=1202549384381&slret urn=20130122133832 (last visited March 25, 2014).

57. *See* Lat, *Biglaw: It's Not All About the Benjamins.*

58. Lattman, *Dewey Bankruptcy.*

59. Lattman, *Culture Keeps Firms Together in Trying Times.*

60. Robert J. Rhee, *On Legal Education and Reform: One View Formed from Diverse Perspectives*, 70 MD. L. REV. 310, 322 (2011).

61. Ashby Jones, *Thinking of Hiking Up Billable Rates? Here's Why You Shouldn't*, WSJ LAW BLOG, January 4, 2010, http://blogs.wsj.com/law/2010/01/04/thinking-of-hiking-up-billable-rates-heres-why-you-shouldnt/.

62. Robert J. Rhee, *On Legal Education and Reform*, at 322

63. Jennifer Smith, *GCs to Law Firms: Pay for Your Own Tuna Fish Sandwiches*, WSJ LAW BLOG, October 22, 2012, http://blogs.wsj.com/law/2012/10/22/gcs-to-law-firms-pay-for-your-own-tuna-fish-sandwiches/

64. ACC, *ACC Value Champions*, http://www.accdigitaldocket.com/accdock et/2012ValueChampions#pg1http://www.acc.com/valuechallenge/about/index.cfm (last visited March 25, 2014).

65. *See* Ribstein, *Death of Big Law*, at 760–1.

66. THOMAS D. MORGAN, THE VANISHING AMERICAN LAWYER 112–23 (2010) has an excellent discussion of these trends.

67. ACC, *Association of Corporate Counsel Census Reveals Power Shift from Law Firms to Corporate Legal Departments*, http://www.acc.com/aboutacc/newsroom/pressreleases/acc_census_press.cfm (last visited March 25, 2014).

68. Ben W. Heineman Jr., The Rise of the General Counsel, HARVARD BUSINESS REVIEW, September 27, 2012, http://blogs.hbr.org/cs/2012/09/the_rise_of_the_general_counsel.html.

69. Roy Strom, *Some Law School Grads Find Their Place In-House*, CHICAGO LAWYER, March 1, 2012, http://www.chicagolawyermagazine.com/Archives/2012/03/In-House-Counsel.aspx.

70. NALP, Jobs & JD's, Class of 2011 15 (2012).

71. Mary Swanton, *Some Law School Grads Head Directly In-House*, INSIDE COUNSEL MAGAZINE, March 1, 2012, http://www.insidecounsel.com/2012/03/01/some-law-school-grads-head-directly-in-house.

72. *See* www.axiomlaw.com (last visited March 25, 2014); William D. Henderson, *More Complex than Greed*, THE AMERICAN LAWYER, May 29, 2012, http//www.axiomlaw.com/Docs/002051210Axiom.pdf.

73. Ron Friedman, *The Rise of Axiom Law*, PRISM LEGAL, July 1, 2012, http://prismlegal.com/the-rise-of-axiom-law/.

74. Kevin Colangelo, *Axiom's $28 Million Knockout Punch: A Little Speculation*, THE BIONIC LAWYER, February 2013, http://www.yusonirvine.com/blogs/1/posts/axioms-28-dollars-million-round-a-little-speculation.

75. *Id.*

76. Valorem, *What's So Revolutionary?*, http://www.valoremlaw.com/what-is-revolutionary (last visited March 25, 2014).

77. Niraj Seth and Nathan Koppel, *With Times Tight Even Lawyers Get Outsourced*, WALL ST. J., November 26, 2008, http://online.wsj.com/article/SB122765161306957779.html.

78. Anuj Agrawal, *In Conversation: Sanjay Kamlani and David Perla, Co-CEO's of Pangea3*, BENCH & BAR, June 27, 2012, http://barandbench.com/content/212/conversation-sanjay-kamlani-and-david-perla-co-ceos-pangea3#.VIhi-tLF8hM.

79. Ashby Jones, *True Believer: Thomson Reuters Betting Big on LPO Boom*, WALL ST. J., November 19, 2010, http://blogs.wsj.com/law/2010/11/19/true-believer-with-purchase-thomson-reuters-bets-big-on-lpo-market/.

80. ABA Standing Committee on Ethics and Professional Responsibility, *Formal Opinion 08–451, Lawyer's Obligations When Outsourcing Legal and Nonlegal Support Services*, August 5, 2008, http://www.aapipara.org/File/Main%20Page/ABA%20Outsourcing%20Opinion.pdf.

81. Jordan Weisman, *iLawyer: What Happens When Computers Replace Attorneys?*, THE ATLANTIC, JUNE 19, 2012, http://www.theatlantic.com/business/archive/2012/06/ilawyer-what-happens-when-computers-replace-attorneys/258688/; Joe Palazzo, *Why Hire a Lawyer? Computers Are Cheaper*, WALL ST. J., JUNE 18, 2012, http://online.wsj.com/article/SB10001424052702303379204577472633591769336.html.

82. Joe Palazzolo, *How a Computer Did the Work of Many Lawyers*, WALL ST. J., January 17, 2013, http://blogs.wsj.com/law/2013/01/17/how-a-computer-did-the-work-of-many-lawyers.

83. Todd Henderson and Daniel Currell, *Can Lawyers Stay in the Drivers Seat*, CHICAGO UNBOUND (2013), http://chicagounbound.uchicago.edu/law_and_economics/94/.

84. Bill Henderson, *From Big Law to Lean Law*, at 19.

85. L.A. Law Wikipedia Entry, http://en.wikipedia.org/wiki/L.A._Law (last visited March 25, 2014).

86. *See 25 Years of the Am Law 100*, AM. LAWYER, May 1, 2012, http://www.americanlawyer.com/PubArticleTAL.jsp?id=1202548514396.

87. *See* ERWIN O. SMIGEL, THE WALL STREET LAWYER 17–21 (1964).

88. 25 Years of the Am Law 100, http://www.americanlawyer.com/PubArticle TAL .jsp?id=1202548514396.

89. The full audio of the interview can be found here, http://www.americanlawyer.com/PubArticleTAL.jsp?id=1202550575945 (last visited March 25, 2014).

90. *Id.*

91. *See, e.g.*, Wray Herbert, *The Perils of Comparative Thinking*, ASSOCIATION FOR PSYCHOLOGICAL SCIENCE, April 28, 2012, http://www.psychologicalscience.org/index.php/news/were-only-human/how-to-win-the-happiness-lottery.html.

92. Jason G. Goldman, *Why Bronze Medalists Are Happier Than Silver Winners*, SCIENTIFIC AMERICAN, August 9, 2012, http://

blogs.scientificamerican.com/thoughtful-animal/2012/08/09/
why-bronze-medalists-are-happier-than-silver-winners/.

93. NANCY LEVIT & DOUGLAS O. LINDER, THE HAPPY LAWYER 86–90 (2010).

94. Ribstein, *Death of Big Law.*

95. Jennifer Smith, *Check Please: Experts Say Apple, Samsung Face Sky-High Legal Fees,* WALL ST. J., August 24, 2012, http://blogs.wsj.com/law/2012/08/24/check-please-experts-say-apple-samsung-face-sky-high-legal-fees/.

96. *See, e.g.,* Francesco Guala, *Reciprocity: Weak or Strong? What Punishment Experiments Do (and Do Not) Demonstrate,* 35 BEHAVIORAL & BRAIN SCIENCES 1 (2012), http://journals.cambridge.org/download.php?file=%2FBBS%2FBBS35_01%2FS0140525X11001221a.pdf&code=ebff5e293473c7c691802b67ab63f032#page=24.

97. *See* IAN AYERS, SUPER CRUNCHERS: WHY THINKING-BY-NUMBERS IS THE NEW WAY TO BE SMART (2008).

98. NATE SILVER, THE SIGNAL AND THE NOISE (2012).

99. *Id.* at 108–41.

100. *Id.* at 128–41.

101. *Id.* at 142–75.

102. *Id.* at 154–62.

103. Andrew Moseman, *First Chess, Now Poker? Computer Programmers Try to Crush Human Competitors,* DISCOBLOG, June 30, 2008, http://blogs.discovermagazine.com/discoblog/2008/06/30/first-chess-now-poker-computer-programmers-try-to-crush-human-competitors/#.USfTf45ubHo.

104. Michael Kaplan, *The Steely Headless King of Texas Hold 'Em,* N.Y. TIMES, September 5, 2013, http://www.nytimes.com/2013/09/08/magazine/poker-computer.html?hp.

105. The facts in the next two paragraphs come from NATE SILVER, THE SIGNAL AND THE NOISE 265–92 (2012); IBM, *Deep Blue,* http://www-03.ibm.com/ibm/history/ibm100/us/en/icons/deepblue/ (last visited March 25, 2014); IBM, *The Science Behind Watson,* http://www-03.ibm.com/innovation/us/watson/the_jeopardy_challenge.shtml (last visited March 25, 2014); Marshall Barin, *How Was IBM's Watson Computer Able to Answer the Questions on Jeopardy,* http://blogs.howstuffworks.com/2011/02/18/how-was-ibms-watson-computer-able-to-answer-the-questions-on-jeopardy-how-did-the-technology-work-how-might-it-be-used/ (last visited March 25, 2014).

106. SILVER, THE SIGNAL AND THE NOISE, at 269.

107. *See* Lex Machina, *Lex Machina Introduces Legal Analytics to Power Data-Driven IP Business Strategy,* October 29, 2013, https://lexmachina.com/media/press/lex-machina-introduces-legal-analytics-to-power-data-driven-ip-business-strategy/.

108. Darrell Etherington, *Judicata Raises $2M from Peter Thiel, Keith Rabois and Others to Give Lawyers Better Research and Analytics Tools,* TECH CRUNCH, December 11, 2012, http://techcrunch.com/2012/12/11/

judicata-raises-2m-from-peter-thiel-keith-rabois-and-others-to-give-lawyers-better-research-and-analytics-tools/.

109. Tony Bartelme, *STORM OF MONEY: Insider Tells How Some Insurance Companies Rig the System*, THE POST AND COURIER, December 2, 2012, http://www.postandcourier.com/article/20121202/PC16/121209871/1165/storm-of-money-insider-tells-how-some-insurance-companies-rig-the-system.

110. *Id.* at 43–4.

111. *Id.* at 163–8.

112. MICHAEL LEWIS, MONEYBALL (2004).

113. Joe Sheehan, *The Moneyball Revolution from Someone Who Helped Make It Happen*, SPORTS ILLUSTRATED, September 23, 2011, http://sportsillustrated.cnn.com/2011/writers/joe_sheehan/09/23/moneyball/index.html.

114. Brooks Barnes, *Solving the Equation of a Hit Film Script, With Data*, N.Y. TIMES, May 6, 2013, http://www.nytimes.com/2013/05/06/business/media/solving-equation-of-a-hit-film-script-with-data.html?hp.

Chapter 5

1. This description generally applies to Big Law as well. Those lawyers have taken advantage of economies of scale by forming large law firms, but these law firms just service bigger cases for bigger clients. Big Law still resists routinization of legal work.

2. *See* CLAYTON CHRISTENSEN, THE INNOVATOR'S DILEMMA: THE REVOLUTIONARY BOOK THAT WILL CHANGE THE WAY YOU DO BUSINESS (2011). The next three paragraphs are a summary of *id.* at xi-xxxvii. Christensen has turned the original 1997 book into something of a cottage industry, including new books entitled CLAYTON M. CHRISTENSEN & MICHAEL E. RAYNOR, THE INNOVATOR'S SOLUTION (2003); CLAYTON M. CHRISTENSEN & CURTIS W. JOHNSON, DISRUPTING CLASS: HOW DISRUPTIVE INNOVATION WILL CHANGE THE WAY THE WORLD LEARNS (2011); and CLAYTON M. CHRISTENSEN & HENRY J. EYRING, THE INNOVATIVE UNIVERSITY: CHANGING THE DNA OF HIGHER EDUCATION FROM THE INSIDE OUT (2011).

3. Christensen first discussed the steel industry briefly in *The Innovator's Dilemma, see id.* at 100–8. He provides a more expanded discussion of the topic in Clayton Christensen, *Disruptive Innovation, in* ENCYCLOPEDIA OF HUMAN-COMPUTER INTERACTION (Mads Soegaard & Rikke F. Dam eds., 2012), http://www.interaction-design.org/encyclopedia/disruptive_innovation.html (last visited March 25, 2014). All of the facts and opinion in this paragraph come from those sources. THE NEW YORKER offers a condensed version of this story, as well as a very interesting profile of Christensen, in Larissa MacFarquhar, *When Giants Fail*, THE NEW YORKER, May 14, 2012, at 85–7.

4. CHRISTENSEN, INNOVATOR'S DILEMMA at xx.

5. William Henderson, *Are We Asking the Wrong Questions About Lawyer Regulation?*, September 19, 2011, http://truthonthemarket. com/2011/09/19/william-henderson-on-are-we-asking-the-wrong-questions-about-lawyer-regulation/.

6. *See* LegalZoom, *at* http://www.legalzoom.com and Rocket Lawyer, *at* http://www.rocketlawyer.com/ (last visited March 25, 2014).

7. Daniel Fisher, *Entrepreneurs v. Lawyers,* FORBES, October 5, 2011, http://www.forbes.com/forbes/2011/1024/entrepreneurs-lawyers-suh-legalzoom-automate-daniel-fisher.html.

8. *Id.*

9. LegalZoom, *About Us, at* http://www.legalzoom.com/about-us (last visited March 25, 2014).

10. LegalZoom still charges as little as $69 for a will or $99 for articles of incorporation. Fisher, *Entrepreneurs.*

11. Unauthorized Practice of Law Comm. v. Parsons Tech. Inc., 179 F.3d 956, 956 (5th Cir. 1999) (vacating the District Court's injunction banning Quicken Family Lawyer after the Texas Legislature amended its 1939 unauthorized practice of law statute).

12. *See, e.g., In re* First Escrow, Inc., 840 S.W.2d 839, 843 & n. 7 (Mo. 1992) ("[T]he General Assembly may only assist the judiciary by providing penalties for the unauthorized practice of law, the ultimate definition of which is always within the province of this Court.").

13. *See* Task Force on the Model Definition of the Practice of Law, *Report,* http://www.americanbar.org/content/dam/aba/migrated/cpr/model-def/ taskforce_rpt_803.authcheckdam.pdf (last visited March 25, 2014).

14. Department of Justice and the Federal Trade Commission, *Comments on the American Bar Association's Proposed Model Definition of the Practice of Law,* http://www.justice.gov/atr/public/comments/200604.htm (last visited March 25, 2014).

15. Department of Justice, *Justice Department and American Bar Association Resolve Charges That the ABA's Process for Accrediting Law Schools Was Misused,* http://www.justice.gov/atr/public/press_releases/1995/0257.htm (last visited March 25, 2014).

16. Gillian Hadfield has an outstanding discussion of how the UPL restrictions affect computerized provision of legal services and choke innovation in Gillian K. Hadfield, *Legal Barriers to Innovation: The Growing Economic Cost of Professional Control over Corporate Legal Markets,* 60 STAN. L. REV. 1689, 1723–6 (2008). For an early analysis of some of the issues, *see* Catherine J. Lanctot, *Scriveners in Cyberspace: Online Document Preparation and the Unauthorized Practice of Law,* 30 HOFSTRA L. REV. 811, 814–5 (2002) (analyzing whether *LegalZoom* type programs violate UPL).

17. *See, e.g.,* Florida Bar v. Stupica, 300 So. 2d 683, 686 (Fla. 1974) (providing divorce forms with advice is UPL); State Ex Rel. Indiana State Bar

Association v. Diaz, 838 N.E.2d 433 (Ind. 2005) (same for immigration forms and advice).

18. *See, e.g.,* Janson v. LegalZoom.com, Inc., 802 F. Supp. 2d 1053, 1062–3 (W.D. Mo. 2011).

19. *Id.*

20. Gillian K. Hadfield, *Higher Demand, Lower Supply? A Comparative Assessment of the Legal Resource Landscape for Ordinary Americans,* 37 Fordham Urb. L.J. 129, 154 (2011). *See also* George C. Harris & Derek F. Foran, *The Ethics of Middle-Class Access to Legal Services and What We Can Learn from the Medical Profession's Shift to a Corporate Paradigm,* 70 Fordham L. Rev. 775 (2001); Deborah L. Rhode, *Access to Justice: Again, Still,* 73 Fordham L. Rev. 1013 (2004).

21. *See* Jonathan G. Blattmachr, *Looking Back and Looking Ahead: Preparing Your Practice for the Future: Do Not Get Behind the Change Curve,* 36 ACTEC J. 1, 19–23 (2010) (arguing that *LegalZoom* service is the unauthorized practice of law and describing his personal, negative experience with *LegalZoom*); Michael S. Knowles, *Keep Your Friends Close and the Laymen Closer: State Bar Associations Can Combat the Problems Associated with Nonlawyers Engaging in the Unauthorized Practice of Estate Planning Through a Certification System,* 43 Creighton L. Rev. 855, 877–81 (2010) (explaining trends in the unauthorized practice of law, including *LegalZoom*); Wendy S. Goffe & Rochelle L. Haller, *From Zoom to Doom? The Risks of Do-It-Yourself Estate Planning,* http://papers.ssrn.com/sol3/papers.cfm?abstract_id=1824425 (last visited March 25, 2014); Rania Combs, *The Problem with LegalZoom (and Other Do-It-Yourself Estate Planning Solutions),* Tex. Wills & Tr. Online: Rania Combs, Att'y at L., Jan. 27, 2010, http://www.texaswillsandtrustslaw.com/2010/01/27/the-problem-with-legalzoom-and-other-do-it-yourself-estate-planning-solutions/.

22. Nathan Kopel, *Seller of Online Legal Forms Settles Unauthorized Practice of Law Suit,* Wall St. J., August 23, 2011, http://blogs.wsj.com/law/2011/08/23/seller-of-online-legal-forms-settles-unauthorized-practiced-of-law-suit/.

23. Daniel Fisher, *Silicon Valley Sees Gold in Internet Legal Services,* Forbes, October 5, 2011, http://www.forbes.com/sites/danielfisher/2011/10/05/silicon-valley-sees-gold-in-internet-legal-services/ (last accessed October 18, 2012).

24. *LegalZoom* does not offer the "Peace of Mind Review" of legal documents by non-lawyers in Missouri. *See* LegalZoom, *Peace of Mind Review,* http://www.legalzoom.com/peace-of-mind-popup.html (last visited March 25, 2014).

25. *Id.*; NASDAQ OMX GlobeNewswire, *LegalZoom Enters into Agreement with State of Washington,* http://www.globenewswire.com/newsroom/news.html?d=201745. The settlement itself can be found here: http://www.atg.wa.gov/uploadedFiles/Home/News/Press_Releases/2010/LegalZoomAOD.pdf (last visited March 25, 2014).

26. Craig Jarvis, *Online Legal Firm in Bar Fight*, CHARLOTTE NEWS OBSERVER, October 5, 2011, http://www.newsobserver.com/2011/ |10/05/1540408/online-firm-in-bar-fight.html.

27. The facts in the next paragraphs all come from LegalZoom's complaint, http://online.wsj.com/public/resources/documents/LegalZoom.pdf (last visited March 25, 2014).

28. *Id.*

29. The letter can be found here: http://www.directlaw.com/LegalZoom%20 20080326%20LOC.pdf (last visited March 25, 2014).

30. *LegalZoom Complaint.*

31. Nate Raymond, *LegalZoom Lawsuit Against NC Bar May Proceed*, THOMPSON REUTERS NEWS & INSIGHT, August 29, 2012, http:// newsandinsight.thomsonreuters.com/Legal/News/2012/08_-_August/ LegalZoom_lawsuit against_NC_bar_may_proceed__judge/. The order itself is available here: http://www.ncbusinesscourt.net/ opinions/2012_NCBC_47.pdf (last visited March 25, 2014).

32. Fisher, *Silicon Valley Sees Gold in Internet Legal Services.*

33. Jennifer Smith, LegalZoom.com *Plans to Pull Its IPO, Sell Stake to Permira*, WALL ST. J., January 7, 2014, http://blogs.wsj.com/law/ 2014/01/07/legalzoom-com-plans-to-pull-its-ipo-sell-stake-to-permira/.

34. Fisher, *Silicon Valley Sees Gold in Internet Legal Services.*

35. *Id.*

36. LegalZoom, Inc., *SEC Form S-1*, http://www.sec.gov/Archives/edgar/ data/1286139/000104746912006446/a2209713zs-1a.htm (last visited March 25, 2014). The facts in the next paragraphs all come from this S-1.

37. *Id.*

38. PR Newswire, *More than 1,700 New Business in South Carolina Use* LegalZoom *Services to Set Up Shop in 2011*, PR NEWSWIRE, November 12, 2012, http://www.prnewswire.com/news-releases/more-than-1700-new-businesses-in-south-carolina-use-legalzoom-services-to-set-up-shop-in-2011-178960041.html.

39. Olivia Oran, *LegalZoom IPO Delayed*, REUTERS, August 3, 2012, http:// newsandinsight.thomsonreuters.com/Securities/News/2012/08_-_ August/LegalZoom_IPO_delayed_-_source/.

40. Richard Granat, *LegalZoom's Achilles' Heel: Free Legal Forms*, ELAWYERING BLOG, August 4, 2013, http://www.elawyeringredux. com/2012/08/articles/free-law/legalzooms-achilles-heel-free-legal-forms/.

41. Carolyn Elefant, *The LegalZoom IPO: Proving That Volume Practice Doesn't Work, Even 21st Century Style*, MYSHINGLE.COM, July 30, 2012, http://myshingle.com/2012/07/articles/trends/the-legalzoom-ipo-proving-that-volume-practice-doesnt-work-even-21st-century-style/.

42. *See* Granat, *LegalZoom's Achilles' Heel: Free Legal Forms.*

43. *Fill Out Legal Forms Faster*, LAW HELP INTERACTIVE, https:// lawhelpinteractive.org/ (last visited March 25, 2014).

44. *See, e.g.,* Utah State Courts, *Online Court Assistance Program,* http://
www.utcourts.gov/ocap/ (last visited March 25, 2014); Maryland
Judiciary, *Family Law Forms,* http://mdcourts.gov/family/forms/index.
html (last visited March 25, 2014).

45. *See* Benny Evangelista, *LegalZoom Sues Rocket Lawyer,* S.F. CHRONICLE,
November 28, 2012, http://www.sfgate.com/business/article/LegalZoom-
sues-Rocket-Lawyer-4075061.php.

46. *Id.*

47. MDFamilylawyer.com, *Fixed Fee Online Legal Services,* http://www.
mdfamilylawyer.com/ (last visited March 25, 2014).

48. SmartLegalForms, *SmartLegalForms vs. LegalZoom,* http://www.
smartlegalforms.com/smartlegalforms-vs-legalzoom.html (last visited
March 25, 2014).

49. *LegalZoom S-1 Form.*

50. RICHARD SUSSKIND, TOMORROW'S LAWYERS 13 (2013).

51. LegalZoom, *Find an Attorney You Can Trust for Your Family,* http://www.
legalzoom.com/attorneys-lawyers/legal-plans/personal.html (last visited
March 25, 2014); Rocket Lawyer, *Get Connected with an On Call Lawyer:
Members Save Thousands of Dollars with Pre-Negotiated Rates,* http://www.
rocketlawyer.com/find-a-lawyer.rl (last visited March 25, 2014).

52. National Law Foundation, *Practical Forms for Attorneys,* http://www.
nlfforms.com/ (last visited March 25, 2014).

53. John G. Locallo, *Behind the Technology Curve? The ISBA Can Help,* 100
ILL. B.J. 124 (2012).

54. DirectLaw, *Virtual Lawyering Made Simple,* http://www.directlaw.com/
(last visited March 25, 2014).

55. All of the facts in this paragraph come from Julia Love, *LegalForce Creator
Shakes Things Up, Again,* THE RECORDER, March 11, 2013, http://www.law.
com/jsp/ca/PubArticleCA.jsp?id=1202591474850 and LegalForce, *Retail,*
http://www.legalforce.com/bookflip/ (last visited March 25, 2014).

56. Cassandra Burke Robertson, *The Facebook Disruption: How Social Media
May Transform Civil Litigation and Facilitate Access to Justice,* 65 ARK. L.
REV. 75, 84–5 (2012) has a great discussion of this site.

57. MetaTalk, IAALBIANYL, = http://metatalk.metafilter.com/15513/
AALAN (last visited March 25, 2014).

58. Stephen Fairley, *Using Avvo to Market Your Law Firm on the Internet,*
THE RAINMAKER BLOG, May 12, 2010, http://www.therainmakerblog.
com/2010/05/articles/law-firm-marketing-1/using-avvo-to-market-your-
law-firm-on-the-internet/.

59. Leena Rao, *Rocket Lawyer Acquires LawPivot To Add A Quora-Like Q&A
Platform To Online Legal Services Site,* TECH CRUNCH, January 14, 2013,
http://techcrunch.com/2013/01/14/rocket-lawyer-acquires-lawpivot-to-
add-a-quora-like-qa-platform-to-online-legal-services-site/.

60. DirectLaw, *Virtual Lawyering Made Simple,* http://www.directlaw.com/
(last visited March 25, 2014).

61. *See* Joseph A. Colquitt, *Hybrid Representation: Standing the Two-Sided Coin on Its Edge*, 38 WAKE FOREST L. REV. 55, 57 & n. 10 (2003).

62. Benjamin H. Barton, *Against Civil* Gideon *(and for* Pro Se *Court Reform)*, 62 FLA. L. REV. 1227 (2010).

63. *See* Letter from Carl Pierce, Chairman, Tennessee Supreme Court Task Force on the Study of Self-represented Litigant Issues in Tennessee, to Marcy Easton, President, Tennessee Bar Association (July 30, 2007), http://www.tba.org/tbatoday/news/2007/prosedivorce_letter_090707.pdf.

64. ABA, *Pro Se Resources By State*, http://www.americanbar.org/groups/delivery_legal_services/resources/pro_se_unbundling_resource_center/pro_se_resources_by_state.html (last visited January 16, 2014).

65. Cybersettle, *About Us,* http://www.cybersettle.com/about-us (last visited March 25, 2014). For an overview of ODR companies, *see* Joseph W. Goodman, *The Pros and Cons of Online Dispute Resolution: An Assessment of Cyber-Mediation Websites*, 2 DUKE L. & TECH. REV. 1–16 (2003), http://scholarship.law.duke.edu/dltr/vol2/iss1/2 (last visited March 25, 2014).

66. Julia Wilkinson, *Colin Rule: From eBay Conflicts to Global Peace Initiatives*, ECOMMERCEBYTES.COM, June 26, 2011, http://www.ecommercebytes.com/cab/abu/y211/m06/abu0289/s05.

67. Wilkinson, *Colin Rule: From eBay Conflicts to Global Peace Initiatives*.

68. Modria, *Our Modular Dispute Resolution System*, http://www.modria.com/resolution-center/ (last visited March 25, 2014); *see also* Thomas Claburn, *Modria's Fairness Engine: Justice on Demand*, INFORMATIONWEEK CLOUD, November 19, 2012, http://www.informationweek.com/cloud-computing/platform/modrias-fairness-engine-justice-on-deman/240142275.

69. Modria, *About,* http://www.modria.com/about/ (last visited March 25, 2014).

70. Eric Johnson, *Modria Wants You to Settle Your Workplace Problems (and Even Patent Disputes) Online*, ALL THINGS D, November 24, 2012, http://allthingsd.com/20121124/modria-wants-you-to-settle-your-workplace-problems-and-even-patent-disputes-online/.

71. Humayun Khan, *Modria Launches Dispute Resolution Tool to Scale Former eBay and PayPal Tech*, BETAKIT, November 19, 2012, http://www.betakit.com/modria-launches-dispute-resolution-tool-to-scale-former-ebay-and-paypal-tech/.

72. *Modria* lists its current investors here: http://www.modria.com/team/ (last visited March 25, 2014).

73. *Divorce Mediation Resources*, http://divorcemediationresources.com/ (last visited March 25, 2014).

74. *Wevorce*, http://www.wevorce.com/#5 (last visited March 25, 2014).

75. Nathaniel Rich, *Silicon Valley's Start-Up Machine*, N.Y. TIMES, May 2, 2013, http://www.nytimes.com/2013/05/05/magazine/y-combinator-silicon-valleys-start-up-machine.html?pagewanted=all&_r=0.

76. Mitu Gulati & Robert E. Scott, *The Three and a Half Minute Transaction: Boilerplate and the Limits of Contract Design* 1–32 (2013).

77. *Id.*

Chapter 6

1. CLIFFORD WINSTON, ROBERT W. CRANDALL, & VIKRAM MAHESHRI, FIRST THINGS WE DO, LET'S DEREGULATE ALL THE LAWYERS 55 (2011).

2. *See* WILLIAM HALTON & MICHAEL MCANN, DISTORTING THE LAW: POLITICS, MEDIA, AND THE LITIGATION CRISIS (2009).

3. *Overlawyered.com* is probably the best-known website for these anecdotes. Philip K. Howard is another master of the damning litigation anecdote. *See* PHILIP K. HOWARD, LIFE WITHOUT LAWYERS (2009).

4. The collateral source rule is a common law rule that prohibits the admission of evidence that a victims' damages were or will be compensated from a source like medical insurance or workers' comp.

5. All of the facts in this paragraph and the next can be found in MARC A. FRANKLIN ET AL., TORT LAW AND ALTERNATIVES 822–6 (9th ed. 2011).

6. Report of the Tort Policy Working Group on the Causes, Extent and Policy Implications of the Current Crisis in Insurance Availability and Affordability, Feb. 1986 (U.S. Gov't Printing Office, 1986-491-510:40090).

7. Joseph Sanders & Craig Joyce, *"Off to the Races": The 1980s Tort Crisis and the Law Reform Process*, 27 HOUSTON L. REV. 207, 217–22 (1990).

8. *Id.*

9. *See* Robert A. Van Kirk, *The Evolution of Useful Life Statutes in the Products Liability Reform Effort*, 1989 DUKE L.J. 1689 (1989).

10. JOHN GOLDBERG ET AL., TORT LAW 517–38 (3rd ed. 2012).

11. ATRA, *State Reforms,* http://www.atra.org/legislation/states (last visited March 25, 2014). ATRA also lists state tort reform enactments by year, from 1986–2012. ATRA, *State Tort Reform Enactments,* http://www.atra. org/Publications/StateTortReformEnactments.

12. 28 U.S.C.A. § 2678 (West 2006) (FTCA cap of 20–25 percent); 42 U.S.C.A. § 406 (West 2006) (Social Security cap of 25 percent); False Claims Act, 31 U.S.C. § 3730(d)(1) (2006) (False Claims Act cap of between 15 and 25 percent); 38 U.S.C. 5904(d)(1) (2006) (veterans' benefits cap of 20 percent).

13. Jim Saunders, *Is State Law Limiting Workers Comp Attorney Fees Constitutional? Fla. Supreme Court May Get Issue*, PALM BEACH POST, April 22, 2011, http://www.palmbeachpost.com/news/news/ state-regional/is-state-law-limiting-workers-comp-attorney-fees-c/nLrqc/.

14. The Private Securities Litigation Reform Act of 1995, Pub. L. No. 104-67.

15. The Securities Litigation Uniform Standards Act of 1998, Pub. L. No. 105-353.

16. All of the facts in this paragraph come from John W. Wunderlich, *"Uniform" Standards for Securities Class Actions*, 80 TENN. L. REV. 167, 174 (2012).

17. *Id.*
18. John Armour et al., *Delaware's Balancing Act*, 87 Indiana L. J. 1345, 1380 (2012).
19. David F. Engstrom, *Harnessing The Private Attorney General: Evidence From Qui Tam Litigation*, 112 Colum. L. Rev. 1244, 1262–4 (2012).
20. The Class Action Fairness Act of 2005, S. Bill 5 (109th Cong., 1st Sess.).
21. Chad M. Pinson & David M. Hunt, *Consumer Class Actions: Texas Trends*, 30 Rev. Litig. 475, 516–20 (2011).
22. Elizabeth Chambliss Burch, *Financiers as Monitors in Aggregate Litigation*, 87 N.Y.U. L. Rev. 1273, 1281–2 (2012).
23. *Id.*
24. *Id.*
25. 131 S.Ct. 1740 (2011).
26. Erin O'Hara O'Connor & Larry E. Ribstein, *Preemption and Choice-of-Law Coordination*, 111 Mich. L. Rev. 647, 698–9 (2013).
27. Discover Bank v. Super. Ct., 113 P.3d 1100, 1110 (Cal. 2005).
28. Concepcion, 131 S. Ct. at 1748–53.
29. American Express Co. v. Italian Colors Restaurant, No. 12-133 (Supreme Court 2013), http://www.supremecourt.gov/opinions/12pdf/12-133_19m1. pdf (last visited March 25, 2014).
30. Michael Orey, *How Business Trounced the Trial Lawyers*, Business Week, January 8, 2007, http://www.businessweek.com/magazine/ content/07_02/b4016001.htm.
31. *Id.*
32. For arguments that the litigation explosion is and was a myth, *see* Marc Galanter, *An Oil Strike in Hell: Contemporary Legends about the Civil Justice System*, 40 Ariz. L. Rev. 717 (1998); Marc Galanter, *Real World Torts: An Antidote to Anecdote*, 55 Md. L. Rev. 1093 (1996); Marc Galanter, *The Day after the Litigation Explosion*, 46 Md. L. Rev. 3 (1986). For the opposite view, *see* Walter K. Olson, The Litigation Explosion (1991).
33. Louise Weinberg, *The Article III Box: The Power of "Congress" to Attack the "Jurisdiction" of "Federal Courts,"* 78 Tex. L. Rev. 1405, 1420–1 (2000) ("One would have to be sleeping the sleep of Rip Van Winkle to be unaware that courthouse doors have been closing (or narrowing) ever since the decline of the Warren Court.").
34. *See, e.g.*, Valerie P. Hans & William S. Lofquist, *Jurors' Judgments of Business Liability in Tort Cases: Implications for the Litigations Explosion Debate*, 26 Law & Soc'y Rev. 85, 94–8 (1992).
35. Lester Brickman, Lawyer Barons: What Their Contingency Fees Really Cost America (2011).
36. Goldfarb v. Va. State Bar, 421 U.S. 773 (1975).
37. Bates v. State Bar of Arizona, 433 U.S. 350 (1977).
38. *In re* Primus, 436 U.S. 412 (1978).
39. Nora Freeman Engstrom, *Attorney Advertising and the Contingency Fee Cost Paradox*, 65 Stan. L. Rev. 633, 662–5 (2013).

40. *Id.*

41. Consider Jim "The Hammer" Shapiro, http://www.youtube.com/watch?v=Q5hn8bhEpMY (last visited March 25, 2014), or Adam Reposa: Lawyer, Patriot, Champion, http://www.youtube.com/watch?v=tBLTW-KLdHA&list=PLD69A038C0E662334 (last visited March 25, 2014).

42. *See, e.g.,* Stephen Daniels & Joanne Martin, *Texas Plaintiffs' Practice in the Age of Tort Reform: Survival of the Fittest—It's Even More True Now,* 51 N.Y.L.S. L. R. 285 (2006), http://www.nyls.edu/center-for-professional-values-and-practice/wp-content/uploads/sites/134/2013/08/nlr208.pdf.

43. *See, e.g.,* Bernard Black et al., *Stability, Not Crisis: Medical Malpractice Claim Outcomes in Texas, 1988–2002,* 2 J. EMPIRICAL LEGAL STUD. 207, 210 (2005) (finding that post–tort reform the number of paid medical malpractice claims in Texas declined from 6.4 per 100 practicing physicians per year in 1990–92 to 4.6 per 100 in 2000–2); David A. Hyman et al., *Estimating the Effect of Damages Caps in Medical Malpractice Cases: Evidence From Texas,* 1 J. LEG. ANALYSIS 355 (2009).

44. *Id.* at 302–4.

45. Daniels & Martin, *Texas Plaintiffs' Practice in the Age of Tort Reform: Survival of the Fittest—It's Even More True Now,* 51 N.Y.L. SCH. L. REV. at 297.

46. Stephen Daniels & Joanne Martin, *The Texas Two-Step: Evidence on the Link Between Damage Caps and Access to the Civil Justice System,* 55 DEPAUL L. REV. 635, 655 (2005).

47. *See* Stephen Daniels & Joanne Martin, *The Strange Success of Tort Reform,* 53 EMORY L.J. 1225 (2004).

48. Orey, *How Business Trounced the Trial Lawyers.*

49. Herbert M. Kritzer, *The Commodification of Insurance Defense Practice,* 59 VAND. L. REV. 2053 (2006).

50. *Id.* at 1059–60.

51. *Id.*

52. *See* EcoPol Project, *Jellyfish and Dead Zones,* ECOPOL, June 9, 2012, http://ecopolproject.blogspot.com/2012/06/jellyfish-and-dead-zones-jellyfish.html.

53. *See* Nora Freeman Engstrom, *Sunlight and Settlement Mills,* 86 NEW YORK UNIVERSITY LAW REVIEW 805 (2011) (Hereinafter Engstrom, *Sunlight*); Nora Freeman Engstrom, *Run-of-the-Mill Justice,* 22 GEORGETOWN JOURNAL OF LEGAL ETHICS 1485 (2009) (hereinafter Engstrom, *Run-of-the-Mill*).

54. Engstrom, *Run-of-the-Mill,* at 1491–2.

55. *Id.* at 1492.

56. *See* Stephen Daniels & Joanne Martin, *"It's Darwinism – Survival of the Fittest:" How Markets and Reputations Shape the Ways in Which Plaintiffs' Lawyers Obtain Clients,* 21 LAW & POL'Y 377 (1999).

57. *Id.* at 1492–3.

58. Engstrom, *Sunlight,* at 817.

59. Engstrom, *Run-of-the-Mill,* at 1543–5.

60. Engstrom, *Sunlight,* at 835–50.
61. 550 U.S. 544 (2007).
62. 556 U.S. 662 (2009).
63. Edward A. Hartnett, *Taming Twombly, Even After Iqbal*, 158 U. Pa. L. Rev. 473, 474–5 (2010).
64. *Twombly*, 550 U.S. at 570; *Iqbal*, 129 S.Ct. at 1949.
65. Elizabeth C. Burch, *There's a* Pennoyer *in My Foyer*, 13 Green Bag 105, 115 (noting that "the old [Rule 8] has not been amended at all" but the Court's interpretation changed nonetheless).
66. *See* Kevin M. Clermont & Stephen C. Yeazell, *Inventing Tests, Destabilizing Systems*, 95 Iowa L. Rev. 821, 823–31 (2010); Arthur R. Miller, *From Conley to Twombly to Iqbal: A Double Play on the Federal Rules of Civil Procedure*, 60 Duke L.J. 1, 3–17 (2010).
67. Twombly, 550 U.S. at 558.
68. Iqbal, 556 U.S. at 684–6.
69. Arthur R. Miller, *From Conley to Twombly to Iqbal: A Double Play on the Federal Rules of Civil Procedure*, 60 Duke L.J. 1, 26 (2010)
70. Elizabeth M. Schneider, *The Changing Shape of Federal Civil Pretrial Practice: The Disparate Impact on Civil Rights and Employment Discrimination Cases*, 158 U. Pa. L. Rev. 517, 518–9 (2010).
71. Jess Bravin, *New Look at Election Spending Looms in September*, Wall St. J., July 1, 2009, at A4, http://online.wsj.com/article/SB124640661014076677.html.
72. *See* Karen Petroski, *Iqbal and Interpretation*, 39 Fla. St. L. Rev. 417, 418 (2012).
73. Twombly, 550 U.S. at 559.
74. BMW v. Gore, 517 U.S. 559, 574–85 (1996).
75. State Farm Mut. Auto. Ins. Co. v. Campbell, 538 U.S. 408, 425 (2003).
76. Robert A. Klink, *The Punitive Damage Debate*, 38 Harv. J. Legis. 469 (2001).
77. Browning-Ferris Indus. of Vt., Inc. v. Kelco Disposal, Inc., 492 U.S. 257, 282 (1989) (O'Connor, J., concurring in part and dissenting in part).
78. Pac. Mut. Life Ins. Co. v. Haslip, 499 U.S. 1, 18 (1991).
79. Exxon Shipping Co. v. Baker, 554 U.S. 471, 499 (2008).
80. Justice Brennan listed more than a hundred in his dissent in *Marek* 473 U.S. 1, 43–51 (1985). A more recent (and longer) list can be found in 3 Mary Derfner & Arthur Wolf, Court Awarded Attorney Fees (2008).
81. *See, e.g.*, Pamela S. Karlan, *Disarming the Private Attorney General*, 2003 U. Ill. L. Rev. 183, 205.
82. Alyeska Pipeline Serv. Co. v. Wilderness Soc'y, 421 U.S. 240, 269 (1975).
83. Civil Rights Attorney's Fees Awards Act of 1976, 42 U.S.C. § 1988.
84. N.C. Dep't of Transp. v. Crest St. Cmty. Council Inc., 479 U.S. 6, 11 (1986) (holding that time spent in an administrative proceeding to enforce Title VI regulations would not entitle successful claimants to an attorney's fee award).

85. Farrar v. Hobby, 506 U.S. 103, 115 (1992) (suggesting that in many nominal damages cases plaintiffs should collect no fees because vindication of an abstract right still does not establish the central element of her claim, compensatory damages).

86. W. Va. Univ. Hosps. v. Casey, 499 U.S. 83 (1991) (holding that plaintiffs cannot recover the costs of experts' services).

87. Buckhannon Board & Care Home, Inc. v. West Virginia Department of Health & Human Resources, 532 U.S. 598 (2001).

88. Jeffrey S. Brand, *The Second Front in the Fight for Civil Rights: The Supreme Court, Congress, and Statutory Fees*, 69 Tex. L. Rev. 291, 373 (1990).

89. Deborah M. Weissman, *Law as Largess: Shifting Paradigms of Law for the Poor*, 44 Wm. & Mary L. Rev. 737, 783 (2002).

90. Steven Eppler-Epstein, *Passion, Caution, and Evolution: The Legal Aid Movement and Empirical Studies of Legal Assistance*, 126 Harv. L. Rev. F. 102, 103–4 (2013).

91. NLADA, *History of Civil Legal Aid*, http://www.nlada.org/About/ About_HistoryCivil (last visited March 25, 2014).

92. LSC, *LSC Funding*, http://www.lsc.gov/congress/lsc-funding (last visited March 25, 2014); Joe Palazzolo, *Legal Services Facing a Big Budget Cut*, Wall St. J., November 15, 2011, http://blogs.wsj.com/law/2011/11/15/ legal-services-facing-a-big-budget-cut/.

93. *See* National Right to Counsel Committee, Justice Denied (2009), http://www.constitutionproject.org/manage/file/139.pdf (last visited March 25, 2014); ABA Standing Committee on Legal Aid & Indigent Defendants, Gideon's Broken Promise: America's Continuing Quest For Equal Justice (2004), http://www.americanbar.org/content/ dam/aba/administrative/legal_aid_indigent_defendants/ls_sclaid_def_ bp_right_to_counsel_in_criminal_proceedings.authcheckdam.pdf (last visited March 25, 2014); Richard Klein & Robert Spangenberg, The Indigent Defense Crisis (1993); ABA Special Committee on Criminal Justice in a Free Society, Criminal Justice in Crisis (1988); Bureau of Justice Statistics, National Criminal Defense Systems Study 22–33 (1986); Norman Lefstein, ABA Standing Committee on Legal Aid & Indigent Defendants, Criminal Defense Services For The Poor, Methods and Programs for Providing Legal Representation and the Need for Adequate Financing (1982); Laurence A. Benner et al., Nat'l Legal Aid & Defender Ass'n, The Other Face of Justice (1973).

94. Heather Baxter, *Gideon's Ghost: Providing the Sixth Amendment Right to Counsel in Times of Budgetary Crisis*, 2010 Mich. St. L. Rev. 341 (2010).

95. Michael S. Nachmanoff, *Sequestration Threatens to Eviscerate Federal Public Defenders*, The Hill's Congress Blog, July 23, 2013, http:// thehill.com/blogs/congress-blog/judicial/312659-sequestration-threatens- to-eviscerate-federal-public-defenders.

96. The ABA/Spangenberg Reports for 2007, 2005, 2003, 2002, and 1999 can be found here: http://www.americanbar.org/groups/

legal_aid_indigent_defendants/initiatives/indigent_defense_systems_
improvement/reports_studies.html (last visited March 25, 2014).

97. Jacqueline B. Dixon, *50 Years After "Gideon,"* 49 TENN. B.J. 3 (February,
2013).

98. *See, e.g.,* ABA, *Resource Center for Access to Justice Initiatives, Legal Aid Funding:
Resources and Technical Assistance,* http://www.americanbar.org/groups/legal_
aid_indigent_defendants/initiatives/resource_center_for_access_to_justice/
funding_civil_legal_services.html (last visited March 25, 2014).

99. See, *e.g.,* ABA, *Indigent Defense/Public Defender Systems,* http://www.
americanbar.org/groups/legal_aid_indigent_defendants/initiatives/
indigent_defense_systems_improvement/policies_guidelines.html (last
visited March 25, 2014).

100. *See* JOHN P. HEINZ ET AL., URBAN LAWYERS 317 (2005).

101. AMERICAN BAR FOUNDATION, 2005 LAWYER STATISTICAL REPORT 7–8 (2005).

102. ABA, *Total National Lawyer Counts,* http://www.americanbar.org/
content/dam/aba/migrated/marketresearch/PublicDocuments/total_
national_lawyer_counts_1878_2011.xls (the number of licensed lawyers
in 1975 was 404,772 and in 2012 it was 1,104,766).

103. ABF & NALP, AFTER THE JD II 43, 54 (2009).

104. Jenna Greene, *Budget Cuts Constrict Lawyers' Routes to Federal Jobs,*
NAT'L L.J., October 11, 2011, http://www.law.com/jsp/article.jsp?id=12025
18453942&slreturn=20130223220233.

105. Greg Bluestein, *State Budget Cuts Clog Criminal Justice System,* CRIME
& COURTS, NBC NEWS, October 26, 2011, http://www.nbcnews.com/
id/45049812/ns/us_news-crime_and_courts/#.UU5gFXBubHo.

106. Stephen Losey, *Retirements Surge, New Hires Plummet,* FEDERAL
TIMES, October 15, 2012, http://www.federaltimes.com/article/20121015/
PERSONNEL02/310150001/Retirements-surge-new-hires-plummet.

107. John Schwartz, *Critics Say Budget Cuts for Courts Risk Rights,* N.Y.
TIMES, November 26, 2011, http://www.nytimes.com/2011/11/27/us/
budget-cuts-for-state-courts-risk-rights-critics-say.html?pagewanted=
all&_r=0.

108. Jason Kotowski, *Budget Cuts, Other Factors Causing Court Delays,*
THE BAKERSFIELD CALIFORNIA, March 9, 2013, http://www.
bakersfieldcalifornian.com/local/x738927226/Budget-cuts-other-
factors-causing-court-delays; Maura Dolan & Victoria Kim,
Budget Cuts to Worsen California Court Delays, Officials Say, L.A.
TIMES, July 20, 2011, http://articles.latimes.com/2011/jul/20/local/
la-me-0720-court-cuts-20110720.

109. Nels Pearsall, Bo Shippen, & Roy Weinstein, *Economic Impact of
Reduced Judiciary Funding and Resulting Delays in State Civil Litigation,*
March 2012, http://www.micronomics.com/articles/Economic_Impact_
of_Reduced_Judiciary_Funding_and_Resulting_Delays_in_State_
Civil_Litigations.pdf (last visited March 25, 2014).

Chapter 7

1. Above the Law, *Lost Generation,* http://abovethelaw.com/tag/lost-generation/ (last visited March 25, 2014).

2. *See, e.g., A Less Gilded Future,* THE ECONOMIST, May 5, 2011, http://www.economist.com/node/18651114.

3. ABA, *Enrollment and Degrees Awarded, 1963–2011,* http://www.americanbar.org/content/dam/aba/administrative/legal_education_and_admissions_to_the_bar/statistics/enrollment_degrees_awarded.authcheckdam.pdf (last visited March 25, 2014).

4. *Id.*

5. Marc Gans, *Not a New Problem: How the State of the Legal Profession Has Been Secretly in Decline for Quite Some Time,* http://papers.ssrn.com/sol3/papers.cfm?abstract_id=2173144, at 34–6 (last visited March 25, 2014).

6. *Id.*

7. ABA, *Lawyer Demographics,* http://www.americanbar.org/content/dam/aba/migrated/marketresearch/PublicDocuments/lawyer_demographics_2012_revised.authcheckdam.pdf (last visited March 25, 2014) (More than 10 percent and as much as 13 percent of the practicing bar has been over sixty-five since 1980).

8. Benjamin H. Barton, *Economists on Deregulation of the American Legal Profession: Praise and Critique,* 2012 MICH. ST. L. REV. 493, 501 (2012).

9. Barry Currier, *The Evolution of J.D. Programs—Is Non-Traditional Becoming More Traditional?,* 38 Sw. L. REV. 635, 636 (2009).

10. James Podgers, *State of the Union: The Nation's Lawyer Population Continues to Grow, But Barely,* A.B.A. J., July 1, 2011, http://www.abajournal.com/magazine/article/state_of_the_union_the_nations_lawyer_population_continues_to_grow_but_bare/.

11. Census Bureau, *Current Population Survey (CPS)—Definitions,* http://www.census.gov/cps/about/cpsdef.html (last visited March 25, 2014).

12. Bureau of Labor Statistics, *Employment Projections, Projections Methodology,* http://www.bls.gov/emp/ep_projections_methods.htm (last visited March 25, 2014).

13. ABA, *Legal Profession Statistics,* http://www.americanbar.org/resources_for_lawyers/profession_statistics.html (last visited March 25, 2014).

14. Gans, *Not a New Problem,* at 4.

15. BLS, Occupational Outlook Handbook, *Lawyers,* http://www.bls.gov/ooh/legal/lawyers.htm (last visited March 24, 2014).

16. The OOH number for 2010 was adjusted downward after Gans finished his research: *id.*

17. The 2010 calculations come from Gans, *Not a New Problem,* at 26. The 2011–12 calculations come from NALP, *Class of 2011 Summary Report,* http://www.nalp.org/uploads/NatlSummChart_Classof2011.pdf and NALP, *Class of 2012 Summary Report,* http://www.nalp.org/uploads/NationalSummaryChart2012.pdf.

18. Elie Mystal, *The 2014 U.S. News Law School Rankings*, ABOVE THE LAW, March 11, 2013, http://abovethelaw.com/2013/03/the-2014-u-s-news-law-school-rankings/.

19. ABF & NALP, *After the JD II: Second Results from a Study of Legal Careers* 54 (2009).

20. Aaron N. Taylor, *Why Law School Is Still Worth It*, THE NATIONAL JURIST, October 11, 2011, http://www.nationaljurist.com/content/why-law-school-still-worth-it.

21. U.C. Hastings College of Law, Office of Career & Professional Development, *Careers Outside of Legal Practice*, http://www.uchastings.edu/career-office/docs/CareersOutsideLegalPractice.pdf (last visited March 25, 2014).

22. NALP, *After the JD II*, at 21.

23. *Id.* at 48.

24. *Id.* at 54.

25. Gans, *Not a New Problem*, at 22.

26. Mark Greenbaum, *No More Room at the Bench*, L.A. TIMES, January 8, 2010, http://articles.latimes.com/2010/jan/08/opinion/la-oe-greenbaum8-2010jan08.

27. ABA, *Enrollment and Degrees Awarded, 1963–2011*, http://www.americanbar.org/content/dam/aba/administrative/legal_education_and_admissions_to_the_bar/statistics/enrollment_degrees_awarded.authcheckdam.pdf (last visited March 25, 2014).

28. BLS, Occupational Outlook Handbook, *Lawyers*, http://www.bls.gov/ooh/legal/lawyers.htm (last visited March 24, 2014).

29. Matt Leichter, *Law Graduate Overproduction*, http://lawschooltuitionbubble.wordpress.com/original-research-updated/law-graduate-overproduction/ (last visited March 25, 2014).

30. Gans, *Not a New Problem*, 16–18; NALP, *Class of 2011 Summary Report*, http://www.nalp.org/uploads/NatlSummChart_Classof2011.pdf (last visited March 25, 2014).

31. Ashby Jones, *New Lawyers, Seeking Jobs, Are Advised to Think Small*, WALL ST. J., June 25, 2012, http://online.wsj.com/article/SB10001424052702303506404577448974083992182.html.

32. Leigh Jones, *Vanishing Act: Year II: For the Second Year in a Row, The NLJ 250 Declined—The Biggest Two-Year Drop in the Survey's 33-Year History*, NAT'L L.J., November 8, 2010.

33. *Id.*

34. Dana Olsen, *Bye Bye Big Firm*, CORPORATE COUNSEL, April 1, 2012, http://www.corpcounsel.com/id=1202545285843/Bye-Bye-Big-Firm?slret urn=20140204170121.

35. Carolyn Elefant, *Is It Really Sayonara to Biglaw This Time?*, MYSHINGLE.COM, March 26, 2012, http://myshingle.com/2012/03/articles/biglaw-to-solo/is-it-really-sayonara-to-biglaw-this-time/

36. *Lawyer 2.0: Technology for Solo Practitioners*, http://www.lawyer2pointo. com/genesis/ (last visited March 25, 2014).

37. NALP, *After the JD II*, at 54.

Chapter 8

1. ROBERT STEVENS, LAW SCHOOL: LEGAL EDUCATION FROM THE 1850S TO THE 1980S 8 (1983).

2. *Id.* at 20–8.

3. *Id.* at 21–2.

4. *See* Russell Weaver, *Langdell's Legacy: Living with the Case Method*, 36 VILL. L. Rev. 517, 517–44 (1991).

5. Bruce A. Kimball, *"Warn Students That I Entertain Heretical Opinions, Which They Are Not to Take as Law": The Inception of Case Method Teaching in the Classrooms of the Early C. C. Langdell, 1870–1883*, 17 L. & HIST. REV. 57, 57–8 (1999).

6. JOHN W. JOHNSON, AMERICAN LEGAL CULTURE, 1908–1940 66–7 (1981).

7. LEGAL EDUCATION AND PROFESSIONAL DEVELOPMENT—AN EDUCATIONAL CONTINUUM 106 (Robert MacCrate ed., 1992).

8. James P. White, *The American Bar Association Law School Approval Process: A Century Plus of Public Service*, 30 WAKE FOREST L. REV. 283, 284 (1995).

9. JEROLD S. AUERBACH, UNEQUAL JUSTICE (1976).

10. Laura I. Appleman, *The Rise of the Modern American Law School: How Professionalization, German Scholarship, and Legal Reform Shaped Our System of Legal Education*, 39 NEW ENG. L. REV. 251, 262 (2005).

11. Christopher Tomlins, *Framing the Field of Law's Disciplinary Encounters: A Historical Narrative*, 34 LAW & SOC'Y REV. 911, 932 (2000).

12. Dorothy E. Finnegan, *Raising and Leveling the Bar: Standards, Access, and the YMCA Evening Law Schools, 1890–1940*, 55 J. LEGAL EDUC. 208 (2005).

13. George B. Shepherd & William G. Shepherd, *Scholarly Restraints? ABA Accreditation and Legal Education*, 19 CARDOZO L. REV. 2091, 2114–5 (1998). *See also* AUERBACH, UNEQUAL JUSTICE at 95 ("Between 1890 and 1910 the number of Harvard style day law schools increased from 51 to 79, while the number of night schools more than quadrupled from 10 to 45.").

14. RICHARD ABEL, AMERICAN LAWYERS 277–8 (1989).

15. Laurel A. Rigertas, *Lobbying and Litigating Against "Legal Bootleggers"— The Role of the Organized Bar in the Expansion of the Courts' Inherent Powers in the Early Twentieth Century*, 46 CAL. W. L. REV. 65, 88 (2009).

16. Rachel F. Moran, *Of Rankings and Regulation: Are the U.S. News & World Report Rankings Really a Subversive Force in Legal Education?*, 81 IND. L.J. 383, 391–2 (2006).

17. Andrew P. Morriss, *The Market for Legal Education & Freedom of Association: Why the "Solomon Amendment" Is Constitutional and Law Schools Are Not Expressive Associations*, 14 Wm. & MARY BILL RTS. J. 415, 419–25 (2005).

18. John O. Sonsteng et al., *A Legal Education Renaissance: A Practical Approach For The Twenty-First Century*, 34 WM. MITCHELL L. REV. 303, 329 (2007).

19. Monica R. Hargrove, *The Evolution of Black Lawyers in Corporate America: From The Road Less Traveled to Managing the Major Highways*, 53 HOW. L.J. 749, 780 (2010).

20. Sonsteng, *A Legal Education Renaissance*, at 329.

21. Carl C. Monk & Harry G. Prince, *How Can an Association of Law Schools Promote Quality Legal Education?*, 43 S. TEX. L. REV. 507, 508 (2002).

22. Michael L. Rustad & Thomas H. Koenig, *A Hard Day's Night: Hierarchy, History & Happiness in Legal Education*, 58 SYRACUSE L. REV. 261, 302 (2008).

23. *Id.*

24. *Id.*

25. STEVENS, LAW SCHOOL, AT 172–8.

26. BENJAMIN H. BARTON, THE LAWYER-JUDGE BIAS IN AMERICAN COURTS 121–2 (2011).

27. *Id.* at 122.

28. William G. Hammond, *Legal Education and the Study of Jurisprudence in the West and North-West*, 8 J. SOC. SCI. 165, 170–5 (1876).

29. The graph comes from Benjamin H. Barton, *An Empirical Study of Supreme Court Justice Pre-Appointment Experience*, 64 FLA. L. REV. 1137 (2012).

30. ABEL, AMERICAN LAWYERS, at 55.

31. *Id.* at 277–8.

32. The total number of law students, including the roughly 1 percent of law students that attended an unaccredited law school in 1983, was 128,742. ABA, *Enrollment and Degrees Awarded,* http://www.americanbar.org/content/dam/aba/administrative/legal_education_and_admissions_to_the_bar/statistics/enrollment_degrees_awarded.authcheckdam.pdf (last visited January 8, 2014).

33. *Id.*

34. *Id.*

35. From 1984 to 2001, law schools grew at an annualized rate of just 0.19 percent. From 2001 to 2011 that percentage rose to 1.5 percent.

36. ABEL, AMERICAN LAWYERS, at 287.

37. I generated this number by subtracting the 8,547 part-time law professors listed from the 35,629 total of law professors, full-time skills training, administrators, and librarians shown here: ABA, *Staff and Faculty Members,* http://www.americanbar.org/content/dam/aba/administrative/legal_education_and_admissions_to_the_bar/statistics/2012_2013_faculty_by_gender_ethnicity.authcheckdam.pdf (last visited January 8, 2014).

38. ABA, *Student Faculty Ratio,* http://www.americanbar.org/content/dam/aba/administrative/legal_education_and_admissions_to_the_bar/statistics/student_faculty_ratio.authcheckdam.pdf (last visited January 8, 2014).

39. BRIAN Z. TAMANAHA, FAILING LAW SCHOOLS 39–53 (2012).

40. *Id.* at 108–9.

41. ABA, *Law School Tuition,* http://www.americanbar.org/content/dam/aba/administrative/legal_education_and_admissions_to_the_bar/statistics/ls_tuition.authcheckdam.pdf (last visited March 25, 2014). All of the remaining statistics in this paragraph come from that source.

42. ABA, *Average Amount Borrowed,* http://www.americanbar.org/content/dam/aba/administrative/legal_education_and_admissions_to_the_bar/statistics/avg_amnt_brwd.authcheckdam.pdf (last visited January 8, 2014).

43. *See* GLENN REYNOLDS, THE HIGHER EDUCATION BUBBLE 12–4 (2012).

44. This post by Brian Tamanaha on Balkinization is particularly heartbreaking, *see* Brian Tamanaha, *The Quickly Exploding Law Graduate Debt Disaster,* BALKINIZATION, March 24, 2012, http://balkin.blogspot.com/2012/03/quickly-exploding-law-graduate-debt.html.

45. Jason Delisle, *The Graduate Student Debt Review: The State of Graduate Student Borrowing,* March, 2014, http://newamerica.net/sites/newamerica.net/files/policydocs/GradStudentDebtReview-Delisle-Final.pdf.

46. This list is generated from the *U.S. News* rankings for indebtedness, http://grad-schools.usnews.rankingsandreviews.com/best-graduate-schools/top-law-schools/grad-debt-rankings (last visited March 28, 2013) and the general *U.S. News* rankings, http://grad-schools.usnews.rankingsandreviews.com/best-graduate-schools/top-law-schools/law-rankings (last visited March 28, 2013).

47. I am quite critical of the *U.S. News* ranking elsewhere and do not think it is the only measure of law school quality. Nevertheless, law students, applicants, and some employers probably do, and for these purposes it is a fair proxy for the worth of a degree.

48. Matt Leichter, *Private Law School Tuition Projections,* LAW SCHOOL TUITION BUBBLE, http://lawschooltuitionbubble.wordpress.com/original-research-updated/tuition-projections/ (last visited March 25, 2014).

49. Paul Campos, *The Crisis of the American Law School,* http://works.bepress.com/cgi/viewcontent.cgi?article=1000&context=paul_campos (last visited March 25, 2014).

50. *See* Yale Law School, *Endowment Funds,* http://www.law.yale.edu/givetoyls/endowmentfunds.htm (last visited March 28, 2014).

51. Jonathan D. Glater, *Harvard Law, Hoping Students Will Consider Public Service, Offers Tuition Break,* N.Y. TIMES, March 18, 2008, http://www.nytimes.com/2008/03/18/us/18law.html.

52. Christopher Danzig, *How Stanford Law School Could Cut Tuition and Save the World,* ABOVE THE LAW, March 9, 2012, http://abovethelaw.com/2012/03/how-stanford-law-school-could-cut-tuition-and-save-the-world/.

53. Paul Campos, *The 30 Percent Solution,* INSIDE THE LAW SCHOOL SCAM, March 7, 2012, http://insidethelawschoolscam.blogspot.com/2012/03/30-per-cent-solution.html.

54. Derek Muller, *The 2014 U.S. News Law School Rankings: Employment Data (Part II)*, TaxProf Blog, March 28, 2013, http://taxprof.typepad.com/taxprof_blog/2013/03/the-2014.html.

55. Law School Transparency, *ABA President Zack: Law School Transparency Needed to Clarify Attorney Salary Misperceptions*, http://www.lawschooltransparency.com/2011/02/aba-president-zack-law-school-transparency-needed/ (last visited March 25, 2014).

56. Tali Sharot, The Optimism Bias: A Tour of the Irrationally Positive Brain (2011).

57. ABA, *2012 Key Facts and Admissions Totals*, http://www.americanbar.org/content/dam/aba/administrative/legal_education_and_admissions_to_the_bar/statistics/2012_key_facts_ad_totals.authcheckdam.pdf (last visited January 9, 2014).

58. A Brian Leiter study of tenure track faculty hired from 1996–2001 showed that roughly three-quarters of the hires came from nineteen schools, with more than one-third graduating from Yale, Harvard, or Stanford. Randolph Jonakait, *The Two Hemispheres of Legal Education and the Rise and Fall of Local Law Schools*, 51 N.Y.L. Sch. L. Rev. 863, 901–2 (2007).

59. *See* Brent E. Newton, *Preaching What They Don't Practice: Why Law Faculties' Preoccupation with Impractical Scholarship and Devaluation of Practical Competencies Obstruct Reform in the Legal Academy*, 62 S.C. L. Rev. 105, 129–30 (2010).

60. *See* Edward N. Wolff, Does Education Really Help?: Skill, Work, and Inequality 12 (2006).

61. *See* NACE, *NACE Salary Survey: Starting Salaries for New College Graduates* 3 (2012).

62. *See* Robert J. Rhee, *The Madoff Scandal, Market Regulatory Failure and the Business Education of Lawyers*, 35 J. Corp. L. 363, 389 n. 110 (2009).

63. *See* Thomas M. Cooley Law School, Reports on Employment in the Legal Profession 2–3 (2011), http://www.cooley.edu/reports/_docs/Report1_Employment_Legal_Profession072511.pdf (last visited July 26, 2013).

64. Rachel M. Zahorsky, *Law Grads "Indentured Servants" to Loans, Law Prof Says; Law School Crisis a Symptom of Weak Economy*, ABA J., June 14, 2012, http://www.abajournal.com/news/article/campos_indentured_servants_law_school_crisis_symptom_economy/.

65. South Texas College of Law, What Can You Do With Your Law Degree?, http://www.stcl.edu/career/handouts/What%20Can%20I%20Do%20With%20A%20Law%20Degree.pdf (last visited July 26, 2013).

66. For an overview of the ABA process, *see* http://www.americanbar.org/groups/legal_education/resources/accreditation.html (last visited March 25, 2014). For an overview of the AALS version, *see* http://www.aals.org/about_handbook_requirements.php (last visited March 25, 2014).

67. William D. Henderson & Andrew P. Morriss, *Student Quality as Measured by LSAT Scores: Migration Patterns in the U.S. News Rankings*

Era, 81 IND. L.J. 163, 197 (2006); *see also* George B. Shepherd, *No African-American Lawyers Allowed: The Inefficient Racism of the ABA's Accreditation of Law Schools*, 53 J. LEGAL EDUC. 103, 133 (2003) (estimating the cost per student of complying with the library standard alone at more than $4000 based on spending by recently accredited schools).

68. AALS, *Member and Fee Paid Law Schools,* http://www.aals.org/about_memberschools.php (last visited March 25, 2014).

69. Monk & Prince, *How Can an Association of Law Schools Promote Quality Legal Education?*, at 511; David E. Bernstein, *Affirmative Blackmail*, WALL ST. J., Feb. 11, 2006, at A9 (Because only graduates of ABA-approved schools can take the bar in the overwhelming majority of states, the ABA has "a legal monopoly on accreditation standards.").

70. For a compilation of the rankings from 1987–2009 (with a Stanford slant), *see* J. Paul Lomio et al., *Ranking of Top Law Schools 1987–2009 by US News & World Report* (2008), http://www.law.stanford.edu/publications/projects/lrps/pdf/lomio_etal-rp20.pdf (last visited March 25, 2014).

71. *See* Gov't Accounting Office, *Issues Related to Law School Cost and Access* 7 (2009).

72. Gene Nichol, *Educating for Privilege*, NATION, Oct. 13, 2003, at 22, http://www.thenation.com/doc/20031013/nichol; *see also* Henderson & Morriss, *Student Quality as Measured by LSAT Scores,* at 165–6.

73. Karen Sloan, *Professor's Book Gives Law Schools a Failing Grade,* THE NATIONAL LAW JOURNAL, June 19, 2012, http://www.law.com/jsp/cc/PubArticleFriendlyCC.jsp?id=1339923145534.

74. TAMANAHA, FAILING LAW SCHOOLS, at 109–44.

75. *See id.* at 135–44. First among Brian Tamanaha's prescriptions is to place limits on the amount any particular institution can offer to students (and add limits if the institution's graduates regularly default) and an individual limit for students themselves. *See id.* at 167–85; Brian Z. Tamanaha, *How to Make Law School Affordable*, N.Y. TIMES, May 31, 2012, http://www.nytimes.com/2012/06/01/opinion/how-to-make-law-school-affordable.html.

76. Political Calculations, *Does It Pay to Go to Law School,* July 20, 2010, http://politicalcalculations.blogspot.com/2010/07/does-it-pay-to-go-to-law-school.html.

77. Philip G. Schrag, *Failing Law Schools—Brian Tamanaha's Misguided Missile*, at 9, http://papers.ssrn.com/sol3/papers.cfm?abstract_id=2179625 (last visited March 25, 2014).

78. *Id.* at 9–10.

79. Equal Justice Works, *New Student Loan Repayment Option Could Help Recent Graduates*, U.S. NEWS, November 7, 2011, http://www.usnews.com/education/blogs/student-loan-ranger/2012/11/07/new-student-loan-repayment-option-could-help-recent-graduates.

80. John Hechinger, *Student-Loan Collection Targeted for Overhaul in Congress*, BLOOMBERG, December 4, 2012, http://www.bloomberg.com/news/2012-12-04/student-loan-collection-targeted-for-overhaul-in-congress.html.

81. Alison Damast, *Obama's New "Pay as You Earn" Plan a Windfall for MBAs*, BLOOMBERG BUSINESS WEEK, November 2, 2012, http://www.businessweek.com/articles/2012-11-02/obamas-new-pay-as-you-earn-plan-a-windfall-for-mbas.

82. Federal Student Aid, *PLUS Loans,* http://studentaid.ed.gov/types/loans/plus (last visited March 28, 2013).

83. Matt Leichter, *How Grad PLUS Loans Sustain Zombie Law Schools*, AM LAW DAILY, February 13, 2013, http://www.americanlawyer.com/PubArticleALD.jsp?id=1202588045076&How_Grad_PLUS_Loans_Sustain_Zombie_Law_Schools&slreturn=20130228213407.

84. Federal Reserve Bank of New York, *Student Loan Debt History,* http://www.newyorkfed.org/studentloandebt/ (last visited March 28, 2014).

85. Paul O'Donnell, *How the Student Loan Crisis Is Hurting Home Prices,* USA TODAY, March 10, 2013, http://www.usatoday.com/story/money/business/2013/03/10/cnbc-student-loans-housing/1969293/.

86. Bill Hardekopf, *More Than Half of Student Loans Are Now in Deferral or Delinquent*, FORBES, February 1, 2013, http://www.forbes.com/sites/moneybuilder/2013/02/01/alarming-number-of-student-loans-are-delinquent/.

87. STEVEN J. HARPER, THE LAWYER BUBBLE (2013).

88. Sharon Jayson, *Who's Feeling Stressed? Young Adults, New Survey Shows*, U.S.A. Today, February 6, 2013, http://www.usatoday.com/story/news/nation/2013/02/06/stress-psychology-millennials-depression/1878295/.

89. Daniel Bortz, *How to De-Stress from Student Loan Debt,* U.S. NEWS, May 11, 2011, http://money.usnews.com/money/personal-finance/articles/2012/05/11/how-to-de-stress-from-student-loan-debt.

Chapter 9

1. Richard A. Matasar, *The Rise and Fall of American Legal Education*, 49 N.Y. L. SCH. L. REV. 465, 475 (2004).

2. Paul Caron, *Indiana Tech's Class of 24 1Ls Is 76% Below Target; On Plus Side, 2:1 Student/Faculty Ratio Will Be #1 in Country*, TAXPROF BLOG, July 29, 2013, http://taxprof.typepad.com/taxprof_blog/2013/07/indiana-techs.html.

3. ABA, *Enrollment and Degrees Awarded*, http://www.americanbar.org/content/dam/aba/administrative/legal_education_and_admissions_to_the_bar/statistics/enrollment_degrees_awarded.authcheckdam.pdf (last visited January 8, 2014).

4. ABA, *ABA-Approved Law Schools*, http://www.americanbar.org/groups/legal_education/resources/aba_approved_law_schools.html (last visited January 8, 2014).

5. 2013–14 in-state tuition was $16,854 for Memphis and $17,678 for Tennessee. University of Memphis Law School, *Tuition and Fees*, http://www.memphis.edu/law/futurestudents/cost.php (last visited July 26, 2013); The University of Tennessee College of Law, *Tuition and Fees*, http://law.utk.edu/financial-services/tuition-and-fees/ (last visited July 26, 2013).

6. Vanderbilt Law School, TOP-LAW-SCHOOLS.COM, http://www.top-law-schools.com/vanderbilt-law-school.html (last visited March 25, 2014).

7. Nashville School of Law, *Tuition, Fees, and Books*, http://nashvilleschooloflaw.net/?page_id=6 (last visited July 26, 2013).

8. The data to support this claim and the rest of this paragraph come from: Joshua Wright, *Data Spotlight: New Lawyers Glutting the Market (Updated)*, June 22, 2011, http://www.economicmodeling.com/2011/06/22/new-lawyers-glutting-the-market-in-all-but-3-states/.

9. Hayes Hickman, *City Hall to be LMU Law School*, KNOXVILLE NEWS SENTINEL, February 13, 2008, http://www.knoxnews.com/news/2008/feb/13/city-hall-be-lmu-law-school/.

10. Belmont University, *Belmont University Announces New College of Law*, October 7, 2009, http://forum.belmont.edu/news/2009/10/07/belmont-university-announces-new-college-of-law/.

11. LMU Duncan School of Law, *Costs of Attendance*, http://law.lmunet.edu/future-students/cost-of-attendance/ (last visited July 26, 2013).

12. Belmont University College of Law, *FAQ*, http://www.belmont.edu/law/admission/faq.html (last visited July 26, 2013).

13. David Segal, *For Law Schools, A Price to Play the A.B.A.'s Way*, N.Y. TIMES, December 17, 2011, http://www.nytimes.com/2011/12/18/business/for-law-schools-a-price-to-play-the-abas-way.html?pagewanted=all.

14. Belmont University College of Law, *FAQ*, http://www.belmont.edu/law/admission/faq.html (last visited July 26, 2013).

15. David Segal, *New Law School Sues Bar Association*, N.Y. TIMES, December 22, 2011, http://www.nytimes.com/2011/12/23/business/duncan-law-school-sues-american-bar-association.html.

16. Martha Nell, *Federal Judge Nixes Duncan Law TRO, Calls School's Future Success in Suit Against ABA "Unlikely,"* ABA J., January 18, 2012, http://www.abajournal.com/news/article/federal_judge_nixes_duncan_law_tro_calls_schools_future_success_in_suit_aga/.

17. Mark Hansen, *Duncan School of Law Drops Lawsuit against ABA over Accreditation Denial*, ABA J., October 30, 2012, http://www.abajournal.com/news/article/duncan_school_of_law_drops_lawsuit_over_accreditation_denial/.

18. Joe Palazzo and Jennifer Smith, *Some Grads Face Longer Odds, Law Schools Lacking ABA Accreditation Put Students under a Tough Job Hurdle*, WALL ST. J., March 10, 2013, http://online.wsj.com/article/SB10001424127887324096404578352473272923326.html.

19. *LMU Law Dean Steps Down as School Gears Up for New Accreditation Bid*, Knox News Sentinel, October 25, 2012, http://www.knoxnews. com/news/local-news/lmu-law-dean-steps-down-as-school-gears-up-for; *Full Court Press: LMU Law School Working Hard on ABA Reapplication*, Knox News Sentinel, December 19, 2012, http://www.knoxnews.com/ news/2012/dec/19/full-court-press-lmu-law-school-working-hard-on/.

20. Megan Boehnke, *Full Court Press*.

21. *Id.*

22. Megan Boehnke, *LMU Law School Earns Accreditation*, Knoxville News Sentinel, December 8, 2014, http://www.knoxnews.com/news/ local-news/lmu-law-school-earns-aba-accreditation_98147036.

23. Belmont University, *College of Law Receives Provisional Accreditation from the ABA*, June 10, 2013, http://forum.belmont.edu/news/2013/06/10/ college-of-law-receives-provisional-accreditation-from-aba/

24. Pierce Greenberg, *In Year Two, Belmont Law School Moves into New Home While Seeking Accreditation*, Nashville Scene, August 19, 2012, http://nashvillecitypaper.com/content/city-news/year-two-belmont-law-school-moves-new-home-while-seeking-accreditation.

25. Elie Mystal, *Belmont (TN) To Open New Law School—Just Because They Can*, Above the Law, October 7, 2009, http://abovethelaw. com/2009/10/belmont-tn-to-open-new-law-school-just-because-they-can/.

26. Top Law Schools, *Vanderbilt Law School,* http://www.top-law-schools. com/vanderbilt-law-school.html (last visited March 25, 2014).

27. *See* Sam Flamigan & Robert Morse, *Methodology: Best Law Schools Rankings*, U.S. News, March 11, 2013, http://www.usnews.com/ education/best-graduate-schools/top-law-schools/articles/2013/03/11/ methodology-best-law-schools-rankings.

28. Belmont's website explicitly makes this claim: Belmont University, *Belmont University Announces New College of Law*, http://forum.belmont. edu/news/2009/10/07/belmont-university-announces-new-college-of-law/ (last visited July 26, 2013).

29. For a full description of the law school scam blog movement, *see* Lucille A. Jewell, *You're Doing It Wrong: How the Anti-Law School Scam Blogging Movement Can Shape the Legal Profession*, 12 Minn. J.L. Sci. & Tech. 239, 263–74 (2011).

30. *Id.*

31. *See, e.g., Third Tier Reality*, http://thirdtierreality.blogspot.com/ (last visited March 25, 2014). For a list of all of Third Tier Reality's law school profiles, *see* Nando's Law School Profiles, http:// lawschoolsewagepitprofiles.wordpress.com/ (last visited March 25, 2014).

32. Law School Transparency, http://www.lawschooltransparency.com/ (last visited March 25, 2014); The Law School Tuition Bubble, http:// lawschooltuitionbubble.wordpress.com/ (last visited March 25, 2014).

33. Mary Beth Marklein, *Grads Taking Law Schools to Task for Poor Job Market*, USA Today (Aug. 24, 2010, 1:28 PM), http://www. usatoday.com/news/education/2010-08-24-1Alawschool24_ST_N. htm?loc=interstitialskip; John Eligon, *Jobs Data More Vital to Her Than Food*, The N.Y. Times City Room Blog (Aug. 27, 2010), http:// cityroom.blogs.nytimes.com/2010/08/27/jobs-data-more-vital-to-her-than-food/; Annie Lowrey, *A Case of Supply and Demand*, Slate Magazine, October 27, 2010, http://www.slate.com/id/2272621/.

34. Campos actually stopped posting on the site in 2013, but all of the posts can still be found here: *Inside the Law School Scam*, http:// insidethelawschoolscam.blogspot.com/ (last visited March 25, 2014).

35. *Welcome to My Nightmare*, Inside the Law School Scam, August 7, 2011, http://insidethelawschoolscam.blogspot.com/2011/08/welcome-to-my-nightmare.html.

36. August, 2011 Posts, http://insidethelawschoolscam.blogspot.com/ 2011_08_01_archive.html (last visited March 25, 2014).

37. Sarah Mul, *Around the Blogosphere: A Law Prof Scamblogger?*, ABA J., August 12, 2011, http://www.abajournal.com/news/article/around_ the_blawgosphere_a_law_prof_scamblogger/

38. Debra Cassens Weiss, *Law Prof Blogging on "Law School Scam" Is No Longer Anonymous*, August 22, 2011, http://www.abajournal.com/ news/article/law_prof_blogging_on_law_school_scam_is_no_longer_ anonymous/?utm_source=feedburner&utm_medium=feed&utm_ campaign=ABA+Journal+Daily+News&utm_content=Netvibes.

39. Paul Campos, Don't Go To Law School (Unless) (2012).

40. Paul Campos, *Goodbye Is Too Good a Word*, Inside the Law School Scam, February 27, 2013, http://insidethelawschoolscam.blogspot.com/ 2013/02/goodbye-is-too-good-word.html.

41. Brian Z. Tamanaha, Failing Law Schools (2012).

42. *See, e.g., id.* at 20–53.

43. *Hitler Learns His Teaching Schedule*, YouTube, http://www.youtube.com/ watch?v=mLC7Q3DTzi4 (last visited March 25, 2014).

44. The complaint can be found here: http://anziskalaw.com/uploads/Filed_ Amended_New_York_Law_School_Complaint.pdf (last visited March 25, 2014).

45. The complaint can be found here: http://anziskalaw.com/uploads/Filed_ Amended_Thomas_Cooley_Law_School_Complaint.pdf (last visited March 25, 2014).

46. Law Offices of David Anziska, *Filed Complaints*, http://anziskalaw.com/ Filed_Complaints.html (last visited March 25, 2014).

47. *See NYLS* Complaint at 20–22, http://anziskalaw.com/uploads/Filed_ Amended_New_York_Law_School_Complaint.pdf (last visited March 25, 2014).

48. Debra Cassens Wiess, *Job Stats Suit against New York Law School Hits Final Roadblock*, ABA J., March 29, 2013, http://www.abajournal.com/

news/article/unsuccessful_job_stats_suit_against_new_york_law_
school_wont_be_heard_by_st/?utm_source=feedburner&utm_
medium=feed&utm_campaign=ABA+Journal+Daily+News&
utm_content=Netvibes.

49. Staci Zaretsky, *Class Action Lawsuit against Thomas M. Cooley Law
School Dismissed*, ABOVE THE LAW, July 23, 2012, http://abovethelaw.
com/2012/07/class-action-lawsuit-against-thomas-m-cooley-law-
school-dismissed/.

50. Ameet Sachdev, *Judge Tosses Job-Placement Suit against John Marshall*,
CHICAGO TRIB., November 9, 2012, http://articles.chicagotribune.
com/2012-11-09/business/chi-judge-tosses-jobplacement-suit-against-
john-marshall-20121109_1_john-marshall-job-market-john-corkery

51. Joe Palazzolo, *Illinois Judge Tosses Consumer Fraud Suit against DePaul
Law*, WALL ST. J., September 12, 2012, http://blogs.wsj.com/law/
2012/09/12/illinois-judge-tosses-consumer-fraud-suit-against-depaul-law/.

52. Joan C. Rogers, *Law Graduates' Consumer Fraud Claims Squeak Past
Alma Mater's Motion to Dismiss*, BLOOMBERG BNA, April 10, 2013, http://
www.bna.com/law-graduates-consumer-n17179873307/.

53. *Id.*

54. *See* Gomez-Jimenez et al. v. New York Law School, *Order*, http://www.
nacua.org/documents/GomezJimenez_v_NYLawSchool.pdf (last visited
March 25, 2014).

55. Maura Dolan, *Law School Graduates Aren't Finding Much on the
Employment Docket*, L.A. TIMES, April 1, 2013, http://articles.latimes.
com/2013/apr/01/local/la-me-law-grads-20130402.

56. Joe Palazzolo & Jennifer Smith, *Law Grads Claim Schools Misled*, WALL
ST. J., February 2, 2102, http://online.wsj.com/article/SB10001424052970
203920204577197471843581532.html.

57. Matthew Shaer, *The Case(s) against Law School*, NEW YORK MAGAZINE,
March 4, 2012, http://nymag.com/news/features/law-schools-2012-3/.

58. LSAC, *LSATs Administered*, http://www.lsac.org/lsacresources/data/lsats-
administered (last visited December 8, 2014).

59. The yearly declines were 10 percent in 2010–11, 16 percent in 2011–12, and
another 13 percent in 2012–13.

60. LSAC, *LSATs Administered*, http://www.lsac.org/lsacresources/data/
lsats-administered (last visited March 25, 2014); Jacob Gershman,
Number of LSAT Test Takers Is Down 45% Since 2009, WALL ST. J.,
October 31, 2013, http://blogs.wsj.com/law/2013/10/31/number-of-
lsat-test-takers-is-down-45-since-2009/.

61. LSAC, *LSAC Volume Summary*, http://www.lsac.org/lsacresources/data/
lsac-volume-summary (last visited December 8, 2014).

62. LSAC, *End of Year Summary 2003–Present*, http://www.lsac.org/
lsacresources/data/lsac-volume-summary (last visited December 8,
2014).

63. Ethan Bronner, *Law Schools' Applications Fall as Costs Rise and Jobs Are Cut,* N.Y. TIMES, January 30, 2013, http://www.nytimes.com/2013/01/31/ education/law-schools-applications-fall-as-costs-rise-and-jobs-are-cut.html.

64. ABA, *Enrollment and Degrees Awarded 1963–2011,* http://www. americanbar.org/content/dam/aba/administrative/legal_education_ and_admissions_to_the_bar/statistics/enrollment_degrees_awarded. authcheckdam.pdf (last visited March 25, 2014).

65. Jennifer Smith, *First Year Law School Enrollment at 1977 Levels,* WALL ST. J., December 17, 2013, http://blogs.wsj.com/law/2013/12/17/ first-year-law-school-enrollment-at-1977-levels/?mod=newsreel

66. TaxProf Blog, *Decline in LSAT Test-Takers Portends 'Death Spiral' for Low-Ranked Schools,* March 20, 2012, http://taxprof.typepad.com/ taxprof_blog/2012/03/decline-in-.html.

67. Glenn Reynolds, *Higher Education Bubble Update, Legal Education Edition,* INSTAPUNDIT, MARCH 20, 2012, http://pjmedia.com/ instapundit/139302/.

68. Philip J. Closius, *American Law Schools in Crisis,* BALTIMORE SUN, June 4, 2012, http://www.baltimoresun.com/news/opinion/oped/bs-ed-law-schools-20120604,0,871544.story.

69. *See* Karen Sloan, *It's a Buyer's Market at Law School,* NAT'L L.J., June 25, 2012, http://www.law.com/jsp/nlj/PubArticleNLJ.jsp?id=1202560485444 &rss=nlj&sreturn=1.

70. Steven R. Smith, *Financing the Future of Legal Education: "Not What It Used to Be",* 2012 MICH. ST. L. REV. 579, 611 (2012).

71. Standard & Poor's, *As Law School Demand Drops, Credit Quality among U.S. Schools Diverges,* http://online.wsj.com/public/resources/documents/ lawschoolcredit.pdf (last visited January 8, 2014).

72. Steven Davidoff Solomon, *Creditors Keep Troubled Law School on Life Support,* N.Y. TIMES, November 4, 2014, http://dealbook.nytimes. com/2014/11/04/worth-nothing-failing-law-schools-are-kept-on-life-support/?_r=0.

73. *About CUA Law,* http://www.law.edu/about/index.cfm (last visited July 26, 2013).

74. Clair Finnegan, *Law School Enrollment Dropoff Causes Departmental Budget Cuts,* THE TOWER, April 14, 2013, http://www.cuatower.com/ news/2013/04/14/law-school-enrollment-dropoff-causes-departmental-budget-cuts/.

75. Taxprof Blog, *WSJ: At Least 10 Law Schools Cut Size of Incoming 1L Class,* June 11, 2012, http://taxprof.typepad.com/taxprof_blog/2012/06/wsj-at-least.html; Ashby Jones, *Top Law School Cuts Admissions,* WALL ST. J., March 11, 2013, http://online.wsj.com/article/SB100014241278873242810045783544901145841444.html?mod=WSJ_hps_MIDDLE_Video_second.

76. Karen Sloan, *Arizona Cuts Law School Tuition, Marking a First,* NAT'L L. J., April 4, 2013, http://www.law.com/jsp/nlj/PubArticleNLJ.

jsp?id=1202594883355&et=editorial&bu=National%20Law%20
Journal&cn=20130405nlj&src=EMC-Email&pt=NLJ.com-%20
Daily%20Headlines&kw=Arizona%20cuts%20law%20school%20
tuition%2C%20marking%20a%20first&slreturn=20130307194721.

77. Ethan Bronner, *Law Schools' Applications Fall as Costs Rise and Jobs Are Cut*, N.Y. TIMES, January 30, 2013, http://www.nytimes.com/2013/01/31/education/law-schools-applications-fall-as-costs-rise-and-jobs-are-cut.html.

78. Brian Leiter, *U of Arizona Law Cuts Official Tuition Rate*, BRIAN LEITER'S LAW SCHOOL REPORTS, April 8, 2013, http://leiterlawschool.typepad.com/leiter/2013/04/u-of-arizona-law-cuts-official-tuition-rate.html.

79. *The Scholarship Game*, INSIDE THE LAW SCHOOL SCAM, January 2, 2012, http://insidethelawschoolscam.blogspot.com/2012/01/scholarship-game.html.

80. Texas Wesleyan University, *Texas Wesleyan School of Law Transitions to Texas A&M*, August 21, 2013, http://txwes.edu/news-and-events/all-news/texas-sized-reputation/texas-wesleyan-school-of-law-transitions-to-texas-am/.

81. Eleanor Tang Su, *UCSD Looking at a Law School*, SAN DIEGO UNION TIMES, January 28, 2010, http://web.utsandiego.com/news/2010/jan/28/ucsd-looking-law-school/.

82. Yvonne Zipp, *Western Michigan University Considers Formal Alliance with Cooley Law School*, MLIVE.COM, April 2, 2013, http://www.mlive.com/news/kalamazoo/index.ssf/2013/04/western_michigan_university_co_8.html.

83. Lincoln Caplan, *An Existential Crisis for Law Schools*, N.Y. TIMES, July 14, 2012, http://www.nytimes.com/2012/07/15/opinion/sunday/an-existential-crisis-for-law-schools.html.

84. *Law Schools Put Hiring Freeze on Faculty*, N.J. BUSINESS, October 12, 2012, http://www.njbiz.com/article/20121012/NJBIZ01/121019932&source=RSS.

85. Sarah Lawsky, *Spring Self-Reported Entry Level Hiring Report 2014*, PRAWFSBLAWG, May 2, 2014, http://prawfsblawg.blogs.com/prawfsblawg/2014/05/spring-self-reported-entry-level-hiring-report-2014.html.

86. Paul Caron, *Appalachian Law School to Lay Off 63% of Its Faculty?*, TAXPROFBLOG, March 21, 2014, http://taxprof.typepad.com/taxprof_blog/2014/03/appalachian-law-school.html.

87. Jon Wolper, *Vermont Law School Gives Buyouts to 10 Workers*, LEBANON VALLEY NEWS, January 18, 2013, http://www.vnews.com/news/3896880-95/buyouts-laid-law-members.

88. Debra Cassens Weiss, *Law Schools Cope with Declining Enrollment by Quietly Cutting Faculty*, ABA J., July 16, 2013, http://www.abajournal.com/news/article/law_schools_cope_with_declining_enrollment_by_quietly_cutting_faculty/.

89. Hollee S. Temple, *Are Digitization and Budget Cuts Compromising History*, ABA J., May 1, 2013, http://www.abajournal.com/magazine/article/are_digitization_and_budget_cuts_compromising_history/.

90. James G. Milles, *Legal Education in Crisis, and Why Law Libraries Are Doomed*, http://papers.ssrn.com/sol3/papers.cfm?abstract_id=2370567 (last visited January 9, 2014).

91. Joe Palazzolo & Chelsea Phipps, *With Profession under Stress, Law Schools Cut Admissions*, WALL ST. J., June 11, 2012, http://online.wsj.com/article/SB10001424052702303444204577458411514818378.html.

92. Elie Mystal, *Cooley Law will Say Anything to Justify Its Behavior*, ABOVE THE LAW, June 11, 2011, http://abovethelaw.com/2012/06/cooley-law-will-say-anything-to-justify-its-behavior/.

93. *See* Gary S. Rosin, *Unpacking the Bar: Of Cut Scores and Competence*, 32 J. LEGAL PROF. 67, 93 (2008) ("For any given cut score [the score needed to pass the bar], bar passage rates not only fall as law school LSAT scores fall, they fall at increasing rates."). Given that both the LSAT and the bar exam have also been found to disadvantage minority applicants, this may mean both tests are flawed.

94. Jacob Gershman, *Law School Deans Question Sharp Drop in Bar Exam Scores*, WALL ST. J., November 26, 2014, http://blogs.wsj.com/law/2014/11/26/dozens-of-law-school-deans-question-drop-in-bar-exam-scores/.

95. ABA, ABA STANDARDS FOR APPROVAL OF LAW SCHOOLS 2012–13, chapter 4, http://www.americanbar.org/content/dam/aba/publications/misc/legal_education/Standards/2013_2014_standards_chapter4.authcheckdam.pdf (last visited March 25, 2014).

96. *See, e.g.*, Elie Mystal, *The American Bar Association Will Have an Online Law School Guy as Its Top Advisor on Law School Education*, ABOVE THE LAW, April 25, 2012, http://abovethelaw.com/2012/04/the-american-bar-association-will-have-an-online-law-school-guy-as-its-top-adviser-on-legal-education/.

97. George B. Shepherd, *Defending the Aristocracy: ABA Accreditation and the Filtering of Political Leaders*, 12 CORNELL J.L. & PUB. POL'Y 637, 639–49 (2003).

98. *See* Douglas K. Rush & Hisako Matsuo, *Does Law School Curriculum Affect Bar Examination Passage?*, 57 J. LEGAL EDUC. 224, 235 n. 40 (2007) ("[T]he Section of Legal Education and Admission to the Bar voted on August 4–5, 2005 to place Whittier Law School and Golden Gate University School of Law on two years probation for, among other issues, their low bar examination passage rates.").

99. The ABA has pulled provisional accreditation, *see* Gary Rosin, *ABA Pulls La Verne's Accreditation*, THE FACULTY LOUNGE, June 14, 2011, http://www.thefacultylounge.org/2011/06/aba-pulls-la-vernes-accreditation.html, but not full accreditation, *cf.* Paul D. Carrington, *Letter to the Wall Street Journal*, http://paulcarrington.com/ABA%20as%20Cartel.htm (last visited March 25, 2014).

100. Elie Mystal, *The American Bar Association Will Have an Online Law School Guy as Its Top Advisor on Law School Education*, ABOVE THE LAW, April 25, 2012, http://abovethelaw.com/2012/04/

the-american-bar-association-will-have-an-online-law-school-guy-as-its-top-adviser-on-legal-education/.

101. *See, e.g.,* Massachusetts School of Law at Andover, Inc. v. Amer. Bar Ass'n, 107 F.3d 1026 (3d Cir. 1997).

102. The Antitrust Division of the Justice Department launched a very public lawsuit against the ABA that ended in a consent decree, which the ABA promptly violated. The case has been dormant since 2007, but the underlying grist of the case is still present and could be revived under sufficient political pressure or interest. *See* BARTON, LAWYER-JUDGE BIAS, at 129.

103. Elie Mystal, *Another Senator Wants to Hop on the Occupy the ABA Bandwagon,* ABOVE THE LAW, http://abovethelaw.com/2011/10/another-senator-wants-to-hop-on-the-occupy-the-aba-bandwagon/.

104. Mark Hansen, *Sen. Grassley Questions ABA's Law School Accreditation Process,* ABA J., July 13, 2011, http://www.abajournal.com/news/article/grassley_seeks_answers_on_abas_law_school_accreditation_process/.

105. *See, e.g.,* BARTON, LAWYER-JUDGE BIAS, at 121–2.

106. National Conference of Bar Examiners, *2012 Statistics,* http://www.ncbex.org/assets/media_files/Bar-Examiner/articles/2013/8201132012statistics.pdf (last visited March 25, 2014).

107. Gary Rosin, *ABA Pulls La Verne's Accreditation,* THE FACULTY LOUNGE, June 14, 2011, http://www.thefacultylounge.org/2011/06/aba-pulls-la-vernes-accreditation.html (LaVerne); Megan Boehnke, *LMU Law School Denied Provisional Approval by American Bar Association,* KNOXVILLE NEWS-SENTINEL, December 20, 2011, http://www.knoxnews.com/news/2011/dec/20/lmu-law-school-denied-provisional-approval-by/.

108. William D. Henderson, *The Calculus of University Presidents,* NAT'L L. J., May 20, 2013, http://www.law.com/jsp/nlj/PubArticleNLJ.jsp?id=1202600579767.

109. Emory History, *School of Dentistry,* http://emoryhistory.emory.edu/places/schools/schoolsDENTIST.html (last visited March 25, 2014).

110. *See, e.g.,* Sara K. Rankin, *Tired of Talking: A Call for Clear Strategies for Legal Education Reform: Moving Beyond the Discussion of Good Ideas to the Real Transformation of Law Schools,* 10 SEATTLE J. FOR SOC. JUST. 11, 14–15 (2011).

111. Reinvent Law Laboratory, http://www.reinventlaw.com/main.html (last visited March 25, 2014).

112. Tax Prof Blog, *Prospective Students Say Law School's U.S. News Ranking Is More Important Than Placement Stats,* June 20, 2012, http://taxprof.typepad.com/taxprof_blog/2012/06/four-times-more-ols.html.

Chapter 10

1. Graduates of elite law schools are disproportionately represented on the federal bench, Grutter v. Bollinger, 539 U.S. 306, 322 (2003); in law school faculties, Brent E. Newton, *Preaching What They Don't Practice: Why Law Faculties' Preoccupation with Impractical Scholarship*

and Devaluation of Practical Competencies Obstruct Reform in the Legal Academy, 62 S.C. L. Rev. 105, 131 (2010); and in law firms. Richard W. Bourne, *The Coming Crash in Legal Education: How We Got Here, and Where We Go Now*, 45 Creighton L. Rev. 651, 665 n. 47 (2012).

2. Richard Sander, *Class in American Legal Education*, 88 Denv. U. L. Rev. 631 (2011).

3. Doug Williams et al., *Revisiting Law School Mismatch: A Comment on Barnes*, 105 Nw. U. L. Rev. 813, 821 (2011).

4. Letter from Felix Frankfurter to Mr. Rosenwald (May 13, 1927) (on file with the Harvard Law School Library).

5. Benjamin H. Barton, The Lawyer-Judge Bias in the American Legal System (2011).

6. Oona A. Hathaway, *Path Dependence in the Law: The Course and Pattern of Legal Change in a Common Law System*, 86 Iowa L. Rev. 601, 604 (2001).

7. James E. Moliterno, The American Legal Profession in Crisis (2013).

8. Andrew Lu, *Pre-Law Students Still Cite Law School Rankings as Most Important*, Findlaw, October 19, 2012, http://blogs.findlaw.com/greedy_associates/2012/10/pre-law-students-still-cite-law-school-rankings-as-most-important.html.

9. Lucille A. Jewel, *Bourdieu and American Legal Education: How Law Schools Reproduce Social Stratification and Class Hierarchy*, 56 Buff. L. Rev. 1155, 1186 (2008); Duncan Kennedy, *Legal Education and the Reproduction of Hierarchy*, 32 J. Legal Educ. 591 (1982).

10. Steven J. Harper, The Lawyer Bubble 69–70 (2013).

11. *See, e.g.*, Citi Private Bank and Hildebrandt Consulting LLC, *2013 Client Advisory*, http://hildebrandtconsult.com/uploads/Citi_Hildebrandt_2013_Client_Advisory.pdf (last visited March 25, 2014).

12. Harper, Lawyer Bubble, at 74.

13. Maulik Shah, *The Legal Education Bubble: How Law Schools Should Respond To Changes in the Legal Market*, 23 Geo. J. Legal Ethics 843, 847 (2010).

14. Brian Tamanaha, Failing Law Schools 71–103 (2012).

15. Ira P. Robbins, *Best Practices on "Best Practices": Legal Education And Beyond*, 16 Clinical L. Rev. 269, 301–2 (2009).

16. Paul Horwitz, *What Ails the Law Schools*, 111 Mich. L. Rev. 955, 961 (2013).

17. Lincoln Caplan, *An Existential Crisis for Law Schools*, N.Y. Times, July 14, 2012, http://www.nytimes.com/2012/07/15/opinion/sunday/an-existential-crisis-for-law-schools.html?_r=0.

18. Bruce MacEwen, Growth Is Dead: Now What? 60–4 (2013)

19. Axiom Law, *Overview*, http://www.axiomlaw.com/index.php/overview (last visited March 25, 2014).

20. William D. Henderson & Rachel M. Zahorsky, *The Pedigree Problem: Are Law School Ties Choking the Profession?*, A.B.A. J., July 1, 2012, http://www.abajournal.com/magazine/article/the_pedigree_problem_are_law_school_ties_choking_the_profession/.

21. *Id.*

22. *See* David Leonhardt, *The Idled Young Americans*, N.Y. Times, May 3, 2013, http://www.nytimes.com/2013/05/05/sunday-review/the-idled-young-americans.html.

23. *Most Depressing Job Interview You'll Ever See Currently Taking Place at a Starbucks Table*, The Onion, http://www.theonion.com/articles/most-depressing-job-interview-youll-ever-see-curre,32020/ (last visited March 25, 2014).

24. *See, e.g.*, Susan Adams, *Why Do So Many Doctors Regret Their Job Choice?*, Forbes, April 27, 2012, http://www.forbes.com/sites/susanadams/2012/04/27/why-do-so-many-doctors-regret-their-job-choice/.

25. Caela J. McKeever, *How the Economy Upended Young Architects' Hopes*, Crosscut, September 25, 2012, http://crosscut.com/2012/09/25/architecture/110494/architectural-jobs-interns-economy-recession-/.

26. Brian Fuller, *Are You Happy? Not Really*, EE Times, March 28, 2011, http://www.eetimes.com/electronics-blogs/social-mania-blog/4214567/Are-you-happy--Not-really.

27. Michael Ryall, *The Business School Tuition Bubble*, HBR Blog, May 2, 2011, http://blogs.hbr.org/cs/2011/05/the_business_school_tuition_bubble.html.

28. Tim Mullaney, *Jobs Fight: Haves vs. The Have-Nots*, USA Today, September 16, 2012, http://usatoday30.usatoday.com/money/business/story/2012/09/16/jobs-fight-haves-vs-the-have-nots/57778406/1.

29. Sherwin Rosen, *The Economics of Superstars*, 71 Am. Econ. Rev. 845 (1981). Support for the rest of this paragraph comes from this source.

30. Robert H. Frank & Philip J. Cook, The Winner Take All Society (1995).

31. Robert H. Frank, The Economic Naturalist's Field Guide, chapter 9 (2010).

32. Glenn Harlan Reynolds, The Higher Education Bubble (2012). The rest of the assertions in the next two paragraphs come from this source. *See also* Glenn Harlan Reynolds, The New School (2014).

33. Meta Brown et al., *Press Briefing on Household Debt and Credit*, Liberty Street Economics: The N.Y. Fed., February 28, 2013, http://libertystreeteconomics.newyorkfed.org/2013/02/just-released-press-briefing-on-household-debt-and-credit.html.

34. Meta Brown et al., *Grading Student Loans*, Liberty Street Economics: The N.Y. Fed., March 5, 2012, http://libertystreeteconomics.newyorkfed.org/2012/03/grading-student-loans.html.

35. Benjamin Ginsberg, The Fall of the Faculty (2013) covers this phenomenon in exceptional detail.

36. Glenn Reynolds, *Higher Education Bubble Update, Legal Education Edition*, Instapundit, April 17, 2013, http://pjmedia.com/instapundit/167222/.

37. TAMANAHA, FAILING LAW SCHOOLS, at 43–4.
38. JONATHAN R. MACEY, THE DEATH OF CORPORATE REPUTATION (2013).
39. MARC GALANTER & THOMAS PALAY, TOURNAMENT OF LAWYERS 22 (1991).
40. Annette Schuller et al., *Doing Business in the European Union: An Overview of Common Legal Issues*, 31 CO. LAWYER 9 (2002).
41. GLENN REYNOLDS, AN ARMY OF DAVIDS (2005); Glenn H. Reynolds, *Small Is the New BigLaw: Some Thoughts on Technology, Economics, and the Practice of Law*, 38 HOFSTRA L. REV. 1 (2009).

Chapter 11

1. R.H. Coase, *The Problem of Social Cost*, 3 J. L. & ECON. 1–44 (1960).
2. Robert Cooter, *The Cost of Coase*, 11 J. L. STUD. 1–29 (1982).
3. R.H. COASE, THE FIRM, THE MARKET, AND THE LAW (1988).
4. Jonathan R. Macey, *Transaction Costs and the Normative Elements of the Public Choice Model: An Application to Constitutional Theory*, 74 VA. L. REV. 471–518 (1988).
5. *Id.* at 7–16.
6. Ronald J. Gilson, *Value Creation by Business Lawyers: Legal Skills and Asset Pricing*, 94 YALE L.J. 239, 243–4 (1984).
7. David M. Driesen & Shubha Gosh, *The Functions of Transaction Costs: Rethinking Transaction Cost Minimization in a World of Friction*, 47 ARIZ. L. REV. 61, 62 (2005).
8. Gillian K. Hadfield, *Higher Demand, Lower Supply? A Comparative Assessment of the Legal Resource Landscape for Ordinary Americans*, 37 FORDHAM URB. L.J. 129, 133, 151 (2010).
9. Alex Kozinski & Misha Tseytlin, *You're (Probably) a Federal Criminal, in* IN THE NAME OF JUSTICE 43, 49 (Timothy Lynch ed., 2009).
10. ROBERT A. KAGAN, ADVERSARIAL LEGALISM: THE AMERICAN WAY OF LAW 6–9 & Table 1 (2001).
11. *Id.* at 14–16.
12. *Id.* at 6–58.
13. Derek C. Bok, *A Flawed System of Law Practice and Training*, 33 J. LEGAL EDUC. 570, 571 (1983).
14. Gillian Hadfield, *The Cost of Law: Promoting Access to Justice through the Corporate Practice of Law*, http://papers.ssrn.com/sol3/papers.cfm?abstract_id=2183978 (last visited March 25, 2014).
15. George C. Harris & Derek F. Foran, *The Ethics of Middle-Class Access to Legal Services and What We Can Learn From the Medical Profession's Shift to a Corporate Paradigm*, 70 FORDHAM L. REV. 775–845 (2001).
16. DEBORAH L. RHODE, ACCESS TO JUSTICE (2004).
17. Deborah Rhode, *Access to Justice: Connecting Principles to Practice*, 17 GEO. J. LEGAL ETHICS 369, 371 (2004).
18. Emily A. Spieler *The Paradox of Access to Civil Justice: The "Glut" of New Lawyers and the Persistence of Unmet Need*, 44 U. TOL. L. REV. 365 (2013).

19. Sarah M. Buel, *Access to Meaningful Remedy: Overcoming Doctrinal Obstacles in Tort Litigation Against Domestic Violence Offenders*, 83 OR. L. REV. 945, 971 n. 148 (2004).

20. American Bar Association, *Civil Gideon Resolution*, http://www.americanbar.org/content/dam/aba/administrative/legal_aid_indigent_defendants/ls_sclaid_105_revised_final_aug_2010.authcheckdam.pdf (last visited March 25, 2014).

21. The ABA Standing Committee on Pro Bono and Public Service, Supporting Justice III: A Report on the Pro Bono Work of America's Lawyers (2013), http://www.americanbar.org/content/dam/aba/administrative/probono_public_service/ls_pb_Supporting_Justice_III_final.authcheckdam.pdf (last visited March 25, 2014).

22. William T. Robinson, *Legal Help for the Poor: The View from the A.B.A.*, N.Y. TIMES, August 30, 2011, http://www.nytimes.com/2011/08/31/opinion/legal-help-for-the-poor-the-view-from-the aba.html.

23. 452 U.S. 18 (1981).

24. 131 S.Ct. 2507 (2011).

25. *See* Jason Boblick, *A Consumer Protection Act?: Infringement of the Consumer Debtor's Due Process Rights under the Bankruptcy Abuse Prevention and Consumer Protection Act of 2005*, 40 ARIZ. ST. L.J. 713, 735 & n. 167 (2008). There have been sporadic, quite limited applications, *see* Martha F. Davis, *In the Interests of Justice: Human Rights and the Right to Counsel in Civil Cases*, 25 TOURO L. REV. 147, 154 (2009), but nothing like the broad, national right that civil *Gideon* advocates are hoping for.

26. Adi Robertson, *Only 2 Percent of Americans Can't Get Internet Access, but 20% Choose Not to*, THE VERGE, August 26, 2013, http://www.theverge.com/2013/8/26/4660008/pew-study-finds-30-percent-americans-have-no-home-broadband.

27. Gretchen Ruethling, *Almost All Libraries Offer Free Web Access*, N.Y. TIMES, June 24, 2005, http://www.nytimes.com/2005/06/24/national/24library.html.

28. A2J, *Access to Justice on a Smartphone*, May 14, 2012, http://www.kentlaw.iit.edu/news/2012/access-to-justice-on-a-smartphone (last visited March 25, 2014).

29. Aaron Smith, *Smartphone Ownership 2013*, PEW INTERNET, June 5, 2013, http://pewinternet.org/Reports/2013/Smartphone-Ownership-2013/Findings.aspx.

30. Legal Information Institute, *About*, http://www.law.cornell.edu/lii/about/about_lii (last visited March 25, 2014).

31. *See* John O. McGinnis & Steven Wasick, *Law's Algorithm* (draft on file with author) at 9–20.

32. LII, *Wex*, http://www.law.cornell.edu/wex/ (last visited March 25, 2014).

33. *See, e.g.*, Wikipedia, *Due Process*, http://en.wikipedia.org/wiki/Due_process (last visited March 25, 2014). This source supports the rest of this paragraph.

34. Tennessee Administrative Office of the Courts, *Court-Approved Divorce Forms*, http://www.tncourts.gov/help-center/court-approved-divorce-forms (last visited March 25, 2014).

35. Tennessee Administrative Office of the Courts, *Order of Protection Forms,* http://www.tncourts.gov/programs/self-help-center/forms/order-protection-forms (last visited March 25, 2014).
36. Tennessee Administrative Office of the Courts, *Court-Approved General Sessions Forms,* http://www.tncourts.gov/node/1436225 (last visited March 25, 2014).
37. National Center for State Courts, *Self-Representation State Links,* http://www.ncsc.org/Topics/Access-and-Fairness/Self-Representation/State-Links.aspx?cat=Court%20Forms (last visited March 25, 2014).
38. ABA, *State Access to Justice Commissions: Lists and Links,* http://www.americanbar.org/groups/legal_aid_indigent_defendants/initiatives/resource_center_for_access_to_justice/state_atj_commissions.html (last visited March 25, 2014).
39. All of the documents described in this paragraph can be found here: Tennessee Administrative Office of the Courts, *Court-Approved Divorce Forms,* http://www.tncourts.gov/help-center/court-approved-divorce-forms (last visited March 25, 2014).
40. LawHelp Interactive, *About LawHelp Interactive,* https://lawhelpinteractive.org/about (last visited March 25, 2014).
41. IIT Chicago-Kent College of Law, *A2J Author,* http://www.kentlaw.iit.edu/institutes-centers/center-for-access-to-justice-and-technology/a2j-author (last visited March 25, 2014).
42. LawHelp Interactive, Illinois Legal Aid, *Automated Form Library,* http://www.illinoislegalaid.org/index.cfm?fuseaction=home.formLibrary (last visited March 25, 2014).
43. LawHelp.org, *Find Help Near You Now,* http://www.lawhelp.org/find-help/ (last visited March 25, 2014).
44. LawHelp.org, *About,* http://www.lawhelp.org/about-us (last visited March 25, 2014).
45. Texaslawhelp.org, *Homepage,* http://texaslawhelp.org/ (last visited March 25, 2014).
46. LegalZoom.com, *Peace of Mind Review,* http://www.legalzoom.com/assets/modals/modal-legalzoom-peace-of-mind-review.html (last visited March 25, 2014).
47. LegalZoom.com, *Legal Document Review,* http://www.legalzoom.com/legal-document-review/legal-document-review-overview.html (last visited March 25, 2014).
48. LegalZoom.com, *Our Products and Services,* http://www.legalzoom.com/products-and-services.html (last visited March 25, 2014).
49. *Id.*
50. LegalZoom.com, *Living Wills Pricing,* http://www.legalzoom.com/living-wills/living-wills-pricing.html (last visited March 25, 2014).
51. LegalZoom.com, *Help Me Compare,* http://www.legalzoom.com/wills-estate-planning/summary-compare-wills.html (last visited March 25, 2014).

52. For a model version provided by *LegalZoom*, *see* http://www.legalzoom. com/samples/Living_Will_IL.pdf (last visited March 25, 2014).

53. LegalZoom, *Divorce Education Center,* http://www.legalzoom.com/divorce-guide/uncontested-contested-divorce.html (last visited March 7, 2014).

54. LegalZoom, *Divorce,* http://www.legalzoom.com/legal-divorce/divorce-overview.html (last visited March 25, 2014).

55. LegalZoom, *Pricing for Chapter 7 Bankruptcy Packages,* http://www. legalzoom.com/bankruptcy/bankruptcy-pricing.html (last visited March 25, 2014).

56. LegalZoom, *All Forms,* https://www.legalzoom.com/legalforms/ (last visited March 25, 2014).

57. LegalZoom, *Legal Forms,* https://www.legalzoom.com/legalforms/bill-of-sale-automobile (last visited November 22, 2013).

58. MDFamilylawyer.com, *Fixed Fee Online Legal Services,* http://www. mdfamilylawyer.com/.

59. *Id.*

60. SmartLegalForms, *SmartLegalForms vs. LegalZoom,* http://www. smartlegalforms.com/smartlegalforms-vs-legalzoom.html.

61. National Law Foundation, *Practical Forms for Attorneys,* http://www. nlfforms.com/; John G. Locallo, *Behind the Technology Curve? The ISBA Can Help,* 100 Ill. B.J. 124 (2012).

62. http://www.google.com/#hl=en&gs_rn=7&gs_ri=psy-ab&qe= aG93IGRvIGkgd3JpdGUgYSB3aWw&qesig=kBqsFOod1_DMnf8JQiP7eQ &pkc=AFgZ2tlfosluMFIskLWyyo6BZ7oZXJJqy8GedMP_ 7nsAcn8cYAQ5mvGO_pwLKTRuH4mwMOy5rXQzTHcAXOgMWKE h5vetYWOZkg&cp=20&gs_id=26&xhr=t&q=how+do+i+write+ a+will+on+my+own&es_nrs=true&pf=p&output=search&sclient= psy-ab&oq=how+do+i+write+a+wil&gs_l=&pbx=1&bav=on.2,or.r_ qf.&bvm=bv.44342787,d.eWU&fp=75966c488fe17396&biw=1033&bih=629

63. http://www.wikihow.com/Write-Your-Own-Last-Will-and-Testament.

64. LegalZoom, *Find an Attorney You Can Trust for Your Family,* http:// www.legalzoom.com/attorneys-lawyers/legal-plans/personal.html; Rocket Lawyer, *Get Connected with an On Call Lawyer: Members Save Thousands of Dollars with Pre-Negotiated Rates,* http://www.rocketlawyer. com/find-a-lawyer.rl.

65. LegalZoom, *Find an Attorney You Can Trust for Your Family,* http:// www.legalzoom.com/attorneys-lawyers/legal-plans/personal.html?utm_ source=pjx&utm_medium=affiliate&utm_campaign=43737&cm_ mmc=affiliate-_-pjx-_-43737-_-na.

66. Rocket Lawyer, *Get Connected With an On Call Lawyer,* http://www. rocketlawyer.com/find-a-lawyer.rl.

67. *LegalMatch,* http://www.legalmatch.com/ (last visited March 25, 2014).

68. *See* Joseph A. Colquitt, *Hybrid Representation: Standing the Two-Sided Coin on Its Edge,* 38 Wake Forest L. Rev. 55, 57 & n. 10 (2003).

69. Benjamin H. Barton, *Against Civil* Gideon *(and for* Pro Se *Court Reform)*, 62 Fla. L. Rev. 1227 (2010).

70. Cynthia Gray, Reaching Out or Overreaching: Judicial Ethics and Self-Represented Litigants 1–2 (2005).

71. *Id.* This list of activities is so basic as to be humorous to a poverty lawyer, but sadly many or most courts addressing *pro se* litigants fail to follow these simple steps.

72. The Self-Represented Litigation Network, Core Materials on Self-Represented Litigation Innovation (2006).

73. Richard Zorza, The Self-Help Friendly Court: Designed from the Ground Up to Work for People without Lawyers (2002), http://www.zorza.net/Res_ProSe_SelfHelpCtPub.pdf. AJS actually has a whole website dedicated to the topic, http://216.36.221.170/prose/home.asp and https://www.ajs.org/key-links/ajs-store/publications-and-resources/pro-se/. *See also* Richard Zorza, *Self-Represented Litigation and the Access to Justice Revolution in the State Courts: Cross Pollinating Perspectives Towards a Dialog for Innovation in the Courts and the Administrative System*, 29 J. Nat'l Assoc. Administrative L. Judiciary 63 (2009).

74. *See* Lois Bloom & Helen Hershkoff, *Federal Courts, Magistrate Judges, and the Pro Se Plaintiff*, 16 Notre Dame J.L. Ethics & Pub. Pol'y 475, 476–7 (2002).

75. *See* Ronald W. Staudt & Paula L. Hannaford, *Access to Justice for the Self-Represented Litigant: An Interdisciplinary Investigation by Designers and Lawyers*, 52 Syracuse L. Rev. 1017 (2002).

76. *See* Anita Davis, *A Pro Se Program That Is Also "Pro" Judges, Lawyers, and the Public*, 63 Tex. B.J. 896 (2000).

77. The Judicial Branch of California, *Online Self-Help Center*, http://www.courtinfo.ca.gov/selfhelp/.

78. Utah State Courts, *Online Court Assistance Program*, http://www.utcourts.gov/ocap/; Maryland Judiciary, *Family Law Forms*, http://mdcourts.gov/family/forms/index.html.

79. Modria, *Resolution Center: Property Assessment Appeals*, https://www.modria.com/assessment/.

80. Consumer Protection BC, *Resolve Your Dispute*, http://www.consumerprotectionbc.ca/odr.

81. There is a short video describing the process available here: http://www.odr.info/node/83.

82. *See* Jill Gross, *Vikki Rogers on UNCITRAL's Working Group III on Online Dispute Resolution*, ADR Prof Blog, July 30, 2012, http://www.indisputably.org/?p=3754.

83. Benjamin H. Barton, *Against Civil Gideon (and for* Pro Se *Court Reform)*, 62 Fla. L. Rev. 1227, 1228–9 (2010).

84. Richard Susskind, Tomorrow's Lawyers 92–5 (2013).

85. Lynn A. Epstein, *The Technology Challenge: Lawyers Have Finally Entered the Race But Will Ethical Hurdles Slow the Pace?*, 28 Nova L. Rev. 721, 737–8 (2004).

86. *Id.*

87. William T. Robinson, *Legal Help for the Poor: The View from the A.B.A.*, N.Y. Times, August 30, 2011, http://www.nytimes.com/2011/08/31/opinion/legal-help-for-the-poor-the-view-from-the-aba.html.

88. Tom Lininger, *From Park Place To Community Chest: Rethinking Lawyers' Monopoly*, 101 Nw. U. L. Rev. Colloquy 155, 158–9 (2007); Clint Bolick, *Access to Legal Services: The Market Provides*, 49 Ariz. Att'y 76 (2012).

89. The complaints against *LegalZoom* and links to the documents are available in chapter 5.

90. LegalZoom, *Perspectives*, http://www.legalzoom.com/perspectives/legalzoom-serves-north-carolina-high (last visited March 25, 2014).

91. Michael Braunstein, *Structural Change and Inter-Professional Competitive Advantage: An Example Drawn From Residential Real Estate Conveyancing*, 62 Mo. L. Rev. 241, 257–8 (1997) has an excellent overview of these arguments.

92. ABA Comm. on Professionalism, In the Spirit of Public Service: A Blueprint for the Rekindling of Lawyer Professionalism 52 (1986), http://www.americanbar.org/content/dam/aba/migrated/2011_build/professional_responsibility/stanley_commission_report.authcheckdam.pdf (last visited March 25, 2014).

93. Deborah L. Rhode, In the Interests of Justice: Reforming the Legal Profession 158–65 (2000).

94. Deborah Rhode et al., Legal Ethics (2013).

95. Lisa J. Frisella et al., *State Bar of California*, 17 Cal. Reg. L. Rep. 339, 343 (2001).

96. Leslie C. Levin, *The Case for Less Secrecy in Lawyer Discipline*, 20 Geo. J. Legal Ethics 1 (2007).

97. Benjamin H. Barton, *An Institutional Analysis Of Lawyer Regulation: Who Should Control Lawyer Regulation—Courts, Legislatures, or the Market?*, 37 Ga. L. Rev. 1167, 1209 (2003).

98. ABA, *Lawyer Population and Agency Caseload Volume 2009*, http://www.americanbar.org/content/dam/aba/migrated/cpr/discipline/09-ch1.authcheckdam.pdf (last visited March 25, 2014).

99. ABA, Total National Lawyer Counts, http://www.americanbar.org/content/dam/aba/migrated/marketresearch/PublicDocuments/total_national_lawyer_counts_1878_2011.xls (last visited March 25, 2014).

100. Percentages from ABA, *Lawyer Demographics*, http://www.americanbar.org/content/dam/aba/migrated/marketresearch/PublicDocuments/lawyer_demographics_2013.authcheckdam.pdf (last visited March 25, 2014).

101. Julie Rose O'Sullivan, *Professional Discipline for Law Firms? A Response to Professor Schneyer's Proposal*, 16 Geo. J. Legal Ethics 1, 86 (2002).

102. ABA, *Lawyer Population and Agency Caseload Volume 2009*, http://www.americanbar.org/content/dam/aba/migrated/cpr/discipline/09-ch1.authcheckdam.pdf (last visited March 25, 2014).

103. *Id.*

104. ABA, *Sanctions Imposed 2009*, http://www.americanbar.org/content/dam/aba/migrated/cpr/discipline/09-ch2.authcheckdam.pdf (last visited March 25, 2014).

105. Daniel Currell & M. Todd Henderson, *Can Lawyers Stay in the Driver's Seat?*, http://papers.ssrn.com/sol3/papers.cfm?abstract_id=2201800 (last visited March 25, 2014).

106. Richard Susskind, Tomorrow's Lawyers 13 (2013).

Chapter 12

1. Patrick Schiltz, *On Being a Happy, Healthy, and Ethical Member of an Unhappy, Unhealthy, and Unethical Profession*, 52 Vand. L. Rev. 871, 874–81 (1999).

2. Monica Parker, The Unhappy Lawyer: A Roadmap for Finding Meaningful Work Outside of the Law (2008).

3. Will Meyerhoffer, Way Worse Than Being a Dentist: The Lawyer's Quest for Meaning (2011).

4. Douglas Litowitz, The Destruction of Young Lawyers: Beyond One L (2006).

5. Nancy Levit & Douglas O. Linder, The Happy Lawyer: Making a Good Life in the Law (2010).

6. *Id.* at 9.

7. Substitute the words "well-being" or "satisfaction" for happiness if you prefer.

8. Elizabeth Dunn et al., *Spending Money on Others Promotes Happiness*, 319 Science 1687–8 (2008).

9. Daniel Kahneman & Alan B. Kruger, *Developments in the Measures of Subjective Well-Being*, J. Econ. Persp. 8–9 (2006).

10. Daniel Kahneman, Thinking, Fast and Slow 396–7 (2011).

11. Levit & Linder, The Happy Lawyer, at 10.

12. Maurice Stucke, *Should Competition Policy Promote Happiness?*, 81 Ford. L. Rev. 2576, 2632 (2013).

13. *Id.* at 2631.

14. *Id.*

15. Daniel H. Pink, Drive (2009).

16. *Id.* at 85–146.

17. Larry E. Ribstein, *The Death of Big Law*, 2010 Wisc. L. Rev. 749, 753–4 (2010).

18. Malcolm Gladwell, The Tipping Point 179 (2000).

19. Pink, Drive at 86–108.

20. *Id.* at 99.

21. Levit & Linder, The Happy Lawyer at 171–3.
22. Michael Trotter, Profit and the Practice of Law 17 (2012).
23. Marc Galanter & Thomas Palay, The Tournament of Lawyers (1991).
24. *Id.* at 20–36.
25. Pink, Drive at 15–81.
26. *Id.* at 42–4.
27. Peter Lattman, *Suit Offers a Peek at the Practice of Inflating a Legal Bill*, N.Y. Times, March 25, 2013, http://dealbook.nytimes.com/2013/03/25/suit-offers-a-peek-at-the-practice-of-padding-a-legal-bill/.
28. Amanda Becker, *Law Firm Associates' Job Satisfaction Down, Survey Finds*, Washington Post, September 13, 2010, http://www.washingtonpost.com/wp-dyn/content/article/2010/09/10/AR2010091006548.html.
29. Jennifer Smith, *Companies Reset Legal Costs*, Wall St. J., April 8, 2012, http://online.wsj.com/article/SB10001424052702304587704577331711808572108.html.
30. Ashby Jones, *Why Don't Women Stay at Law Firms? Here's One Take*, Wall St. J., March 19, 2010, http://blogs.wsj.com/law/2010/03/19/why-dont-women-stay-at-law-firms-heres-one-take/.
31. Rachel Rodgers, *You Don't Have to Quit Lawyering to Have a Life: 5 Steps to a Virtual Practice*, Forbes, December 11, 2012, http://www.forbes.com/sites/yec/2012/12/11/you-dont-have-to-quit-lawyering-to-have-a-life-5-steps-to-a-virtual-practice/.
32. Levit & Linder, The Happy Lawyer at 53–77.
33. Bartlit, Beck, Herman, Palenchar, Scott LLP, About, http://www.bartlit-beck.com/about.html (last visited March 25, 2014).
34. Michael H. Trotter, Declining Prospects xvi (2012); Tucker Ellis LLP, http://www.tuckerellis.com/ (last visited March 25, 2014).
35. Rosa Brooks, *Should I Go to Law School?*, Foreign Policy, April 25, 2013, http://www.foreignpolicy.com/articles/2013/04/25/should_you_go_to_law_school.
36. *Id.*
37. Tucker Max, *Why You Should Not Go to Law School*, Huffington Post, February 18, 2013, http://www.huffingtonpost.com/tucker-max/law-school_b_2713943.html.
38. Steven J. Harper, *Law School Is a Sham*, Salon, April 6, 2013, http://www.salon.com/2013/04/06/law_school_is_a_sham/.
39. J. Maureen Henderson, *Why Attending Law School Is the Worst Career Decision You'll Ever Make*, Forbes, June 26, 2012, http://www.forbes.com/sites/jmaureenhenderson/2012/06/26/why-attending-law-school-is-the-worst-career-decision-youll-ever-make/.
40. The website below contains some graphic pictures of filthy toilets. If you have a strong stomach, *see* Third Tier Reality, http://thirdtierreality.blogspot.com/ (last visited March 25, 2014); *Dear Me,*

Don't Go to Law School (alternate), YouTube, http://www.youtube.
com/watch?annotation_id=annotation_566398&feature=iv&src_
vid=ShliKfsLQoo&v=yo5HnXomG88 (last visited March 25, 2014);
Don't Go to Law School—Find Out Why, YouTube, http://www.youtube.
com/watch?v=ZhjhHuMKqgs (last visited March 25, 2014).

41. *See, e.g.*, Eric Weiner, *Lowered Expectations*, N.Y. Times, July 19, 2009,
http://opinionator.blogs.nytimes.com/2009/07/19/lowered-expectations/.

42. Chelsea Phipps, *More Law Schools Haggle on Scholarships*, Wall St. J.,
July 29, 2012, http://online.wsj.com/article/SB1000087239639044130304
577557182667927226.html.

43. Roger E. Schechter, *Changing Law Schools to Make Less Nasty Lawyers*, 10
Georgetown J. Leg. Ethics 367 (1997).

44. Deborah Rhode, In Pursuit of Knowledge (2006).

45. James B. Levy, *SCOTUS Chief Justice Roberts Criticizes Legal Scholarship
for Being Out of Touch with Practicing Bar*, Legal Skills Prof Blog,
July 7, 2011, http://lawprofessors.typepad.com/legal_skills/2011/07/
scotus-chief-justice-roberts-criticizes-legal-scholarship-for-being-out-of-
touch-with-practicing-bar.html.

46. Arthur Allen Leff, *Economic Analysis of Law: Some Realism about
Nominalism*, 60 Va. L. Rev. 451, 469 (1974).

Chapter 13

1. Jacob Gershman, *California Bar Wants More Power to Crack Down on
Unlicensed Lawyers*, WSJ Law Blog, April 29, 2014, http://blogs.
wsj.com/law/2014/04/29/california-bar-wants-more-power-to-
crack-down-on-unlicensed-lawyers/.

2. Deborah L. Rhode, Access to Justice 88 (2004); Gillian K. Hadfield,
*Legal Barriers to Innovation: The Growing Economic Cost of Professional
Control over Corporate Legal Markets*, 60 Stan. L. Rev. 1689, 1692–5 (2008).

3. Laurel A. Rigertas, *Stratification of The Legal Profession: A Debate in Need
of a Public Forum*, 2012 Prof. Law. 79, 128–9 (2012).

4. Stephen Gillers, *How to Make Rules for Lawyers: The Professional
Responsibility of the Legal Profession*, 40 Pepp. L. Rev. 365, 396–7 (2013).

5. Alfred Z. Reed, Training for the Public Profession of the Law
(1921).

6. *Id.* at 281.

7. Roy Stuckey et. al, Best Practices For Legal Education (2007).

8. William M. Sullivan et al., Educating Lawyers: Preparation for
the Practice of Law (2007).

9. Robert Stevens, Law School 155–7 (1983); Felix S. Cohen, *Transcendental
Nonsense and the Functional Approach*, 35 Colum. L. Rev. 809 (1935).

10. *See, e.g.*, John Elson, *The Regulation of Legal Education: The Potential
for Implementing the MacCrate Report's Recommendation for Curricular
Reform*, 1 Clinical L. Rev. 363 (1994).

11. Deborah Rhode, *Legal Education: Rethinking the Problem, Reimagining the Reforms*, 40 PEPP. L. REV. 437, 455–8 (2013); Richard Posner, *Let Employers Insist If Three Years of Law School Is Necessary*, S.F. DAILY J., Dec. 15, 1999, at A4; Mitu Gulati, Richard Sander, & Robert Sockloskie, *The Happy Charade: An Empirical Examination of the Third Year of Law School*, 51 J. LEGAL EDUC. 235 (2001).

12. BRIAN Z. TAMANAHA, FAILING LAW SCHOOLS 172–6 (2013).

13. Ruth Tam, *Obama: Law Schools Should Think About Being "Two Years Instead of Three,"* WASH. POST, August 23, 2013, http://www. washingtonpost.com/blogs/post-politics/wp/2013/08/23/obama- law-schools-should-think-about-being-two-years-instead-of- three/?wprss=rss_election-2012&clsrd.

14. Karen Sloan, *Law School Two-Year Option Intrigues New York's Top Judge*, NAT'L L. J., January 18, 2013, http://www.law.com/jsp/nlj/ PubArticleNLJ.jsp?id=1202585130033&Law_school_twoyear_option_ intrigues_New_Yorks_top_judge_.

15. John O. McGinnis & Russell D. Mangas, *First Thing We Do, Let's Kill All the Law Schools*, WALL ST. J., January 17, 2013, http://online.wsj.com/ article/SB10001424052970204632204577128443306853890.html?mod=dje mEditorialPage_h.

16. Brent E. Newton, *The Ninety-Five Theses: Systemic Reforms of American Legal Education and Licensure*, 64 S.C. L. REV. 55 (2012).

17. Ray Worthy Campbell, *Rethinking Regulation and Innovation in the U.S. Legal Services Market*, 9 N.Y.U. J. L. & BUS. 1, 36 (2012), *citing* Deborah L. Rhode, *The Delivery of Legal Services by Non-Lawyers*, 4 GEO. J. LEGAL ETHICS 209 (1990).

18. David R. Barnhizer, *The Purposes and Methods of American Legal Education*, 36 J. LEGAL PROF. 1 (2011).

19. David Lat, *Bring Back Apprenticeships*, N.Y. TIMES, February 2, 2012, http://www.nytimes.com/roomfordebate/2011/07/21/the-case-against- law-school/bring-back-apprenticeships-in-legal-education.

20. John J. Farmer, *To Practice Law, Apprentice First*, N.Y. TIMES, February 17, 2013, http://www.nytimes.com/2013/02/18/opinion/to-practice-law- apprentice-first.html.

21. I wrote a whole book about this, BENJAMIN H. BARTON, THE LAWYER JUDGE-BIAS IN AMERICAN COURTS (2011).

22. Dan Slater, *Law School in 2 Years (Same $$)—Assessing Northwestern's Program*, WALL ST. J., June 20, 2008, http://blogs.wsj.com/law/ 2008/06/20/law-school-in-2-years-same-price-assessing-northwesterns- program/.

23. TAMANAHA, FAILING LAW SCHOOLS, at 8.

24. Katherine Mangan, *As They Ponder Reforms, Law Deans Find Schools "Remarkably Resistant to Change,"* CHRON. HIGHER ED., February 27, 2011, http://chronicle.com/article/As-They-Ponder-Reforms-Law/126536/.

25. Ethan Bronner, *A Call for Drastic Changes in Educating New Lawyers*, N.Y. TIMES, February 10, 2013, http://www.nytimes.com/2013/02/11/ us/lawyers-call-for-drastic-change-in-educating-new-lawyers. html?emc=eta1&_r=0.

26. *See, e.g.*, Matt Bodie, *Notice to All Law Faculty: Read This Report*, PRAWFSBLAWG, September 20, 2013, http://prawfsblawg.blogs.com/ prawfsblawg/2013/09/notice-to-all-law-faculty.html.

27. Karen Sloan, *Law Professors Give ABA an Earful on Tenure's Future*, NAT'L L. J., January 6, 2014, http://www.nationallawjournal.com/ id=1202636468913.

28. Washington State Bar Association, *Supreme Court Adopts Limited License Legal Technician Program*, http://www.wsba.org/News-and-Events/ News/Supreme-Court-Adopts-Limited-License-Legal-Technician-Rule (last visited March 25, 2014).

29. *See* Deborah L. Rhode, *Policing the Professional Monopoly: A Constitutional and Empirical Analysis of Unauthorized Practice Prohibitions*, 34 STAN. L. REV. 1 (1981); Ralph C. Cavanagh & Deborah L. Rhode, *The Unauthorized Practice of Law and Pro Se Divorce: An Empirical Analysis*, 86 YALE L.J. 104 (1976).

30. ABA COMMISSION ON NONLAWYER PRACTICE, NONLAWYER ACTIVITY IN LAW-RELATED SITUATIONS (1995), http://www.americanbar.org/ content/dam/aba/migrated/cpr/clientpro/Non_Lawyer_Activity. authcheckdam.pdf.

31. Nathan M. Crystal, *Core Values: False and True*, 70 FORDHAM L. REV. 747, 764–5 (2001).

32. Mathew Rotenberg, Note, *Stifled Justice: The Unauthorized Practice of Law and Internet Legal Resources*, 97 MINN. L. REV. 709, 709–10 (2012).

33. Catherine J. Lanctot, *Scriveners in Cyberspace: Online Document Preparation and the Unauthorized Practice of Law*, 30 HOFSTRA L. REV. 811, 822–36 (2002).

34. For an overview of international deregulation and re-regulation of lawyers, *see* Nuno Garoupa, *Globalization and Deregulation of Legal Services*, http://www. masonlec.org/site/rte_uploads/files/Garoupa%20GLOBALIZATION%20 AND%20DEREGULATION%20OF%20LEGAL%20SERVICES%20 -v6%20FINAL.pdf (last visited March 25, 2014).

35. Chris Bonjean, *ISBA Submits Resolution Regarding ABA's Ethics 20/20*, ILLINOIS L@WYER, http://iln.isba.org/blog/2012/06/20/isba-submits- resolution-regarding-abas-ethics-2020.

36. Bill Henderson, *Connecting the Dots on the Structural Shift in the Legal Market*, THE LEGAL WHITEBOARD, August 3, 2012, http://lawprofessors. typepad.com/legalwhiteboard/2012/08/connecting-the-dots-on-the- structural-shift-in-the-legal-market.html.

37. Gillian Hadfield, *The Cost of Law: Promoting Access to Justice through the Corporate Practice of Law*, http://papers.ssrn.com/sol3/papers. cfm?abstract_id=2183978 (last visited March 25, 2014).

38. *See* Stephanie L. Kimbro, *Regulatory Barriers to the Growth of Multijurisdictional Virtual Law Firms and Potential First Steps to their Removal*, 13 N.C. J.L & Tech. On. 165 (2012), http://www.ncjolt.org/sites/default/files/3Art_Kimbro_165_226.pdf.

39. *See* Ted Schneyer, *"Professionalism" as Pathology: the ABA's Latest Policy Debate on Nonlawyer Ownership of Law Practice Entities*, 40 Fordham Urb. L.J. 75 (2012).

40. *See, e.g.*, John Wallbillich, *This Week in Legal Schadenfreude*, Wired GC, April 20, 2012, http://www.wiredgc.com/2012/04/20/this-week-in-legal-schadenfreude/.

41. M. E. Bradford, Founding Fathers: Brief Lives of the Framers of the United States Constitution (1994).

42. Dan Slater, *Barack Obama: The U.S.'s 44th President (and 25th Lawyer-President!)*, WSJ Law Blog, November 5, 2008, http://blogs.wsj.com/law/2008/11/05/barack-obama-the-uss-44th-president-and-24th-lawyer-president/.

43. Jennifer E. Manning, Membership of the 113th Congress: A Profile 3 (2013), http://www.fas.org/sgp/crs/misc/R42964.pdf (last accessed May 7, 2013).

44. *Id.*

45. Alexis De Tocqueville, Democracy in America and Two Essays on America 313 (Gerald E. Bevan trans., 2003).

46. *Id.* at 315.

47. *Id.* at 313.

48. Lawrence M. Friedman, A History of American Law 634 (2nd ed. 1985).

49. *Id.*

50. ABA, *Total National Lawyer Counts,* http://www.americanbar.org/content/dam/aba/migrated/marketresearch/PublicDocuments/total_national_lawyer_counts_1878_2011.xls (last visited July 26, 2013).

51. Richard L. Abel, American Lawyers 159 (1989).

52. Bryant Garth, *Crises, Crisis Rhetoric, and Competition in Legal Education: A Sociological Perspective on the (Latest) Crisis of the Legal Profession and Legal Education*, http://papers.ssrn.com/sol3/papers.cfm?abstract_id=2166441 (last visited March 25, 2014).

53. James P. Gifford, *Lawyers and the Depression*, 137 Nation 236–9 (1933).

54. ABA, *U.S.-India Trade Relations: Challenges and Opportunities*, http://www.americanbar.org/content/dam/aba/uncategorized/GAO/2013mar27_usindiatraderelations_1.authcheckdam.pdf (last visited March 25, 2014).

55. Ryan W. Hopkins, *Liberalizing Trade in Legal Services: The GATS, The Accountancy Disciplines, and The Language of Core Values*, 15 Ind. Int'l & Comp. L. Rev. 427, 427–8 (2005).

56. Laurel S. Terry, *From GATS to APEC: The Impact of Trade Agreements on Legal Services*, 43 Akron L. Rev. 875, 881 n. 23 (2010).

57. ABA, *U.S.-India Trade Relations: Challenges and Opportunities.*

58. 18 U.S.C. § 2333 (2013).

59. Id.

60. Ross Todd, *Arab Bank Ruling Is Bright Spot for Terrorism Plaintiffs*, THE AM LAW LITIGATION DAILY, April 25, 2013, http://www.americanlawyer. com/digestTAL.jsp?id=1202597580290&Arab_Bank_Ruling_Is_ Bright_Spot_for_Terrorism_Plaintiffs&slreturn=20130428172955; Lanier Saperstein & Geffrey Sant, *The Anti-Terrorism Act: Bad Acts Make Bad Law*, N.Y. LAW JOURNAL, September 5, 2012, http://www. newyorklawjournal.com/PubArticleNY.jsp?id=1202570071497&The_ AntiTerrorism_Act_Bad_Acts_Make_Bad_Law

61. Holmes v. Buss, 506 F.3d 576 (7th Cir. 2007).

62. BENJAMIN H. BARTON, THE LAWYER-JUDGE BIAS IN THE AMERICAN LEGAL SYSTEM 259–83 (2011).

INDEX